International Financial Integration

Also by Anthony M. Endres

NEOCLASSICAL MICROECONOMIC THEORY: The Founding Austrian Version

INTERNATIONAL ORGANIZATIONS AND THE ANALYSIS OF ECONOMIC POLICY: 1919–1950 (*co-authored*)

GREAT ARCHITECTS OF INTERNATIONAL FINANCE: The Bretton Woods Era

International Financial Integration

Competing Ideas and Policies in the Post-Bretton Woods Era

Anthony M. Endres

First published 2011 by
PALGRAVE MACMILLAN

Palgrave Macmillan in the UK is an imprint of Macmillan Publishers Limited, registered in England, company number 785998, of Houndmills, Basingstoke, Hampshire RG21 6XS.

Palgrave Macmillan in the US is a division of St Martin's Press LLC, 175 Fifth Avenue, New York, NY 10010.

Palgrave Macmillan is the global academic imprint of the above companies and has companies and representatives throughout the world.

Palgrave® and Macmillan® are registered trademarks in the United States, the United Kingdom, Europe and other countries

ISBN 978-0-230-23226-6   hardback

This book is printed on paper suitable for recycling and made from fully managed and sustained forest sources. Logging, pulping and manufacturing processes are expected to conform to the environmental regulations of the country of origin.

A catalogue record for this book is available from the British Library.

A catalog record for this book is available from the Library of Congress.

10   9   8   7   6   5   4   3   2   1
20   19   18   17   16   15   14   13   12   11

Printed and bound in Great Britain by
CPI Antony Rowe, Chippenham and Eastbourne

Contents

List of Tables and Figures

Tables

Figures

Abbreviations

BIS	Bank for International Settlements
BW	Bretton Woods
CPI	consumer price index
EC	European Community
ECB	European Central Bank
ECU	European currency unit
EMU	European Monetary Union
EMS	European Monetary System
ERM	European exchange rate mechanism
EU	European Union
FAO	Food and Agriculture Organization
GDP	gross domestic product
GNP	gross national product
IBRD	International Bank for Reconstruction and Development
IFI	international financial institution
IFIAC	International Financial Institution Advisory Commission
IFO	international financial order
IFS	international financial system
ILLR	international lender of last resort
IMF	International Monetary Fund
LDC	less developed country
LLR	lender of last resort
NBER	National Bureau of Economic Research
OCA	optimum currency area
OECD	Organisation for Economic Cooperation and Development
SDR	special drawing rights
WB	World Bank
WHO	World Health Organization

Preface

This book is the outcome of five years' research and reflection. It represents a sequel to my *Great Architects of International Finance: The Bretton Woods Era* (London and New York: Routledge, 2005). The present volume takes up the intellectual history and comparative ideas approach from the demise of the Bretton Woods System in 1971 until the end of 2000. For the post-Bretton Woods era, I employ a different procedure than the chapter-by-chapter individual-economist focus in my study of the Bretton Woods era. Here the chapter treatment is by major questions and issues in the international financial system. The topics chosen for the following chapters are as follows: the reactions of leading economists to the collapse of the Bretton Woods system; exchange rate regime choice; capital account convertibility issues; international financial and economic crises; ideas on the changing role of the IMF in the post-BW era and currency consolidation issues.

Each chapter draws on significant contributions by economists to the debate on international financial integration and international monetary reform. The ideas of economists are reviewed and compared, including those of nine Noble Laureates: Milton Friedman, Friedrich Hayek, Paul Krugman, Robert Lucas, James Meade, Robert Mundell, Paul Samuelson, Joseph Stiglitz and James Tobin.

I will compare and contrast the diverse ideas, practical proposals and policy implications arising from the work of prominent economists in the field of international finance and international monetary economics. Different and oftentimes competing ideas will be organized into 'trajectories of thought' – a notion introduced in Chapter 1 that is intended not only to capture economists ideas, philosophical and methodological orientations at any particular point in the post-Bretton Woods era; it also functions to establish commonalities with other economists and trace movements in various lines of thought over time.

The main purpose of this monograph, from my own perspective, is to underscore the importance of intellectual structures in the quite modern history of international finance. The subjects of international finance and international money are now highly technical sub disciplines in economics and are not easily accessible to non-specialists. The most popular methodologies in these fields are formal modelling, usually coupled with sophisticated empirical and econometric testing of propositions about one or other relationship in the international realm. By contrast, it is unusual to employ a comparative ideas approach in these fields. In the final chapter I set out in more detail what I mean by 'intellectual structures' and compare this idea with other more popular methodologies used when historically-minded economists treat international monetary problems. Here I am thinking of economic historians' bread-and-butter techniques for studying historical structures: reasoning by historical analogy and counterfactual analysis. These techniques will not be employed here.

By comparison with the contributions of economic historians, this book is unashamedly focused on comparisons of economic doctrines in historical perspective. By 'doctrines' I mean, following Joseph Schumpeter (1954), economists' explanations of the workings of the international financial system or particular dimensions of that system, based on some unifying principles, reasoning styles and research methodologies. What finally turns economists' explanations into a fully-fledged doctrine is a set of policies advocated on the basis of those principles, reasoning styles and methodologies.

Early drafts of some parts of this book have been presented at the History of Economic Thought Society of Australia Conference, University of New England, 2003; the Society for Heterodox Economics Conference, University of New South Wales, 2007; the Colloquium on Market Institutions and Economic Processes, New York University, 2008; Monash University Economics Seminar Series, 2006 and the Freedom to Choose Conference, University of Notre Dame, Fremantle, 2010. I am greatly obliged to conference and seminar participants for comments and advice. I am also indebted to Grant Fleming for previous joint work on economic thought and research agendas in international agencies which has especially benefited discussion in Chapter 6 on the IMF. Certain parts of the book draw on previously published work. I acknowledge permissions granted for use of this material from the following: Duke University Press for 'Frank D Graham's Case for Flexible Exchange Rates: A Doctrinal Perspective', *History of Political Economy*, 40(1), 2008, 133–67, and John Wiley and Sons for 'Currency Competition: A Hayekian Perspective on International Monetary Integration', *Journal of Money Credit and Banking*, 41(6), 2009, 1251–64.

I have also had the benefit of working with David Harper at NYU on developments in the theory of capital, and it is out of this joint work that the idea of 'thought trajectories' arose and was found useful in the following chapters. More broadly, I am indebted to the support of colleagues in the History of Economic Thought Society of Australia over a period of 25 years. In many different ways they have underscored the importance of studying the intellectual history of economics at a time when that subfield has been unjustly relegated to minor status in university economics curricula and, in many cases, it has disappeared altogether. The present fad of locating economics faculty in business schools rather than either the humanities or social sciences, seems largely to have been responsible for this trend.

As usual I am indebted to friends and family who have variously suffered and in some cases benefited, from my self-enforced social isolation while working on this study. I am especially grateful to the two Amandas: Amanda Tong for research assistance and for preparing the bulk of the manuscript and Amanda Sun for efficiently reshaping and formatting the final manuscript into a form suitable for publication.

Melbourne, April 2010

1
A Qualitative Framework

The political economy of international monetary organization

The ideas of economists proposing either to construct, or change or reform international financial arrangements are by their very nature informed by underlying doctrines. Those doctrines make assertions about how the international economy functions, and incorporate methodological preconceptions on how to collect, interpret and evaluate evidence on the international economy. As well, economic doctrines usually embody specific policies and practical suggestions for change and reform. For economists the 'political economy' of international monetary organization differs sharply in content from 'international political economy' – a subject of prime concern to political scientists intent on analysing international monetary relations, international politics and diplomacy, and the deeply political aspects of inter-governmental relations that play vital roles in making international monetary systems (Best 2005; Cohen 2008a and 2008b).

The ideas of economists on international monetary organization are classifiable as 'political economy' in the sense that term is used by Joseph Schumpeter (1954, p.38). Our orientation in this work is inspired by Schumpeter's notion of economic doctrine as a form of political economy. The practice of Schumpeterian political economy involves articulation of economic doctrines about the international economy. Economic doctrine is constituted by a 'comprehensive set of economic policies' advocated by their proponents, 'on the strength of certain unifying principles'. The choice of 'unifying principles' will entail some selection, some judgements as to what is correct, right or appropriate for certain reasons and (perhaps) as to what is suggested (or even compelled)

1

by the evidence in any real case. Naturally, policy prescriptions and suggestions have a normative ('what should be done') orientation. Various 'unifying principles', belonging to what Schumpeter calls different economic doctrines, will imply correspondingly different methodologies ('how to analyse', 'how to interpret' etc) and core philosophies that turn on beliefs and conventions (rather than resolvable, fully testable, scientific propositions) held by a particular economist.

The political economy of international monetary organization comprises ideas on the:

1. core framework of an international financial order (IFO) and
2. structure and operating details (the everyday rules, conventions etc) of an actual international financial system (IFS).

> When we speak of the international monetary system we are concerned with the mechanisms governing the interactions between trading nations, and in particular the money and credit instruments of national communities in foreign exchange, capital, and commodity markets (Mundell 1972, p.92).

When economists consider an IFO they usually address the

> framework of laws, conventions, regulations and mores that establish the setting of the system and the understanding of the environment by the participants in it. A monetary order is to a monetary system somewhat like a constitution is to a political or electoral system (Mundell 1972, p.92).

The dictates of the IFO in the abstract are not always followed or matched in an observable, real, operating, IFS (Gilbert 1980). For example, the Bretton Woods IFO established in 1944 and revised during the 1944–1971 period, differed markedly from the way the Bretton Woods IFS in fact operated (Bordo 1993, p.37; James 1996; McKinnon 1996a, pp.42–4, 77).

Harry Johnson (1972a), a leading 'Chicago School' monetary economist in the 1970s, distinguished two traditions of international monetary analysis. The first, akin to Schumpeterian political economy, is the 'political-economic approach', though it goes beyond Schumpeter's narrower conception of normative economic doctrines. Johnson's 'political-economic approach' to the subject allows for national and international politics and diplomacy in the formation of ideas and policies on international monetary organization. The second tradition of thought identified by Johnson is concerned with 'scientific-theoretical' work in the realm of international finance. The 'scientific' approach enables economists who are 'usually clever enough at concealing their emotions within the trappings of scientific analysis to pass for dispassionate experts' (Johnson 1972a, p.408). For example, the concept of an automatic, self-disciplining international financial system guided by underlying, stable market processes may have been 'discovered' or at least elaborated scientifically by David Hume over two centuries ago. It could be regarded as a description of the operation of the classical gold standard IFS (Hume's celebrated 'price-specie flow' mechanism). As such it was a scientific theory, proposing causal connections in that classical IFS though it presupposed (some would say, advocated) certain central bank policies or rules that allowed such an automatic system to operate. The scientific theory of the IFS based on the gold standard imposed (or advocated) automatic rules for the conduct of monetary policy by central banks. Similarly, original architects of the Bretton Woods IFO established in 1944, held an underlying doctrine about the workings of the international economy that lead to presupposing, imposing (or indeed advocating) the 'fictitious equality' of national currencies (Johnson 1972a, pp.409–10).

Unlike Johnson, we are not especially interested in the ideas of the international monetary economists surveyed in the following chapters that wish to expand and elaborate the pure logic of the IFO and an associated, evolving IFS, in a vacuum; establishing key causal relationships in the international economy is one thing, suggesting reforms and changes quite another. These two thought operations – so-called 'scientific' knowledge generation and policy analysis – are rarely, if ever prosecuted independently, especially in respect of the economists surveyed in the following chapters. More usually the scientific approach is used actively to inform policy analysis. The economists' ideas we wish to focus on do not comprehend all the new developments, policies, policy options and so on, in a completely dispassionate manner, that is, without any advocacy whatsoever. While informed by research using modern measurement techniques, improved data collection methods and creative imagination, the views of economists will always be propounded from a viewpoint. For instance, economists will target key components for reform in an existing IFS, or will identify defects in aspects of the IFS that other economists may regard as virtues. Alternatively, economists will always see trade-offs when assessing different proposals for the IFS: trade-offs between one reform and another, between immediate dangers or postponed dangers in persisting with a particular international financial rule, operation or convention, or between risks in a particular arrangement or practice – some economists perceiving the risks to be small and less serious, others appreciating the risks as large and more consequential. In any case, the viewpoints of economists include underlying, preferred methodological and philosophical positions on the core, inherently untestable beliefs about aspects of international, cross-border, financial interactions and their ongoing integration or disintegration.

The following chapters will draw on prominent contributions by economists to the debate on international financial organization and system reform. The principal objective is to provide a historical perspective on the political economy of international financial organization, on the ideas, plans, schemes, and policies offered by a selected group of economists. Emphasis will be placed on comparing alternative viewpoints, on providing an account of competing ideas and policies on the basis of what they claim to do, rather than on what they should do or what is right or wrong with those ideas and policies. The reader is left to decide these questions, that is, to judge what proposals and plans are superior or preferable. As Schumpeter (1954, p.40) tells us in connection with studying different doctrines in political economy:

> There would be no sense in speaking of a superiority of Charlemagne's ideas on economic policy as revealed by his legislative and administrative actions over the economic ideas of, say, King Hammurabi; or of the general principles of policy revealed but the proclamations of the Stuart kings over those of Charlemagne; or of the declarations of policy that sometimes preface acts of Congress over those Stuart proclamations. We may of course sympathize with some of the interests favoured in any of those cases rather than with the interests favoured in others, and in this sense array such documents also in a scale of preference. But a place of any body of economic thought in any such array would differ according to the judge's value judgments, and for the rest we shall be left with our emotional or aesthetic preference for the various schemata of life that find expression in those documents. We should be very much in the same position if we were asked whether Gauguin or Titian was the greater painter...And the same thing applies of course to all systems of political economy.

In Schumpeterian spirit, the following discussion will be motivated by the idea that the comparative study of economists' viewpoints is fruitful. Directly judgemental comparisons will be avoided in favour of illuminating and comparing philosophical undercurrents and specific orientations toward the 'facts' thrown up by the international financial system. As such, comparative research of this kind can assist in reasoned reflection on disagreements among economists over the operation and organization of the IFS. As well, comparing alternative viewpoints will enlarge our understanding of the deeper bases of certain policies and reforms proposed by the economists concerned. In this field, the main purpose of taking a comparative ideas approach is therefore

> to find out whether we can identify the differences in factual and normative assumptions that can explain the differences in prescription for solving the problems of the international monetary system. Presumably we all use logic. Hence, if we arrive at different recommendations, we must differ in the assumption of fact or in the hierarchy of values. To identify and formulate these assumptions would...be a major step toward a better understanding of the conflict of ideas (Machlup and Malkiel 1964, p.7).

International financial integration: Meaning and implications

What has been stated so far is that the scope of this book will be restricted to doctrinal issues treated in a comparative-historical perspective. There is no intention here to offer a comprehensive account of the main events in the IFS, its changing organizational form and structure, during the period 1971–2000. There is no doubt that the ideas, proposals and policies of economists will be influenced by, and frequently are reactions to, those events. Economic historians have already documented these events fully for the period under review (e.g. Solomon 1999; Gray 2005). Knowledge of main events in the IFS post-1971 will be taken for granted. The contest of ideas will be the focus of attention. We intend to do intellectual history not economic history.

The purpose of this investigation is to uncover the central tenets underlying the main ideas on reform of the IFS in an era marked by increasing cross-border financial integration. Popular discussion during the period 1971–2000 became fixated with the term 'globalization' to describe a wave of quite liberal economic and social reforms that included freer international trade and capital movements; increasing cross-border harmonization and coordination of macroeconomic and social policies; greater coordination of financial and securities market regulation, media and communications regulation, labour and consumer safety standards, the integration of global business supply chains and so forth. The catch-all term 'globalization' therefore went well-beyond international financial integration. The post-BW era brought with it

> improvements in communication and transportation technologies [that] undermined the old [BW] regime by making international economic integration easier. International trade agreements began to reach behind national borders; for example, policies on antitrust or health and safety, which had previously been left to domestic politics, now became issues in international trade discussions. Finally there was a shift in attitude toward openness, as many developing nations came to believe that they would be better served by a policy of openness (Rodrik 2000, p.184).

Rather than 'globalization' economists have more usually opted for the term 'economic integration' and 'international economic integration'. The latter describes the process relevant to economists' domain of interest. In practice, economic integration can take many different forms. Broadly defined, international economic integration is a harmonizing process operating across national borders, coordinating or unifying economic practices and policies: monetary policy, currency policy, fiscal policy, financial market regulations, industrial competition policy, tax systems, legal codes etc. By policy harmonization and coordination we mean the management and occasionally significant modification of national policies in recognition of economic interdependencies among nations. Integration may describe a process of giving freer scope to markets in allocating labour, capital, goods and services across borders but that is a liberal idea (Rodrik 2000). In general, economic integration suggests a phenomenon with continuous gradation and many dimensions (Haberler 1964; Belassa 1969; Machlup 1977; Rodrik 2000).

The term 'integration' in practice is in one sense neutral because it could mean increasing use of governmental, administrative controls across borders or increasing reliance on market forms of resource allocation. International economic integration may imply less intergovernmental intervention in economic affairs or more intervention. Furthermore, policy coordination between nations could simply turn on practical measures creating common economic goals, sharing economic information, collaborating on economic forecasts, and jointly choosing the timing and magnitude of particular policy actions

(Cooper 1985, p.1222). In these instances there would be a degree of economic integration; it may not, however, imply more or less government interference, more harmonized policy rules, or policy activism in the international realm. Equally, it need not entail exclusive use of market processes in trade and capital flows (Bryant 1995). As Jeffrey Sachs and Adam Warner (1995, p.2) explain, integration 'means not only increased market-based trade and financial flows, but also institutional harmonization with regard to trade policy, legal codes, tax systems, ownership patterns, and other regulatory arrangements'. The terms of any economic integration proposal or policy have to be carefully defined, since they would not always or only include more market-based liberalizations; they may quite possibly involve sophisticated trade-offs between market-based and administrative mechanisms. Yet it should be noticed that Sachs and Warner conclude by observing that the actual trend in international economic integration during the post-Bretton Woods era had been toward adopting market-based processes:

> The world economy at the end of the twentieth century looks much like the world economy at the end of the nineteenth century. A global capitalist system is taking shape, drawing almost all the regions of the world into arrangements of open trade and harmonized institutions. As in the nineteenth century, this new round of globalization promises to lead to economic convergence for the countries that join the system (1995, pp.62–3).

There is also a sense in which 'integration' could be regarded as a value-loaded term. Sachs and Warner mention the danger of assuming that the choice of market processes as a vehicle for integration is a guaranteed route to higher levels of economic performance and ultimately economic convergence. They document the 'profound risks for the consolidation of market reforms in Russia, China, and Africa' and the loose, fragile nature of various international economic and financial agreements among the major industrial nations (unlike the more solid nature of the BW Agreement). Other economists might envisage cross-border policy harmonization as potentially counterproductive, indeed disintegrating if it meant creating more artificial barriers to the movement of capital, labour or international trade in goods and services. Others may object to a prominent role for the operation of market forces across national borders because they consider them as disintegrating over some chosen time horizon or disintegrating insofar as their anticipated consequences would be: harmful to a national or regional policy objective (employment, growth, income distribution, reduction of sovereign debt etc); deleterious to social conditions or social outcomes; suboptimal in their impact on domestic financial markets (particularly free capital movements) or ultimately disruptive because they distribute the burdens of adjustment to trade and payments imbalances in an inequitable manner. The above list could be greatly extended. The point is that economic 'integration' is not a universal, Holy Grail – it all depends on how it is defined and implemented.

Even if economic integration in the international realm was considered productive and desirable, that is if the broad idea of harmonizing economic interdependencies between nations was acceptable, achieving integration is not straightforward. Economists would have plenty of room to differ even on this broad matter. Integration could be effected if stable, harmonious economic arrangements across borders were allowed to develop spontaneously or organically. In this view no international blueprint (such as a Bretton Woods-type agreement) would be needed. Individual nations would adopt their own policies in the economic sphere that stabilize their own economies first and then integrate more fully with others of the same type. Alternatively, economic integration could be effected by establishing clear rules for monetary policy, currency regimes, fiscal policy and so forth – rules that could be consciously designed by leading, hegemonic industrialized nations. Other nations would, as they saw fit, adopt such rules, or possibly even contract with international financial hegemons over such rules, thereby integrating their economies with others.

Finally, in practice, there are limits to international economic integration. If market processes are chosen predominantly as the vehicle for integration, these are presumably 'limited by the reach of jurisdictional boundaries'. Such boundaries pose obstacles, in one form or another, to complete economic integration which in the limit we could imagine as consisting in: free international trade in goods and services, free international capital mobility, free international labour mobility and one world money. Integration in this sense is tantamount to the dissolution of national economies though not necessarily national politics. National sovereignty limits complete integration in this 'ideal' sense. In this connection, Dani Rodrik (2000, p.180) poses questions economists tend to avoid: 'does it not follow that national sovereignty poses serious constraints on international economic integration? Can markets become international while politics remain local?'.

Trajectories of thought on international financial integration

Studying comparative schools of thought in modern economics is a relatively new field (e.g. Mair and Miller 1991). It is common procedure adopted by specialist researchers in the history of economic thought to distinguish definite 'schools' of economic thought. More usually 'schools' of thought are established and defined well after (in some cases many decades after) ideas have been articulated and have coalesced around a particular set of fundamental insights. The notion of 'schools' assumes a static character; a theory or idea propounded long ago becomes fossilized and recognized by later generations of economists as being embodied in a distinctive approach.

This study devotes attention to ideas only very recently articulated; the ideas are still quite close and fresh in a temporal sense. These fresh ideas defy easy categorization into separate schools of economic thought. Instead, ideas can be represented along trajectories (or paths) consistent with the view that knowledge grows in an evolutionary process. Modern work on the principles of evolutionary economics is helpful in this regard (Dopfer and Potts 2008, pp.11–14). Trajectories of thought containing particular ideas can move from one state of comparative order to another as those ideas confront the contemporary environment, as they are applied to practical problems and actualized (if not implemented). However, the 'hard core' propositions – styles and rules of reasoning, methodologies for collecting and assessing evidence, and inherent belief systems – upon which trajectories of thought depend, remain identifiable. These propositions may sometimes appear as 'quite woolly "grand generalities" somewhat in the nature of cosmological beliefs' (Leijonhufvud 1976, p.72). As such, hard core propositions are irrefutable.[1] A trajectory of thought may then be likened to a path built on a solid foundation of core ideas. Three distinct phases of a trajectory of thought may be distinguished.

1. The idea is articulated by leading, prominent, persuasive economists; it need not be new or original but its presentation may be innovative, given contemporary circumstances.

---

[1] The term 'hard core' proposition was originally due to the philosopher of science, Imre Lakatos. The term refers to empirically irrefutable beliefs. See Blaug (1992, p.34) and the essays in Latsis (1976).

2. The idea is adopted more widely by a population of followers, imitators and commentators.
3. Over time the idea is retained, extended and defended in practice over a significant length of time among a larger group of economists.

This three phase process is not always observable in practice. Nonetheless, the trajectory notion has the potential to map out a path of ideas on international financial integration; it embodies both principles and practical prescriptions for international financial organization and reform.

A trajectory of thought captures the process by which economists articulate (if not originate), adopt and retain core ideas in an iterative, interactive process with events, circumstances and evidence. The core proposition of this book is that doctrinal roots run deep; trajectories of thought do not stray significantly from their bedrock, from their well worn paths of reasoning notwithstanding the likelihood that data collection will continue to expand and econometric techniques for using data will continue to become more sophisticated. Doctrines will endure even though knowledge of contemporary circumstances and causal connections between policies and outcomes in the international economy will alter over time. Suggested organizational changes in the IFO or IFS will reflect the thought trajectories underwriting them.

Don Patinkin (1982, pp.16–17) tells us that the task of rendering accounts of competing economic doctrines is an empirical exercise. Like statisticians and econometricians, doctrinal researchers fit regression lines to a range of observations concerning the manifold statements, questions posed and policy prescriptions of economists. A central tendency is then found in the relationship between all these statements, questions and prescriptions. Some of these statements can be set aside as outliers – noise rather than signal in a debate or controversy – that are not consistent with the central message of the economist concerned. It is in the identification of the central doctrinal messages, moving over time like trajectories, that this study intends to concentrate. We will identify a trajectory of thought by uncovering selected economists' main concepts, the functional relationships among those concepts, the principal analytical conclusions and their changes over time. Altogether, when isolated and stated in its strongest form, a relevant trajectory of thought will be constituted by distinctive groups of insights and concepts, relationships between those concepts and links to specific conclusions relating to a real case. Certainly, among identified central ideational positions, circumstantial changes will motivate practical policy changes and operational changes over time. Like any evolutionary process we should expect differential growth in the modification, adoption and retention of a thought trajectory. Trajectories of thought will wax and wane in terms of their acceptance among economists as evidence and circumstances change, with the persuasiveness of individuals' contributions promoting a particular line of thought, and because of broader forces operating in the sociology of the economics profession.

Key dimensions of thought trajectories on international financial problems: Stylized examples

The dimensions of economic thought trajectories on the IFO and the operation of any particular IFS divide into two groups. Firstly, seven illustrative, rather stylized, core doctrines are outlined; they contain preconceptions, presuppositions and sets of substantive beliefs on the workings of an IFS and they also contain philosophical views on the nature of an IFO required to underwrite, or act as a framework for, the IFS. These core viewpoints are not meant to be an exhaustive set. Along with their counter-viewpoints (in parentheses below) they occupy pivotal positions in any thought trajectory that we might choose to follow. Generally, core propositions about the IFS and the associated IFO originate from doctrinal beliefs about a 'properly' operating international economy. In reviewing economists' ideas and policies on various aspects of the actual IFS, we shall find that they will not normally make doctrinal beliefs clear and explicit. The objective in this study will demonstrate that doctrinal elements lurk beneath the surface of economists' interpretation of empirical evidence on the international economy and their subsequent policy suggestions.

Secondly, it is necessary to outline broad inferences, policy implications and operational connotations commonly arising from the various stylized doctrines. The origination, adoption and ongoing retention of a doctrine in the field of international financial arrangements and institutions cannot be understood without an appreciation of the policy implications. These are often matters provoking controversy among economists. Political and ideological factors are also inextricably bound-up in each doctrine: they presuppose how the IFO should be organized or what parts of the IFS should be modified in the interests of particular participants in the international economy.

What specifically do we mean by 'doctrines' in a more applied sense? In the realm of international financial arrangements, the doctrinal bases of the illustrative thought trajectories are enumerated in the boxes below. As we may see, core statements identifying each doctrine can be expressed quite bluntly and without qualification. Supplementary inferences on more practical, policy-related matters often emanating from these core doctrines are listed immediately below each stated doctrine, along with counterpoint inferences in parentheses, as the case demands.

Doctrine 1: Stability of the Post-BW IFS

The IFS is Self-stabilizing
(contra: is not self-stabilizing)

Inferences:
  i. Exchange rates: variations are not violently unstable (contra: are unstable)
  ii. Balance of payments adjustment: current account imbalances adjust in an orderly manner (contra: disorderly adjustment, crisis prone)
  iii. Capital flows: beneficial and stabilizing in the long run (contra: often damaging and destabilizing)

Doctrine 2: Exchange Rates and Currency Consolidation

Currency Exchange Rates are Unlike Other Prices
(contra: are like other prices)

Inferences:
  i. Macroeconomic impacts: currency crises – output and employment respond to destabilizing exchange rate changes (contra: impacts are transitory)
  ii. Currency management: manage key world currencies, use exchange market intervention (contra: currency management unnecessary)
  iii. Currency consolidation: create currency unions; plan currency trans nationalization, use gold as currency anchor (contra: deliberate design of currency consolidation unnecessary)

Doctrine 3: International Financial Markets

International Financial Markets are Inherently Stable in the Long Run
(contra: are inherently unstable)

Inferences:
  i. International exchange in capital is like trade in goods and other services (contra: is unlike trade in goods)
  ii. Capital controls: unnecessary (contra: necessary)
  iii. Short-term financial market disturbances: insignificant impact on world output, employment and trade (contra: significant impact)
  iv. Financial sector regulation: allow greater self-regulation and regional variation (contra: require greater cross-border harmonization of regulations)

Doctrine 4: Post-BW functions of the IMF

IFIs: Essential Global Public Goods

Inferences:
  i. Efficiency and stabilizing functions: crisis managers, project lenders, lenders of last resort
  ii. Liquidity functions: organize and redistribute (not just recycle) financial capital
  iii. Economic intelligence role: monitor world economy; collect and disseminate information to avoid crises

---

Doctrine 5: IMF Operational Issues

IFIs: Fail or are Perennially Ineffective

Inferences:
  i. Enforcement: reform conditionality rules and procedures regularly
  ii. Governance: revise regularly, reduce bureaucracy
  iii. Moral hazard: develop new instruments to reduce or diminish role of IFIs or abolish IFIs

---

Doctrine 6: Creating a Formal IFO

IFO Requires Policy Coordination

Inferences:
  i. Policy (monetary, fiscal etc) rules: IMF and/or G3, or G7 or G20 to formalize or loosely cooperate over
  ii. Conditionality: apply regularly revised sectoral and structural reforms using IMF loan conditionality
  iii. Increase IMF funding: recycle capital toward emerging industrial economies; buy-in private capital flows

---

Doctrine 7: International Economic Policy in the IFS

IFI's: use **Either** to
(a) Promote Liberal Economic Policy Reforms

Inferences:
  i. Apply or slightly modify Washington Consensus
  ii. Make IMF loans conditional on market-oriented policies
  iii. Promote freer trade, abolition of capital controls, market-determined exchange rates

Or to
(b) Promote Redistribution of Global Capital

Inferences:
  i. Discard Washington Consensus; emphasize quality of IFI lending
  ii. Use IFI's to allocate capital more equitably
  iii. Promote institutional reforms in small open economies and developing economies

---

We should expect economists who are thinking and writing about the issues in the boxes above to show broad adherence to one or more of these core doctrines; their thought trajectories will be differentiated in part by the inferences drawn and the specific policy prescriptions they focus on. Economists interested in the IFO and IFS will naturally give their attention to different elements, thereby encouraging other economists to adopt and retain similar core doctrines along with supporting ideas and policies.

While our comparative ideas perspective can illuminate major differences between thought trajectories we should be mindful that only a comparative, historical analysis can judge the success or failure of a set of ideas. That is, the enduring ideas and doctrines can only be judged 'successful' by being implemented, by being confronted with economic reality. Most of the ideas and policy proposals surveyed in the following chapters will not have seen the light-of-day; they will have had no contact with reality in the sense of having in fact been actualized in any real IFS. As such, some economic thought trajectories on the subject of international economic integration will remain as thought experiments and take the form of general abstractions.

While discussions among economists is often couched in terms of exchange rate regimes, capital account regimes, international financial crises, the role of the IMF and so on, deep philosophical beliefs underwrite their practical and policy concerns. When doctrinal debate in the period 1971–2000 turned to the big questions of international financial organization and reform we shall see that answers to these questions often revealed these deeper beliefs. For example, does the configuration of the IFO matter in the sense that it should be formally planned and set out in a blueprint for all participating countries to follow? Does that configuration expose participating nations to integrated financial markets that raise long-run growth prospects at the national level? Or are national economies thereby rendered more vulnerable to violent fluctuations in integrated international financial markets that lower growth? If so, how can national policymakers reduce risk (or achieve economic stability) through a well-designed IFO or through operating changes in the IFS? Some economists argue that vague, half-hearted answers to any of these questions could weaken resolve for global economic integration however it is precisely conceived, threaten the otherwise strong case for freer world trade and diminish prospects for the more appropriate composition of international capital flows in particular, and for more efficient and/or equitable allocation of world capital in general.

2
Economists' Initial Reactions to the Demise of the Bretton Woods System

Introduction

The international financial system as it is presently configured, including the international use of currencies, has evolved in a manner that no prominent economist predicted during or at the end of the Bretton Woods era (Solomon 1999; Endres 2005). Following the collapse of the Bretton Woods system some economists viewed the ensuing international financial arrangements either as fragile or precarious because they did not constitute a genuine, planned IFO. The resulting IFS was considered a 'non-system' (e.g. Williamson 1976). By the end of the period under review Robert Mundell (2000, p.339) was still referring to the existence of a non-system; the last quarter of the twentieth century had witnessed, in his view, the wholesale 'destruction' of any semblance of an IFS. Much earlier Max Corden (1983 and 1994, p.165) observed that there was indeed an IFS in existence post-1971 but it was 'unplanned and uncoordinated'. By contrast, another distinguished commentator, James Tobin (1982, pp.115–16) likened the international financial arrangements in the 1970s to 'monetary anarchy'. Ever since, a plethora of proposals have focused on producing a range of plans deliberately to redesign the international financial 'architecture' and avoid or remove supposed endemic features such as financial instability, speculative capital flows, and financial crises; they also discuss various provisions for an international lender of last resort (e.g. Tobin 1978; Bank for International Settlements 1998; Eichengreen 1999a; Fischer 1999a, 2003a and Isard 2005).

We shall begin the second chapter of the present volume by reviewing the initial reactions of prominent economists to the unravelling of the BW IFS in the years after 1971. It will be assumed that readers are familiar with both the main features of the BW IFO and the corresponding IFS as it evolved (after 1945 up to 1971) in respect of exchange rate policy, international payments arrangements, international reserves arrangements and the role of the IMF.[2]

The obvious starting point is the set of articles in the *Journal of International Economics* (1972) especially organized to respond to the pending collapse of BW. What distinctive proposals for international reform and monetary reconstruction were promulgated? What was the underlying mind set associated with those proposals? We should expect that questions about international financial reform would be different (or, if not the answers would have shown some variation), in 1972 as against those questions that might have been posed (say) in 1992. The protagonists in this early *Journal of International Economics* discussion included many economists who had closely observed and analysed the BW IFS including its various modifications during the 1945–71 period: Robert Triffin (Yale), J. Marcus Fleming (IMF), Paul Samuelson (MIT), Harry Johnson (Chicago) and Charles Kindleberger (MIT). One younger economist, Richard Cooper (Yale) also contributed; as we shall see in later chapters, Cooper completed substantial work on the problem of international financial reform. Elsewhere, two other prominent economists entered the debate: Gottfried Haberler (1973) (Harvard) and Robert Mundell (1972, 1977) (Columbia). We shall proceed by expositing and comparing the ideas of all these economists – ideas and proposals that were eventually to become widely known in the 1970s.

The case for a new synthetic international money

Robert Triffin offered the most comprehensive set of reform policies encompassing both restructuring of the IMF and national macroeconomic policy guidelines. His views were developed over many years before 1971 and were widely acknowledged at the time (Fellner 1972). Triffin had long predicted the dissolution of the BW IFO that had provided the basis for the international financial architecture from 1945–71.

Triffin's ideas were developed in the following context. By 1971, large US dollars holdings had been accumulated by foreign central banks. Positive net capital flows out of the US during the 1960s were fuelled in part

---

[2]On the breakdown of the BW IFS as an historical phenomenon the best sources are Scammell (1975), Solomon (1977), De Grauwe (1989), Bordo (1993) and James (1996). On the key ideas underwriting the BW IFO as a doctrinal phenomenon see Endres (2005, pp.14–34).

by domestic savings which exceeded domestic investment. The US had the world's most liquid capital markets and the most widely used currency in international trade and payments. According to Barry Eichengreen (2007, p.12) 'other countries welcomed their ability to acquire dollar reserves and valued their access to a buoyant American export market'. The US was able to sell low-yielding US dollar denominated debt securities abroad while its business corporations accumulated higher yielding direct investments abroad. In this environment foreign nations' reluctance to revalue their currencies against the US dollar was widespread, ostensibly because both their export-led growth prospects and international financial stability might be threatened (the latter, because of the relative decline in the value of the US dollar and foreign held US dollar debt securities) (Eichengreen (2007, pp.10–16). There was rising uncertainty about whether the US dollar could maintain its relative value given: increasing US dollar reserve holdings in foreign central banks and declining US gold reserves that were supposed to add backing to US dollar supplies. These events formed the background to, and practical support for, Robert Triffin's ideas. Furthermore, by 1972 the US trade deficit began to increase significantly, adding further to net foreign US dollar claims on US domestic assets, and raising doubts about the stability of the US dollar.

The breaking of the US dollar – other major currency link came in the early 1970s; it was a central pillar of the BW IFO. And it was sometimes called the exchange rate 'par value' system. This breaking was assisted by widening inflation differentials between the US and other major industrial nations. Triffin (1972, p.380) was critical of the BW system since it had developed to the point where it had become so dependent on 'the super-sovereignty of a dominant country', namely the United States. He wanted the world to avoid dependence on the US dollar standard (at that point no longer linked to gold) and make existing, large dollar reserves held internationally insurable in some ways against sudden loss in value. The precariousness and uncertainty created by these reserves was uppermost in his mind. For instance, they could suddenly be abandoned for other currencies and perhaps even gold. The consequences may then be catastrophic for the international economy. Somewhat surprisingly, given the debate that was to follow in which there was patently no consensus, he asserted that '[e]veryone agrees today in recognizing that a system which permits such absurdities is finally and irrevocably intolerable' (p.381).

The dissolution of US dollar-gold convertibility in 1971 and the par value system by 1973 coincided with a period of increasing dollar oversupply in the sense that the US trade deficit was financed by surpluses (i.e. liquidity reserves) held elsewhere. Thus, the 'richest and most highly capitalized country in the world finds its deficit financed in one continuous stream by the banking systems of foreign countries' (p.379). The imbalances indicated by current account deficits on the balance of payments were matched by liquidity problems to the extent that world reserves (of liquidity) could, in Triffin's view easily be held back, reallocated, or shrink in real value, causing a major economic crisis. Foreign liquidity depended on the stability of the US dollar. The composition of foreign reserves was problematic because it was the result of fairly orderly growth in the holdings of gold and very 'disorderly' stocks of major world currencies. Reserves held and regulated by the IMF would and should come to the rescue. The liquidity constraint of the old BW system should be maintained; it was originally caused by the immobility of financial capital (usually deliberately created by controls). For Triffin, that constraint possessed a positive social function in that it disciplined domestic macroeconomic policy, and doubtless enabled the IMF to play a leading role in this regard. The IMF would be reformed and play a decisive role in regulating the new post-BW IFS; it would rationally monitor, analyse and then control the world stock of liquidity reserves and adapt it to 'the expansion potential of world production and trade' (p.380).

Experience during the BW era had shown the putative 'hazards' in trying to reconcile the stock of reserves in the world with the recognized requirements of international trade in goods and services when the world 'supply of reserve currencies' obtained 'through the deficits of issuing countries' was almost singularly dominated by one country, namely the United States (p.385). In assisting this task of reconciliation and adaptation, Triffin made a case for consolidating existing IMF financial facilities into a new international reserve asset that would ultimately replace the US dollar as the key currency used to settle international payments imbalances. There should be reformation and simplification of the definitions and rules associated with reserve positions that nations held with the IMF. The IMF's deposits entitled holders to an unconditional right to use those means of payment for settling international obligations. Possibly a new reserve instrument should be created for this general purpose, encompassing existing SDR (special drawing rights) facilities at the IMF, various gold tranches, and formal conditional lines of credit all previously used by the IMF (pp.382–4). In summary, the IMF, rather than some key currency country would become the central international monetary stabilizer and corrector of major current account imbalances in the world economy.[3] And the automatic, immediate conversion of the key country deficit (notably the US, which would lose reserves of US dollars to foreign monetary authorities) would entail that there would be no net increases of officially held, key currencies.

Now the new Triffin rules governing international liquidity regulation would specify a ceiling of 'working balances' of (say) 15% of total reserves that each surplus country could hold for foreign exchange rate intervention purposes, amounting to approximately 5% of annual exports (pp.386–7). Foreign currency holdings in excess of that amount would be deposited with the IMF, would earn interest (unlike gold holdings) and would then be drawn upon by countries whose working balances fell as a result of an ongoing external, current account deficit.

Liquidity reserves would be compulsorily 'pooled' at the IMF. The dollar surfeit or overhang developing in 1972 would then become less threatening to world financial stability. The IMF may also require some proportion of credit lines advanced to deficit countries to be financed through gold remittances if those countries held a disproportionate amount of gold in their official reserves (the average gold proportion was about 33% in 1971 outside the US). Otherwise no rules on gold reserves would apply. Indeed, by 1972, the international monetary importance of the dollar had altogether eclipsed gold. Gold reserves would be unaffected even though gold had lost its monetary function in 1971. Triffin's proposal embodies a deep distrust of the extensive use of the US dollar, the 'dollar standard' as it was then known. Moreover, his was a step further toward turning the IMF into a genuine international bank with 'deposits' and 'credit-creating' capacity.

Triffin's ideas for settling payments imbalances between nations were predicated upon a fixed adjustable exchange rate regime or, failing that, a managed exchange rate regime in which monetary authorities were intervening regularly to keep exchange rates within a predetermined band. Similar ideas were formulated for both international settlements and exchange rate management, by Marcus Fleming (1972) at the IMF.

---

[3]Eventually, in Triffin's vision, the IMF would control the financing of other IFI's, such as the World Bank, and even the World Health Organization. Furthermore, in a novel, far-sighted suggestion, Triffin wanted to use the IMF as a source of funds for 'the international war on pollution' (p.383).

As for balance of payments adjustment, Triffin's reforms involved (pp.389–94):

1. The use of monetary and fiscal policy in a flexible manner to target aggregate internal, domestic demand, subject to the constraints of exchange rate policy under (3) below;
2. The application of price and incomes policies to keep the internal price level from inflating and thereby preserving the competitiveness of export industries;
3. The use of active exchange rate policy (rather than market-determined exchange rates) so as to enhance external adjustment.

His rationale for rejecting market-determined exchange rates seemed in part due to the impact of 'an inflationary error in national monetary policies' (p.391). In that unhappy and conceivably quite regular situation, a market-determined currency would quickly depreciate in value, raising the domestic cost of living and thereby adding to upward wage pressures. Given the institutional arrangements in labour markets at the time, Triffin predicted that the outcome would not be a fall in wages 'but recession and unemployment'. His trenchant view against market-determined exchange rates was also partly based on the prevailing consensus against them, both among economists and policymakers:

> Some economists – very few, it is true – see a panacea in the compulsory and daily readjustment of exchange rates by the total abstention of the central banks from intervention in the market. The market itself would determine the daily level of freely fluctuating exchange rates, at the whim of supply and demand influenced by speculators assumed to be wiser than the country's monetary authorities.... The application of a dogmatic 'laisser faire' to the foreign exchange system is unthinkable in a world in which no government would agree to leave it to market forces alone to determine interest rates or to renounce other and multiple forms of intervention in the country's finances and economy (Triffin 1972, pp.390–1).

No mention is made of capital controls. Indirectly, as a secondary objective, monetary policy would support exchange market interventions by central banks: money and credit would be tightened when a national currency is weak against the US dollar, and loosened when a national currency is strong.

Understandably, the IMF line of thinking at the time, as represented by Fleming (1972) supported Triffin's general argument because it assured a significant role for the IMF. In particular, the IMF favoured Triffin's macroeconomic policy assignments and the IMF's role in supervising temporary, reversible payments imbalances. It was argued that 'free floating of exchange rates' do not necessarily buffer external pressures on an economy and its monetary system. Demand, output and employment instability would be experienced first, especially in the tradeable goods sector. Presumably this view was founded on believing that there was a sufficient degree of rigidity in national, internal wages and prices as well as inelastic supply side responses to changes in relative prices eventually brought about by regular exchange rate changes. Therefore, there was a 'trade-off between insulating and disturbing effects' of market-determined exchange rates (p.368). In Triffin's view, only wider margins in exchange rate flexibility should be permitted to secure adjustment to temporary external payments imbalances.

Immediately before the collapse of the BW system, Robert Mundell (1969a, p.648 and 1972, p.101) proposed a scheme substantially equivalent to Triffin's. As Mundell stated the problem – and it was a statement repeated by him in many different forms during the post-BW era:

> the Federal Reserve System acts like a world central bank, and…the US dollar has most of the attributes of a world currency. The path toward a better integrated order leads, in my opinion, in the direction not of stripping the dollar of these roles, but increasingly internationalizing them. More specifically, it means creating a world currency freely exchangeable into dollars, and a sharing of the responsibilities of US monetary policy in an international consultative committee operating through the IMF (p.100).

Again, the objective was to create a new, synthetic international monetary unit to reduce the world's dependence on US dollars. Mundell wanted to create a world currency (an 'intor') standard to replace the dollar standard. The IMF would supervise the intor standard; the intor would be exchanged by the IMF for all gold and unwanted dollars. The US would be required to adopt a fixed exchange rate: the dollar would have a fixed price in terms of intors. (On the operational detail of this scheme see Endres 2005, pp.199–200). In offering this proposal Mundell showed his preference for a completely new IFO; a new set of rules governing each country's use of foreign exchange (Mundell 1973b, p.372). He was adamant that 'the interests and rights of other members of the world economy' should be harmonized with the US economy. The existing IFO, as of 1971, had led to US dollar hegemony and US financial imperialism. In his words, the existing system had evolved into a form of 'Darwinism expressed in the dollar standard and exposed power of the dominant country'. The alternative was in the direction of creating a new IFO that would 'harmonize, where it is possible, the interests and rights of other members of the world community with the vital interests of the dominant economy' (Mundell 1972, p.100). The interests of the 'dominant economy', namely the United States, was to maintain internal economic balance – high employment and price stability. Mundell continued rather hopefully:

> It would do no good to devise an international monetary order that attempted to force unwanted inflation or deflation upon the United States. If this were attempted the US would probably retreat outside the domain of the order and establish its own dollar area. Subject to this accommodation, however, the US can and probably would find it in its own interest to submit to discipline intelligently administered (p.100).

Both the Triffin and Mundell plans betrayed a preference for fixed, occasionally adjustable exchange rates, that is, for the old 'par value' system. The IMF also figured prominently in both plans. Both plans were also motivated by a desire deliberately to reduce US dollar dominance in the international realm, and especially in its roles as an exchange market intervention and reserve currency. From the position of the use of the dollar as a unit of account and as a vehicle currency for invoicing and settling international trade transactions, Triffin and Mundell were convinced that the dollar's influence would prevail until a new IFO was created (e.g. Mundell 1973a, p.394).

Alternatives to an IFO based on synthetic international money

The IMF would be subject to considerable economic and political pressure if it were able to create and manage a synthetic international money (e.g. a new international reserve asset) of the kind proposed by Triffin and Mundell in the early 1970s. The 'strong inflationary pressures' attendant to such proposals was something that, as Gottfried Haberler (1973, p.79) warned, would be most difficult to control internationally. Nationally, in the case of the United States, there was some hope that an (inflationary) oversupply of US dollars would ultimately meet strong resistance within the US. However, to rely exclusively on uncertain political forces in the US would leave the rest of the world in a state of limbo. Unlike Triffin, Haberler was confident that economic forces would come into play to avoid the wholesale dumping of US dollar reserves held by foreign central banks:

> from an economic standpoint, the[situation]...is manageable and viable. In my opinion it does not pose a burden on other countries, provided the United States keeps inflation under control. True, even under this assumption some countries, probably only a few, may find themselves with unwanted surpluses, either because their inflation control is better than in the United States or because international demand for their exports happens to be exceptionally favourable. Such countries then have a choice of floating (or appreciating) their currency or inflating their economy a little bit (p.70).

Paul Samuelson (1972, p.441) brought some realism to the discussion; he had little patience for international monetary policy and admitted to having 'heretical doubts' about the way international financial mechanisms were portrayed by contemporary economists. Samuelson surmised that the primacy of the dollar as an international vehicle currency, reserve currency and investment currency would decline over time. The most influential trend in this regard would be the expected declining US share of world output (GNP). He estimated that the US share of world GNP was 50% at the beginning of the BW era and 33% in 1972 (p.447). Of course the 'brute fact' of economic size created asymmetries in the IFS but as the relative size of the US economy diminished, the relative value of the US currency would depreciate, thereby leading to reduction in the foreign use of US dollars at least as an investment currency and a liquidity reserve. These asymmetries could not be removed by international agreements and major international monetary blueprints. This view was also expressed by Haberler (1973, p.75). Because of the depth of the world US dollar market, it may still be the case that the use of the US dollar could still persist as a vehicle currency in settling transactions in international trade. In any event, Samuelson implied that the dollar had grown naturally to become the international money *de facto*, without any deliberate planning by the IMF or the US government.

Harry Johnson (1972a, p.410) expressed scepticism about any scheme that attempted to make national currencies symmetrical *à la* the original objectives of the BW IFO. Furthermore, consolidating or pooling reserve assets into a non-national, IMF-managed currency into which all national currencies would be convertible, required 'far more radical change in the existing international monetary system' than supposed by architects of such schemes. Triffin and Mundell 'did not really offer much of an argument' other than that they wanted to reduce the US dollar to equality with all other currencies. The US dollar's 'natural growth' was preferable to 'an artificial new instrument to be created at the Fund' (Johnson 1972a, p.413). He continued:

> It is true that most of us who have thought about international monetary reform have always had at the back of our minds the ideal of a world bank and a new basic world money; but it may be that this is lust for academic perfection which is anti-historical in spirit, and that it would be more natural for the dollar to evolve into the basic international money with the Federal Reserve – an improved Federal Reserve, one would hope – managing it in the interests of the world economy. In that case the world would obtain...stability...and most of the current objections to the dominance of the dollar would cease to be relevant (p.413).

Two reasons were adduced for Johnson's scepticism. First, the international currency markets were implicitly assumed (by architects of pooling schemes) to be atomistically competitive. At least, they thought that such markets could be returned to such a state.

> The 'atomistic' benchmark is misleading because it encourages the notion that institutional devices can be found to reduce large national oligopolies to the status and performance of atomistic firms... – a notion embodied in the original structure of the International Monetary Fund until it was modified to recognize the special status of the dollar as an intervention currency...It is further misleading because it ignores the crucial difference between legislation and institutionalization; in the national economy laws can be passed and enforced...; in the international system, institutions must rest on general consent to their fairness and there is no central sovereign authority to penalize transgressors (Johnson 1972a, p.406).

Altogether, the international financial system in 1972 was structured more along the lines of 'oligopolistic competition'.

Secondly, the existing dominant reserve currency, the US dollar, was a natural, inadvertent, unplanned outcome of economic size, wealth, productivity and financial organization in which the world's largest financial centre was domiciled. Moreover, the US had no moral obligation to sacrifice its domestic policy objectives to preserve the IFS as it presented itself in 1971. Johnson favoured a typically Chicagoan view originally propounded by Henry Simons in the 1930s.[4] In this view, the IFS could function satisfactorily, even if it were composed of participating nations of substantially different economic size. The key to IFS stability was the application of national monetary policy rules targeting price level stability. The Chicagoans, including Johnson, believed that 'gold derived its value from the dollar and not vice versa' (p.412). The guarantee of US dollar gold convertibility (at US $35 per ounce) for all foreign dollar reserve assets was not vital to national monetary authorities. Stability in the purchasing power over goods and services of the reserve assets was in fact the most important requirement. Therefore, in an economically dominant nation such as the US which was producing the most currency, a policy of price level stability would have the positive spillover effect of creating monetary and price stability elsewhere – this was the key to a viable IFS (p.413).

> In an important and relevant sense, one can say that the international monetary system functioned satisfactorily for the world economy's prosperity and economic growth up until 1965 or so because the United States for one reason or another conformed to Simons's prescription and preserved a reasonable degree of price stability, thus providing other countries with an international asset of relatively stable purchasing power superior to gold because it yielded enough interest to compensate for the effects on real purchasing power of the creeping inflationary trend (p.412).

The simple Chicagoan principle enunciated by Johnson in his 1972 article glossed over some practical complications. As Ronald McKinnon (1996a, pp.78–80) was later to demonstrate, international monetary policy coordination must pin down the 'common price level' that is to be targeted by cooperating monetary authorities (assuming cooperation was viable). If the price level was definable and policy imple-

---

[4]On Simons's ideas in the pre-BW era and his views on the BW IFO see Endres (2005, pp.128–33).

mentable, exchange rates between major currencies could remain stable or even be set on a fixed 'par value' basis. Thus, cooperating countries could announce a common price index whose stabilization is the domestic objective of each national central bank. McKinnon concluded that a new IFO could be based on a binding rule to stabilize a common producer price index.

In principle, the existence of global price stability would be central to international economic integration; it would be compatible with stable currencies (whether fixed, fixed-adjustable, or floating). Reserve assets required to honour fixed or various forms of managed, adjustable exchange rates would remain stable in value. Destabilizing shifts would not normally arise in these conditions. The centrepiece of proposals by Triffin and Mundell to consolidate reserve currencies in some central IMF fund or create some new synthetic international money, was founded on the presumption that destabilizing shifts in reserves were inevitable. Now that inevitability could only be posited if national economic policies, especially among major industrial nations, were not harmonized. In particular, if the monetary policies of more dominant currency producers were not well-coordinated, reserve asset destabilization may occur. That the US had a special position in the IFS in the 1970s, and its domestic economy was in the verge of a significant inflationary phase, motivated many leading economists to produce some quite fanciful schemes for international financial reform (Johnson 1972b, pp.132–4). So much, then, for the views of Harry Johnson which had long pedigree in the Chicagoan tradition.

The following table illustrates several possible IFOs discussed in the years immediately pursuant to the collapse of BW in 1971. Each combination across the three columns implies a 'particular set of rules or conventions governing monetary and financial relations between countries' (Cooper 1975, p.66). All were alternatives to an IFO based on new, synthetic international money.

In interpreting this table, consider the classical gold standard: it may be described as 'I. A. 1' that is, a combination of fixed exchange rates, with gold used internationally as the reserve asset for settling international transactions, and fully mobile international capital flows. Combination II. C. 3. is a description of the original BW IFO, and gradually this changed to II. C. 3 and II. B. 3. Gold was the ultimate reserve asset backing the fixed US dollar ($35 per ounce) against which other countries set par values. The onus was placed on national monetary authorities to intervene in foreign exchange markets as residual buyers and sellers of their national currencies after private markets had traded those currencies at a fixed

Table 2.1   **Alternative IFOs (or regionally-based IFOs) as at 1975**

Role of exchange rates in balance of payments adjustment	*Reserve asset*	*Degree of market convertibility for capital flows*
I. Fixed exchange rate	A. Gold	1. Full/Free
II. Adjustable parities	B. SDRS[5]	2. Dual market
III. Gliding parities	C. US dollars, gold and other national currencies	3. Controlled/Limited
IV. Managed float	C. As above	
V. Floating	D. None	

Source: Cooper (1975, p.67) with some emendations.

price. Some adjustment in parities was allowable under specific rules administered by the IMF. Later in the BW era, II. B. 3 was instituted. The combination III. C. 3 was popular among economists (Triffin, Cooper, Samuelson) in 1972. Certainly a 'gliding parity' system of exchange rates in which currency values move in a prespecified band, embodied more continuously flexible exchange rates than permitted by BW. By 1971, the late-BW era combinations of II. A. 3, (with the USA in particular holding the world's largest official stockpile of gold implicitly as a major reserve asset) and II. B. 3, gave way, almost by default to a 'gliding parity' system, III. C. 3. (coinciding with softer controls on capital movements). System IV. C. 3. placed less stringent conditions on the composition of official holdings of reserve assets, while V.D.I did not require any reserve assets whatsoever. During the BW era there was, of course, regional variation. Canada was distinctive: it chose IV. C. 1 and used the US dollar as the main reserve asset, partly because of its overwhelming trading relationship with the US. As we shall see in the following Chapter 3 in this volume, Friedman, Johnson, and Hayek favoured IFO combination V.D.I. A European currency union, as it was later formed, constituted I.D.I. A mixed, multi-polar IFO in which different orders were developed on a regional basis, was also established in different parts of the world economy in the last part of the twentieth century. The multi-polar option was not something considered at

---

[5]SDRs refers to 'Special Drawing Rights', a limited synthetic 'monetary' instrument created by the IMF in 1970. On the nature, technical structure and role of SDRs see Endres (2005, pp.180–4). On the possible place of the SDR in reconstructing the IFO in the post-BW era, see Mundell (1995, pp.490–1).

the original BW meeting in 1944 and did not figure in discussions in 1972. That discussion may well have considered whether or not different combinations represented in Table 2.1 above were compatible, durable or sustainable. As Cooper (1975, p.67) remarked, unfortunately without elaboration, a mixed set of combinations forming an IFO 'must still meet certain consistency requirements'.

During the 1972–75 period, only II and III were widely debated among leading economists working on the future of the IFO. That debate was motivated by: (i) the desire to reduce a perceived, potential instability in the existing post-BW system turning on the possibility that the composition of foreign reserves of US dollars could change dramatically, leading to wholesale dumping of those dollars; (ii) doubts about the financial and monetary discipline of the major reserve currency nation (i.e. the US). Would it produce currency at will to finance military expenditures? And (iii): anxiety about the inability of the US and other major currency issuing nations to change parities, that is to respond to persistent international payments imbalances by changing exchange rates. In particular, the US was in an invidious position; it was restrained by 'a whole range of inhibiting factors not present for other countries' (Cooper 1972, p.326). Those 'inhibiting factors' included the impact of vast issuance of US dollars to the rest of the world in settling a growing current account deficit on the US balance of payments. In addition, the widespread use of the US dollar as an intervention currency to maintain exchange rates made it impossible to set rules, and difficult to set guidelines for other nations initiating changes in their currency values – their 'dollar parities' as they were then known. Destabilizing speculation could exacerbate these difficulties just when foreign exchange market derivative instruments and products were becoming more sophisticated. The US was also gifted with the various asymmetries of scale, depth and sophistication in its financial markets relative to many smaller nations.

Richard Cooper's (1972) contribution to the debate in the *Journal of International Economics* canvassed all the arguments for and against various combinations under II and III in the first column of Table 2.1 above. He examined several operational complications associated with each of these and identified the background problems necessitating the design of relatively rigid exchange rate regimes under I or II. In this connection he recognized the intractable nature of asymmetries in the existing IFS.

> Symmetry can be either legal or actual. Actual symmetry among all currencies is out of the question, if only because nations differ greatly in economic size. This fact automatically accords their cur-

rencies differences in actual importance. I therefore take the desire for symmetry to be a desire for legal symmetry, which is here taken to mean an inability to distinguish legally or formally between any two national currencies in official arrangements, despite their differences in actual importance. Under legal symmetry, all currencies are subject to the same rules (Cooper 1972, p.327).

Now, according to Cooper, attempts either to construct an IFO based on II or III carried with them possible internal contradictions. Exchange rates that were fixed but adjustable, or managed in 'gliding hands', were difficult to maintain as long as official international payments clearing arrangements made extensive use of a single key reserve asset such as the US dollar or if private markets widely used such a currency as a unit of account, vehicle currency or as an investment currency (p.332). 'Legal symmetry' as Cooper called it, cannot coexist if either of these practices persisted. Indeed, legal symmetry 'is not possible' under these conditions. Radical changes would be required (as Johnson had also argued). The creation of a completely 'new, non-national private international currency' was of first importance among these changes. (Compare the role of gold in the capacity of international currency under an IFO designed with a fixed exchange rate regime).

Charles Kindleberger's (1972) contribution to the early post-BW debate was informed by a lifelong historical study of the world economy. His expertise in economic history made him non-committal about the way forward although he was determinedly opposed to simplistic arguments in favour of an international order based on V.D.I. Fully floating, market-determined exchange rates were uncertainty-creating because they often fluctuated violently, thereby implying the 'abandonment of the use of money as a unit of account for calculating comparative advantage' (p.434). They were also costly to hedge against – a factor often forgotten by proponents of flexible rates and forward exchange market contracting. While these remarks seemed somewhat exaggerated his conclusion was more dramatic. The consequences of adopting an IFO based on flexible exchange rates would entail 'cynicism or despair that the public good of international monetary stability cannot be achieved' (p.435). Like Ragnar Nurkse in the pre-BW era, and possibly heeding experience with highly flexible exchange rates in that era, Kindleberger could not bring himself to side with those (including Friedman) who relied on 'stabilizing speculation' to calm currency markets, many of which he presumed were thin and illiquid:

> The assumption of a large pool of stabilizing speculation with excellent prevision of the future solves the problem of providing inter-

national money as a store of value by assuming it away. In fact it reduces the flexible-exchange-rate standard to a fixed-rate system which is adjusted immediately upon the occurrence of any event which will permanently change the structure of trade and payments, and is impervious to any change which is transitory or short-lived (p.436).

Yet the benefits of international money, as chosen by private financial market participants, were emphatically not 'derisory' (p.442), if only such money could be found and widely accepted. Certainly, historical research had shown that the fixed exchange rate system under the classical gold standard that was a spontaneously chosen by the market was vastly superior to anything that a market-determined, flexible exchange rate regime could offer. The economies of scale enjoyed in deep, liquid currency markets where there is one generally accepted international money, reduces transaction costs and enhances incentives for international trade and for the more efficient use of scarce global financial capital. However, from his long-run view of the history of international financial arrangements and institutions, Kindleberger was convinced that it was the 'market, not governments' that ultimately determines what will be widely used as international money. Thus, he outlines the case of the role of the US dollar in the BW era:

That until 1971 the dollar has been the world's numeraire, and not gold, is illustrated by the fact that other countries could change the price of their currencies, but not the price of gold, and the United States alone could change the price of gold, but could not change the price of the dollar. The gain in reduced transaction costs in using a national currency as international money is reached for by the market, however much it may be deprecated by economists, bankers or politicians (p.429).

Kindleberger's research demonstrated how many doctrines on international finance promoting 'a synthetic, deliberately created international medium of exchange' missed this crucial point. He complained that economists were too often formulating unrealistic schemes for international money; these schemes 'share a basic weakness that they do not grow out of the day-to-day life of markets as the dollar standard based on New York has done' (Kindleberger 1967, p.10). Later he was driven to repeat this important historical generalization: 'the market will create additional money, or moneys to suit its needs... If officials decree only one international money the market will produce more' (Kindleberger

1989, pp.55–6). At the national level, the creation of legal tender is not sufficient to cause its use in the international realm. Kindleberger confesses to preferring 'the old-fashioned treatment of money' stating that he 'belongs to the school that money is what is used in the discharge of the functions of money, rather than what is declared by government or governments to be legal tender' (p.426). An identical conclusion applies at the international level: the creation of the SDR or some new international reserve asset administered by the IMF will have limited impact. Official monetary mediums are not readily acceptable as international money by dint of the fact that they are managed by an international agency.

What, then, was made of international orders based on IV or V? Here we wish to consider this question from the vantage point of economists' main doctrines in the period under review – the immediate years following the collapse of BW. Certainly, symmetry in the official use of currencies would broadly obtain with fully market-determined exchange rates. Again the bogey in the discussion was the sheer size of the US dollar market. It was generally thought that market-determined exchange rates 'might increase rather than diminish private international use of major national currencies, especially the dollar' (Cooper 1972, p.336). Would that outcome have been so dangerous? Of course it may not have, going on Paul Samuelson's perspective recounted earlier in this chapter. Nonetheless, this bogey seemed to loom disproportionately in the minds of leading protagonists for creating a new, formalized IFO in the period 1972–75.

Choosing an IFO post-1971: Broad criteria

Both Marcus Fleming and Richard Cooper devoted considerable thought to general criteria required to harmonize both national and international objectives when choosing either an overall IFO or a special national or regional combination along the dimensions listed in Table 2.1 above. What rules should be adopted for the exchange rate regime, the reserve assets held by central banks for exchange market intervention purposes (if any) and for capital account convertibility? That these objectives or rules may conflict made the choice extremely problematic. Fleming (1972, p.345) and Cooper (1975, p.68) both began with the need presumably to preserve some national economic policy independence. Fleming asserted that any financial order should allow national governments to choose a level of output recognizing the national trade-off ('compromise' as he stated it) between full employment and price stability. He presumes, consistent with the intellectual consensus at the time, that the trade-off between unemployment and inflation was incontrovertible with particular, permissible policy relevant ranges over of each of those variables. Cooper wanted to accommodate 'local diversity' of macroeconomic policy objectives. In line with his IMF role, Fleming was concerned to include among relevant IFO criteria rules that helped countries avoid large persistent current account imbalances – deficits or surpluses. As well, it was crucial, he believed, to foster the 'optimal international movement of capital'. The term 'optimal' was not defined. Both economists emphasized cooperation and harmonization of economic interdependencies between nations, going well-beyond financial relationships and including the promotion of freer trade. Additionally Cooper (1975, p.68) observed a need for distributional criteria 'to achieve a desired distribution of the gains, both between countries and within countries, that arise from one regime over another'. Efficiency gains from organizing a stable IFO should be distributed in an agreed manner. Obviously some institutional framework would be needed to achieve that goal. Ostensibly, distributional considerations of this sort would require resolution of detailed, technical issues in order to define and measure gains in the first place.

Neither Fleming nor Cooper preferred an IFO organized on the foundations of V.D.I. They had no confidence that such an order would meet their established criteria for a stable order. For Cooper (1975, p.64) V.D.I appeared to be 'a regime in which governments agree not to interfere either with transactions or with the foreign exchange market in any way, [though] it is definitely not a system without rules; indeed in involves extraordinarily stringent proscriptions'. There is also the possibility of a completely 'free-for-all' structure that is not captured by any combination in Table 2.1. Such a structure was not a prescription for an 'order' at all since it allowed governments, central banks and private market participants to act without any coordinating rules or established conventions:

A free-for-all regime does not commend itself. It would allow large nations to exploit their power at the expense of smaller nations. It would give rise to attempts by individual nations to pursue objectives that were not consistent with one another (e.g. inconsistent aims with regard to a single exchange rate between two currencies), with resulting disorganization of markets. Even if things finally settled down, the pattern would very likely be far from optimal from the viewpoint of all the participants (p.65).

This view was also shared by John Williamson (1976, 1977) a distinguished commentator on the BW system and international financial relations. Williamson (1985a, p.78) later expressed the 'free-for-all' in a capsule summary: '[i]f only each country would look after its own fundamentals the system would look after itself'. He agreed with Cooper: 'international regimes are to be sought to protect countries not only from competitive behaviour by their peers, but also from their own short-sighted follies'. Like many of his economist-contemporaries, Williamson appeared to be under the sway of founding ideas embodied in the original BW doctrine some 30 years earlier. In this connection, Fritz Machlup (1972, p.88) did not regard V.D.I as unstable. In a portentous remark, Machlup continued:

> Keynes believed in the power of ideas but he knew that each gener-
> ation of practitioners and politicians is influenced by the ideas they
> learned in their youth. The time lag is sometimes shorter than thirty
> years, but I do not think that the time for acceptance of the idea of
> freely floating exchange rates as an enduring system has come. It is
> futile to try now to sell this idea to the men in power or the men of
> influence.

Similarly, Ronald McKinnon (1996a, p.58) observed: 'still under the sway of Keynes' views...academic economists in 1973–74 had not really changed their mind-set for 30 years'. Yet we cannot impound Paul Samuelson, a leading economist commonly associated with Keynesian ideas in the BW era, in the group referred to by McKinnon. Samuelson (1972, p.451) escapes such a categorization since he pays tribute to Friedman's dissension from one core idea informing the BW IFO:

> What was essentially wrong about Bretton Woods at its core, we had
> to re-learn from Dr. Friedman, a lone voice braying for so long in the
> wilderness that you can't peg exchange rates in a changing world
> where prices and wages are not two-ways flexible and in which people
> will not subject themselves to the discipline of the exchanges.

In the 1970s it was not widely understood or believed that the IFO need not be centrally planned, or coordinated by international diplomacy, negotiations and rule-setting (Corden 1983, 1994). The actual IFS was becoming more decentralized by the 1970s, partly due to the failure of international negotiations. Mostly, it would seem, growing decentralization was due to increasing private capital mobility and the associated decline in the proportion of world capital passing through, and being managed by, IFIs, including the WB and IMF (Krueger 1998, p.1991).

The Johnson-Machlup view (and also Milton Friedman's, though he contributed very little in the 1970s to debate on this subject), was enunciated initially in reaction to the breakdown of BW in August 1971. This view was implicitly founded on the idea that completely free international capital movements and market-determined exchange rates could be adopted internationally without too much difficulty. (We shall discuss the details of arguments concerning different exchange rate regimes in the next chapter). In the Johnson-Machlup approach, access to balance of payments financing would not be circumscribed by liquidity issues; and reserve assets for this purpose would not therefore be mediated by national monetary authorities or the IMF. One clear implication is that a stable IFO can only develop as major industrial nations adopt appropriate policies that stabilize their domestic economies. A demonstration effect will follow: as these nation's inflation rates become low and less dispersed, frequent changes in these nations' currency exchange rates, as determined by demand and supply in private foreign exchange markets, will not be so volatile. Naturally, quite the opposite may occur. Accelerating inflation in a major industrialized economy such as the US could undermine economic stability elsewhere. In the Johnson-Machlup view, if exchange rates were much more flexible than they were during the BW era, this prospect would be minimized.

By contrast Cooper (1975, p.84), among others, maintained that the US in the 1970s had an incentive to inflate its price level relative to other countries, especially if the value of the US dollar was to remain fixed. Dollars were used extensively in international reserves of foreign monetary authorities. By the mid-1970s the US was importing financial capital from the rest of the world to finance its growing external deficit and borrowing that finance at subsidised (i.e. artificially low) interest rates. On the one hand, this was tantamount to imposing an inflation tax on foreign dollar holdings. On the other hand, the US paid interest on foreign holdings of dollars and this tended to offset the seigniorage benefits of issuing the surfeit of dollars to pay for the rising US external deficit (Fellner 1972, p.742).[6]

---

[6]Seigniorage is the benefit in value terms that accrues to a currency issuer when the rising supply of that cheaply produced currency is offered in return for more expensive foreign goods and services. For a technical definition of seigniorage see Mundell (1969b, p.37).

The essence of the arguments among economists in the 1970s over both the state and reform of the international financial system could be reduced to views on the extent to which more flexible exchange rates could limit the impact of inflation in the US and elsewhere. The majority of economists did not favour complete exchange rate flexibility; they preferred a different approach. Only the national policies of the dominant nations in the world economy (in terms of economic size) could be generally autonomous under (say) an IFO represented by V.D.I. Only those nations could in fact choose a desired inflation-unemployment trade-off. Other countries (by far the majority) would have the choice imposed on them *de facto*. So the degree of international financial integration, and the policies appropriate to that degree, should be within the control of all nations. The IFO needs to be deliberately negotiated to establish agreed rules of the game. The rules could then be enshrined in a binding legal agreement, like the original BW agreement, committing all contracting parties to rules administered by an international institution such as the IMF.

In the 1970s, the notion of deliberately designing and choosing an IFO was taken extremely seriously. Deliberate design could encompass a combination of regional groupings of diverse orders (e.g. including monetary and currency unions), that were highly integrated. It was thought that integration was only assured by rational management under an international agreement. That agreement would contain a rule-based, coordinating architecture to ensure cooperation over exchange rate regimes, monetary policy and liquidity arrangements. Monetary governance instantiated in a formal, binding agreement was still taken as indispensable by most leading economists. The idea of a self-regulating IFO was anathema to all but a small minority. In his book entitled *The Failure of World Monetary Reform 1971–74*, John Williamson (1977) ruefully outlined the experience during that period. High expectations, due mostly to the spirit and success of the BW order, were dashed. The BW doctrine

> embodied...a comprehensive set of rules for assigning macro-economic policies: exchange rates to medium-run external balance, fiscal-monetary policy to short-run internal balance, and reserves to provide a buffer stock (as distinct from a monetary base) that would allow short-run departures from external balance. This is the intellectual position that Keynes had developed in the interwar years (Williamson 1985, p.75).

Obviously this position could not be re-established in the 1970s. As we have seen, new ideas were formulated, and these were mostly based on creating formal and binding international economic policy agreements between nations in the post-BW years. In practice, a negotiated IFO proved to be illusory. As Ronald McKinnon (1996, p.58) accurately observed, prominent economic doctrines in the years immediately pursuant to the collapse of BW in 1971 erroneously reasserted 'the principles of international symmetry and greater national macroeconomic autonomy while still trying to establish par values for exchange rates'.

The underlying mind set of the supporters of a new international monetary blueprint to replace BW were disposed mostly to think about the positive experience of the previous 25 years. To be sure, BW delivered international stability (by comparison with the inter war years 1919–39), steady growth and high levels of employment. In short, as Mundell (1972, p.91) acknowledged, BW succeeded in making the world 'depression-proof'. By the mid-1970s the problem of accelerating inflation began to present itself. The international financial plans and blueprints we have surveyed so far did not directly address this problem. Many economists' reactions to the collapse of BW attended to inflationary effects of their proposed schemes and reforms, though mostly as an afterthought. Only Haberler made inflation a direct concern. Others seemed to regard bouts of inflation as one-time (rather than persistent) events. And they regarded inflation as easily controllable with national demand management tools and incomes policies (national controls on wages and prices). At the same time, they generally preferred agreements on managing, if not fixing, exchange rates as the international policy tool that would keep inflation under control. Intergovernmental cooperation, in this view, should result in higher (real) global growth and lower inflation compared to a situation that allowed governments to develop independent policies. We turn next to a more detailed examination of the exchange rate regime discussions among leading economists in the post-BW era.

3
Controversy Over Choice of Exchange Rate Regime

A tripolar choice problem

The trend toward growing international financial integration using market-based processes in the last quarter of the twentieth century was accompanied by a distinctive parallel trend in thinking among economists about exchange rate regimes. Our focus in this chapter will be on the policy choice of exchange rate regimes; it will not be exhaustively surveying the more technical and theoretical concerns of economists with exchange rate determination in the short run or long run. The purpose of the following discussion is to explain the main features and dimensions of the exchange regime choice – a choice informed by events, long-run historical research, more technical econometric research, and by more subterranean philosophical and doctrinal factors.

Currency exchange rates are prices; each 'rate' represents the price of one currency in terms of another. One flaw in the original BW system was the determination of fixed, adjustable exchange rates – the 'rule' which charged the IMF with maintaining those rates between member nations' currencies. The mechanism for correcting inappropriate exchange rates under the BW 'rule' was subject to considerable criticism during the BW era. In general, very few countries heeded the IMF requirement to devalue their exchange rate when circumstances clearly required such a move (Krueger 1998).

With the breakdown of the BW fixed, adjustable exchange rate mechanism in 1971, the IMF and many economists continued to seek the best rules or at least policy guidelines for controlling or managing exchange rates in a more flexible manner than transpired under the old BW arrangements. In this group we may include economists who envisaged an exchange regime choice for a particular nation having ramifications beyond national borders, all the more so if it was a nation of some considerable economic size. This group regarded exchange rate choice as being inseparable from creating a full-blown IFO in which international agreements and compromises would need to be reached on the most appropriate regime (or regimes). The principal assumption here was that different countries may be suited to different regimes depending on their economic size, industrial structure, level of development and so on. Nonetheless, all exchange rate regime choices would need to be made in consultation and coordination with other nations. By comparison, other economists favoured the choice of regime along the lines of completely fixed, government decreed exchange rates; still others proposed completely flexible, market-determined regimes; others suggested zones or bands of allowable flexibility especially among the currencies of large, advanced industrial economies, and finally there were some who were inclined to creating formal monetary and currency unions.

In fact we may simplify the exchange regime choice problem in the tripolar structure represented in Figure 3.1 below. Box 1 is a condition of full international financial integration in which capital 'markets' are fully controlled by national or international agencies.

In such conditions exchange rates are more easily fixed. Intergovernmental management and/or IFI management of capital movements is comprehensive. Here there is no risk of exchange rate fluctuations. In Box 3 we have fully flexible exchange rates determined by the interplay of market forces on foreign exchange markets. In this situation national monetary authorities have complete autonomy to conduct monetary policy with domestic objectives in view – such as

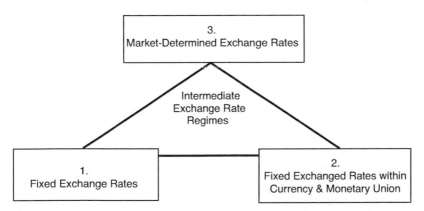

Figure 3.1 A Tripolar Exchange Rate Structure (inspired by Frankel 1999, p.7).

the internal level of prices; they do not directly take account of the need to support a fixed exchange rate. In Box 1 we would have a fixed exchange rate regime, and at Box 2 either a gold standard-type regime or a full currency and monetary union. Capital would flow freely in a gold standard system and within the currency union, though nations within the union would lose autonomy or sovereignty in conducting monetary policy.

It might be expected that, over time, a currency union could be developed regionally and later, in the limit, it could encompass the world as a whole. The same scenario could occur at Box 3, with widespread adoption of flexible market-determined exchange rates. This process could occur gradually as leading industrial nations make the regime choice and are followed in time by other nations. In the limit if all nations adopted such a regime, Boxes 2 and 3 would be substantially equivalent, except that, as long as different national currencies were retained (at Box 3), monetary policy autonomy would also be retained. A wide range of possible intermediate regimes are of course imaginable and feasible and, as depicted in Figure 3.1, they imply some trade-offs between monetary policy independence, capital mobility, and the degree of variation of actual exchange rates. We shall leave aside the currency union option until Chapter 7 where the European currency union debate will be one main feature. We shall proceed by expositing the idealized free floating, market-determined exchange regime and trace the trajectory of ideas on this option throughout the post-Bretton Woods period up until the end of the 1990s. Ideas on various intermediate regime choices will also be examined in detail.

An idealized, market-determined system for exchange rates

Few economists were in the mood to embrace fully flexible, market-determined or 'floating' exchange rate regimes in the 1970s. In the BW era Frank Graham (1943), Milton Friedman (1953) and Harry Johnson (1969) had been strong advocates of floating rates, especially among major industrial nations' currencies. However, they were in the minority and their arguments were not given much credence even though by the mid-1970s exchange rate policy choices amongst major industrial nations had been made in favour of floating exchange rate regimes. The fact that governments in the world's major economies moved to adopt market-determined exchange rates ran against the prevailing, more cautious and sceptical views of many prominent economists specializing in international finance. The essence of the Graham-Friedman-Johnson trajectory of thought on this subject will act as a useful benchmark here; it retained its force throughout the period under review. This line of thought may be summarized in 14 key propositions.

(A) General

1. Currency exchange rates are like any other commodity price; they should be market-determined. The supply of a currency (and there-fore its price) is affected by the national production of money – in short, domestic monetary policy in any particular case. The demand for a currency is affected by, among other things, how much is pro-duced – if too much is produced then the demand may decline because buyers will expect that the purchasing power of that cur-rency will decline in world terms. Monetary forces (demands and supplies of national money and other financial assets denominated in that money) can determine the value of a currency and influence the general direction (in time) of a currency exchange rate. Monetary forces impact on the pressures to change fixed exchange rates and on movements in flexible exchange rates in the long run. Indeed, expectations of ongoing domestic monetary expansion (or contraction) and associated changes in cross-border inflation differ-entials ultimately subvert governmental attempts to fix the value of a national currency in terms of other currencies.

(B) When exchange rates are market-determined they:

2. Change in a manner that does not connote instability (including instability in the overall economic structure).
3. Will encourage development of hedging facilities in forward exchange markets to reduce exchange rate risk.
4. Will be conducive to freer trade since they do not create artificial obstacles to trade. For example, they do not lend themselves to being artificially undervalued for prolonged periods of time thereby inviting claims of unfair advantage and encouraging trade policy retaliation.
5. Do not cause inflation so long as domestic monetary policy is stable, predictable and generally non-inflationary.
6. Confer national monetary policy independence so that developed industrial nations can respond unilaterally to the impact of busi-ness cycles given their unique economic circumstances.
7. Reflect price level changes, specifically inflation differentials, between countries in the long run.

8. Are a more efficient, speedy, automatic means of responding to external shocks affecting particular economies, some of which, depending on national economic structures, are more severe than those affecting other countries.
9. Cast doubt on the future role of the IMF in being involved in national exchange rate management.

(C) When exchange rate regimes involve some intermediate degree of management or exchange rate fixing:

10. Whether or not they are adjusted regularly or set within particular bands, they invite speculative attacks by private foreign exchange market participants because
   a. the reserves of monetary authorities are not infinite and
   b. monetary policy credibility can sometimes be doubted.
11. Exchange rates can occasionally be adjusted by official decree. If there is an official exchange rate devaluation this may well indicate the failure of monetary policy inasmuch as excessive domestic inflation relative to inflation elsewhere has been accommodated by monetary policy.
12. They are often defended by a plethora of exchange controls, capital controls and trade restrictions, all of which are used to reduce the demand for foreign currency.
13. When anchored or pegged to a major foreign currency, they will only be sustainable as long as monetary policy is kept in line with the relevant foreign country's monetary policy.
14. If adjusted continuously under some internationally agreed rule, they will be sustainable only as long as national monetary policy is harmonized among those countries bound by that rule.

One unlikely supporter of the Graham-Friedman-Johnson doctrine summarized in the foregoing list of 14 points was James Meade, who was aptly described as a 1970s 'Keynesian' (McKinnon 1981, p.536). During the BW era Meade (1955) made a case for a flexible exchange rate regime in the context of policies that first ensured internal balance, that is, domestic macroeconomic stability. Subsequently, market-determined exchange rates could be adopted to manage the balance of international payments. Meade repeated this preference in his Nobel Memorial Lecture delivered in 1977, claiming that national governments in the main industrial nations 'had failed to find appropriate national institutional ways of combining full employment with price stability'. If they could design such policies, with 'full employment and price stability at home the balance of payments could with much more confidence be left to the mechanism of flexible foreign exchange rates' (Meade 1993, p.9). He added a dire warning: 'Yet we seem now to be faced with the possibility of a gigantic tragedy' presumably because of the coexistence, in 1977, of high and accelerating inflation and historically high and rising levels of unemployment ('stagflation' as it was then dubbed) in all major industrial economies.

By contrast, in the 1970s advocates of floating exchange rates, indeed relatively stable floating rates for that matter, considered such stability to be pursuant to non-inflationary economic conditions. The full employment objective was a longer-term outcome following the achievement of a low rate and variability of inflation; it should not rank preeminently in the list of major economic policy objectives. The philosophical gulf between Meade and these advocates was wide: Meade was a proponent of active fiscal policy and carefully designed incomes policy – the latter to contain wage and price inflation. In his Nobel Lecture he defined

Full employment as that level of employment at which the supply-demand conditions would lead to attempts to push up the real wage rate more rapidly than the rate of increase in labour productivity if there were perfect competition in the labour market – no monopsonistic employers, no monopolistic trade unions, no social benefits to the unemployed, no obligations on employers to make compulsory severance or redundancy payments to dismissed workers, and so on, – though I am not at all sure whether this extreme form of definition has much meaning. However, in so far as full employment could be defined somewhere along these lines, one would end up with price stability and full employment as separate macro-economic objectives in any real world situation with wage-fixing arrangements as one of the instruments of policy. This is the way in which I like to think of macro-economic problems (Meade 1993, p.4).

With wage fixing acting as an additional policy instrument, a flexible exchange rate could be assigned to dealing with imbalances in the current account of a nation's balance of payments. In addition, flexible exchange rates allow policymakers to use monetary policy freely to choose higher inflation rates and correspondingly lower unemployment if they so desired. Meade's view relied on conventional wisdom in the 1970s which broadly accepted an empirically demonstrated (though always disputed) inverse relationship or 'trade off' between the level of inflation and the level of unemployment. Meade's macroeconomic policy assignment mix, and his ranking of policy objectives giving full employment prime position at the top, would need to be adopted in all major industrial economies in the first instance. International macro policy coordination and some degree of harmonization over policy objectives and priorities would be crucial. That is, by 'crucial' we mean that only then could flexible exchange rate regimes operate widely and be supported by, rather than conflict with, freer trade and freer capital movements between nations. Contra the Graham-Friedman-Johnson trajectory of thought on market-determined exchange rates, 'the supervision of international institutions' was fundamental to the system of flexible exchange rates in the long transition – perhaps many decades – to fully floating currency exchange rates internationally (Meade 1993, p.9). As we shall see later, the case for strengthening international policy coordination in order to support the adoption of floating exchange rates was taken up by other leading economists in the 1980s and 1990s.

Those who took up the Graham-Friedman-Johnson line on exchange rate regimes in the 1970s (apart from further popularizing of flexible rates by Friedman and Johnson), included Friedrich Hayek (Chicago), Fritz Machlup (Princeton) and Gottfried Haberler (Harvard). These economists mostly set aside the problem of transitioning to flexible exchange rates over the long term. In their view, the polar case of fully market-determined exchange rates was the only sustainable option in the long term as long as national macroeconomic policies diverged and many national fiat currencies existed. In these circumstances they understood the power of internationally mobile private capital which was growing in magnitude in the 1970s coextensive with a rising degree of financial asset substitutability across national borders.

Hayek's perspective on currency internationalization and exchange rate regimes

We shall focus this section on Friedrich Hayek, a Nobel Laureate in 1975 who belatedly accepted the flexible exchange rate idea but also appreciated the case for fixed exchange rates. He had always generally accepted the general propositions made by Graham, Friedman and Johnson listed earlier in this chapter. He went further only on one point: currency exchange rates were like any other commodity price except that Hayek considered the underlying service rendered by a currency to be something more complex than that which could be offered by any ordinary commodity. Currencies were objects offering their holders a range of potential services including a liquidity reserve, a unit of account, an investment reserve and a vehicle for trading purposes (Hayek 1978b).

In the 1970s Hayek wavered between fixed and fully flexible exchange rates. He also added an 'outlier' regime not represented in Figure 3.1 – the privatization of currency and the complete replacement of national, government-created fiat monies. In terms of the implications of his idealized case for currency privatization, an international money (or monies) would emerge from such a process that would be spontaneously chosen rather than planned by any government or IFI (Hayek 1979).

Hayek's more realistic proposals in the 1970s deviated from the idealized case for private money. Government-created fiat monies could compete to some extent especially if foreign exchange controls were abandoned. In that situation government monies could be freely chosen as international money, specifically as a vehicle currency, unit of account in international commodity trading or as an investment medium. Hayek was critical of monetary authorities with local monopolies over the production of legal tender money that appeared to be maximizing revenue from inflation and coveting seigniorage. In this far from '*laissez faire*-in-money' environment, he formulated a second-best preference involving competition between government-created currencies.

Hayek understood the international dimension and potentialities of global currency competition, currency choice and currency consolidation. His 'Choice in Currency' (1978a) was originally and pointedly based on an address in 1975 entitled 'International Money'. In this address he condemned the 'wholly Keynesian Bretton Woods agreement' and the purported inflation biased international monetary system that the agreement created (p.116). There is no allusion to an alternative, deliberately constructed international financial architecture; he denied the usefulness of 'an international agreement to adopt a particular mechanism or system of policy' for currency creation and management (p.120). Instead he held that the day-to-day life of markets operating across borders and national jurisdictions would ultimately result in stable or 'good' money and at least to some extent protect money from politics. The first substantive question in the 1975 address was generic in that it was not restricted to any brand of money produced by governments or private interests: 'why should we not let people choose freely what money they want to use?' (p.121). He insisted that individuals ought to be able freely to choose any currency or commodity (such as gold) for the purposes of enjoying the liquidity services provided. The second point in his 1975 address was historically contingent and did not exclude government fiat money as a choice option if it was responsibly produced. The necessary and sufficient check on responsible behaviour in the production of money was that it was subjected to the discipline of competition. Thus Hayek contends that

> the best thing we could wish governments to do is for, say, all the governments of the Atlantic Community, to bind themselves mutually not to place any restrictions on the free use within their territories of one another's – or any other – currencies, including the purchase and sale at any price the parties decide upon, or on their use as accounting units (1978a, p.121).

In the light of this passage, there was nothing original in Friedman's (1984, p.46) 'alternative' (to Hayek's other more radical preference for fully privatized currencies) which was to 'permit different national currencies to compete with one another'. Writing in an era which was just beginning to witness a diminution of the potency of government exchange controls, fewer restrictions on capital movements and free currency convertibility, Hayek pleaded for free choice in national currencies and completely free cross-border financial capital mobility. He suspected that the so-called government monopolies in the production of currency were already rather circumscribed. Exchange controls were certainly one monopoly bolstering factor as were legal restrictions on the use of specific currencies within national borders. A government's receipts and outlays were obviously going to be compulsorily denominated in that government's fiat money. Nevertheless the idea of isolated groups of residents in a national economies holding one currency for all possible liquidity services was anathema to Hayek, though it was the norm during most of the Bretton Woods era. If the financial borders between national economies were more permeable, currency competition would occur spontaneously within and through other legal restrictions that might remain in place.

Following financial liberalization, various currencies issued by governments pursuing 'responsible monetary policy' would tend to displace gradually those of a 'less reliable character' (p.123). Hayek then mentions monetary policy credibility, that is, the 'reputation of financial righteousness' enjoyed by monetary policymakers.[7] Competition in the realm of currency production would 'impose the most effective discipline on governments'. Furthermore, consistent with competition as a discovery process, 'people would soon learn to hold the government responsible for the value of money in which they were paid' (p.123). And in circumstances where national fiat currencies were related by a system of flexible, market-determined exchange rates, national monetary policies were subject to further competitive discipline (p.125n13). Friedman (1984, p.46) agreed and went further: 'In a world of floating, market determined exchange rates, good money will drive out bad money'. Again portentously, Hayek envisioned a time when '[e]lectronic calculators which in seconds would give the equivalent of any price in any currency at the current rate, would...be used everywhere' (1978a, p.123).

In this new financial world there was no place for an international monetary authority such as the IMF in the Hayekian international financial architecture. Hayek expressed scepticism toward any type of planned international monetary policy coordination either by direct intergovernmental agreements or by international financial institutions as proposed by James Meade. Presumably this scepticism derived from observing the putative inflationary bias built-in to international coordination, such as it was, in the Bretton Woods era. Deliberate international monetary policy coordination can reduce the degree of currency competition and reduce the anti-inflation credibility of government currency issuers. Later this view found support in the contributions of Roland Vaubel (1983) and Kenneth Rogoff (1985) who demonstrated the inflation-generating risks of formal policy coordination among colluding monetary authorities.

At the micro-level the international dimension in Hayek's work turns on allowing individuals to participate in a competitive process in which they are able to switch between national and foreign fiat currencies without government prohibition. He wished to unleash the discovery potential of free choice: unrestricted opportunities to substitute currencies may 'lead to the discovery of yet unknown possibilities in currency' (1978b, p.223). That there may be transaction costs involved in substitution is recognized, though Hayek again portentously (in the

---

[7]Hayek (1978b, pp.208–9) was naturally sceptical of the possibility that 'very wise politically independent' central bankers would retain a responsible reputation for any prolonged period.

1970s) predicted an era when almost instant currency electronic conversion minimizes these costs. In the event, the necessity of having just one currency circulating in a particular national jurisdiction is obviated by advances in communications and currency market trading technology.

The theory of international money was much extended in the 1980s and 1990s; it identified factors contributing to the use of national fiat currencies as domestic financial instruments and as international financial instruments by both residents and non-residents (Chrystal 1984). In this now vast theoretical corpus, Ronald McKinnon (1996b) offered useful conceptualizations of international currency substitution:

i) direct currency substitution: residents in a national jurisdiction are able freely to use multiple currencies for transactions within that domain – they hold transaction balances in various currencies and substitute among them; and

ii) indirect currency substitution: residents in a national jurisdiction choose investment and store of value balances (financial assets etc) denominated in different currencies – this choice indirectly affects the demand for transaction balances in that jurisdiction.

McKinnon (1996b, p.44) was concerned with the macro policy consequences: what if 'currency substitution tends to undermine domestic monetary control?' Hayek's positive answer was that either direct or indirect currency substitution (which he conflated) would weaken national monetary policy; normatively he was convinced that currency substitution should be undermining of any one government's monopoly over the production of money. That national jurisdictions, currency and monetary policy are coextensive and instruments of control are something Hayek inveighed against in his search for 'good money' (Kresge 1999, p.12). In the 1970s he focused on an era (then hypothetical) when these national phenomena were eroded and in which so-called independent national monetary policies were no longer viable in a fully integrated international economy. Therefore, for Hayek, there would be nothing disturbing in McKinnon's (1996b, p.57) conclusions:

> Monetary authorities in an open economy cannot easily distinguish direct from indirect currency substitution. They simply observe pressure for the nominal exchange rate to move up or down depending on portfolio shifts in currency preferences. International investors continually change their relative risk assessments of future price inflation, political stability, the terms of trade, and so forth, and all

of this is (potentially) telescoped back into fluctuations in the spot exchange rate if it is left untethered. At any point in time, the central bank cannot know with any confidence what is dominating the demand for its (base) money.

So much, then, for the allure of monetary policy independence or sovereignty, as promoted by a long line of mid-twentieth century floating exchange rate advocates including Graham, Friedman and Johnson. Being able to pursue an independent monetary policy is one thing; exercising independence was completely another – it was emphatically not costless. This was Hayek's main point.

Much later, in the 1990s, Barry Eichengreen, James Tobin and Charles Wyplosz (1995, p.162) made the costs of exercising independent monetary policy clear: 'modest uncertainty about whether or not monetary authorities are inclined to make use of their theoretical independence can lead to significant financial market volatility. If currencies are fluctuating, they fluctuate widely'. Hayek too was concerned about the effects of such fluctuations in distorting resource allocation, trade and investment as well as creating transaction costs which would be higher in order to cover for exchange rate variability.

A floating market-determined exchange rate regime makes inflation a national problem when there is only one currency produced for domestic use and substitution is prohibited or tightly circumscribed by government restrictions. Certainly, in principle, the trend, rate and variability of inflation may be targeted directly by monetary authorities under floating exchange rates (or indirectly by targeting the interest rate relationship between national and foreign rates). However, there is scarcely any freedom remaining for monetary authorities if one of the prime external influences on national monetary policy is the 'risk' of free currency substitution whether direct or indirect. Individuals will be induced to reassess both the degree of liquidity, and nature of liquidity services provided by a national fiat currency in the light of internal and cross-border monetary disturbances and inflation expectations. Accordingly they realign currency portfolios and their disposition of financial assets denominated in various currencies.

That national currencies produced by governments are distinct (as brands) is unexceptionable; that they are completely independent is questionable even when exchange rate regimes are market-determined and when capital mobility and currency choice is free and transaction costs in currency exchange are quite minimal. In fixed exchange rate regimes buttressed by international currency exchange controls, independence holds strongly within particular 'monetary frontiers' (Hayek 1978b, p.213). Prior to the 1970s Hayek supported fixed currency exchange rates on the grounds that flexible rates between genuinely independent national currencies would too easily spread monetary disturbances in the world economy. Fixed rates might be preferable from Hayek's point of view because of the discipline they impose on monetary authorities – they could not choose an inflation rate with impunity under the influence of day-to-day politics. Fixed exchange rates would act as a nominal anchor, as a disciplining anti-inflation measure for national macroeconomic policy. As Hayek (1994, p.150) related in an interview with Axel Leijonhufvud, 'my defence of fixed exchange rates was, in a way, limited'. He opposed flexible rates only where they were to be used 'in order to make inflation easier'. On this point Robert Mundell and Hayek were in full agreement since on Mundell's (1993, pp.608–11) reading of twentieth century financial history, unanchored flexible exchange rates accommodated monetary policy excesses and allowed too much fiscal profligacy (see also Mundell 2000, p.338).

By contrast, therefore, fixed exchange rates would conceivably act as a good nominal anchor, as an anti-inflation measure for national monetary policy. A national currency could be tied or 'pegged' to another and the peg would be sustainable only so long as monetary policy in the anchor currency country was sufficiently credible. Otherwise, the pegged rate could be subjected to what became known as a speculative attack. Alternatively, taking this view one step further, a nation may want to abandon its currency altogether in favour of one produced more credibly by an anchor country. It would then have no exchange rate regime choice to make.

Hayek wavered among the choices of exchange rate regimes depicted in Figure 3.1 above. Floating market-determined currency exchange rates did not guarantee good, stable international money; this depended on something more fundamental that was absent when Hayek favourably contemplated fixed exchange rates. Choice in currency was a vital condition for a successful floating rate regime. Fixed exchange rates were 'no longer necessary when they [official producers of money] have to submit to the discipline of competition with other issuers of money equally current in their own territory'. He added that the breakdown of monetary frontiers meant users and holders of currency were not constrained by exchange controls 'within their territory' of residence; they were afforded currency choice depending on their requirements for differentiated services that a currency provided. Under these conditions, as Hayek observed, objections to floating exchange rates completely evaporate (1978a, p.125n13).

Three sets of conditions were required to meet Hayek's standard for a viable currency and currency exchange rate regime: (i) absence of capital controls and exchange controls; (ii) 'greater trust...in an internationally reputed issuer of money than in one [producer]...for local circumstances', and (iii) potential for competition which was 'nearly as effective as competition *in esse*' (Hayek 1978b, pp.214–15). The potential for competition rests on enabling market participants to obtain and act on a continuous flow of information about the performance of government currency issuers (Endres 2009). In connection with (i) above, the context in the 1970s and 1980s was one of ongoing restrictions on currency convertibility. Free convertibility was still unusual; its merits and demerits were widely canvassed and discussed in the literature of economics (see e.g., McKinnon 1979). Stanley Black's (1985, p.1157) authoritative survey also discusses currency convertibility in the contemporary conditions of a multi-currency world, as if free convertibility was a relatively new phenomenon. He noted that as of (1978), only 43 out of 141 national currency issuers (amongst IMF members) allowed their national residents free access to foreign exchange markets to buy and sell foreign currency in exchange for domestic currency.

The use of international vehicle currencies illustrates Hayek's position; it denies any need for economists to think in terms of national territories on the one hand, and in terms of deliberately choosing an optimal international currency on the other. Tradable goods producers in one national jurisdiction can account for their trades and settle receipts in currencies other than the dominant national currency used within the territory of origin. This practice became commonplace from the 1970s; vehicle currencies are used for quoting prices, as accounting units, and for settling trades across national borders (Hartmann 1999, pp.14–15). In this process of currency internationalization individuals and financial institutions residing in a particular jurisdiction accept and use 'foreign' fiat currencies. In the limit, every national currency is potentially able to play a role as an international vehicle depending on the outcome of competition and substitution in their use and demands for their respective services. The theory of international currency substitution incorporating these considerations was not completely delineated as a branch of literature in economics until the early 1980s (Giovannini and Turtelboom 1994). That literature developed the distinction between different types of international currency, that is, between vehicle currencies, official reserve currencies and investment currencies. In principle in respect of these various functions, drawing sharp distinctions between currency and noncurrency was not worthwhile (Hayek 1978b, p.161). Currencies were just objects offering various services and fixing their rate of exchange with other currencies was not as crucial as allowing free flow of capital across national borders and free choice in currency for various purposes. In practice, the favoured vehicle or central bank reserve or private investment currencies in any circumstance could not be fully planned by governments, by IFIs, or be determined by the exchange rate regime. In the long history of money used in the international economy, no government or economist has been able to define, once-and-for-all, a single currency or choose an optimal currency exchange rate regime that would satisfy all prospective users' requirements, even though some have tried.[8]

Early arguments against intermediate regimes

In the light of Hayek's important contributions in the 1970s, the points in Figure 3.1 presented earlier in this chapter may now be extended and elaborated. See Table 3.1 below in which there are only two polar cases in column two headed: 'Appropriate Exchange Rate Regime', or as Frankel

Table 3.1   Polar Cases for Exchange Rate Regimes

Domestic purchasing power of national currencies (as determined by national price levels)	*Appropriate exchange rate regime*	*Monetary policy implications*
1. Moves independently among nations	Proportionately fluctuating: market-determined	Monetary sovereignty, national choice of price level
2. Moves in unison – same direction and magnitude in given time periods	Fixed	Policy bound by international covenant as in a monetary union OR policy sovereignty, fortuitously coordinated
3. Moves in some nations and not in others	Proportionately fluctuating: market-determined	Monetary sovereignty, national choice of price level
4. Remains stable in all nations	Fixed	Policy coordination bound by international covenant, or by monetary union

---

[8]For example, at Bretton Woods Keynes wished to create a new international currency. In the Bretton Woods era Robert Triffin and Jacques Rueff made attempts to define a generic international currency (Endres 2005, pp.102–26, 158–62).

(1999, p.7) called them, two 'dreamed-of sanctuaries' that could blunt speculative forces threatening to create exchange rate stability.

Obviously either polar case is acceptable and sustainable; it all depends on whether or not monetary policy can be bound by international agreements or by monetary union. The rare case of fortuitous policy coordination cannot genuinely be associated with a choice of optimal exchange rate regimes for the world economy as a whole or for any group of countries or regions. Clearly, from Table 3.1, all exchange rate regime choices must be made in the knowledge that the real value of currencies, that is, the domestic purchasing power of national currencies, and the conduct of monetary policy in relation to those currencies crucially affects the viability and feasibility of any choice.

The fundamental outlook on exchange rate choices common to Hayek (1978a and 1978b), Johnson (1969 and 1972a), Machlup (1972), Haberler (1980), and Friedman (1984) was formed in the knowledge that cross-border capital movements were (or should be) completely free. In that circumstance exchange rate choices must be based on real not nominal exchange rates. There was, in this view, no really intermediate exchange rate regime that could be chosen for long-run stability; only market-determined or fully fixed exchange rate regimes were viable in the long run. Much later in the period under review, the removal of any middle ground choice is also supported by Barry Eichengreen (1994) following extensive historical research on the performance of alternative exchange rate regimes. Later, US Treasury secretary Lawrence Summers (2000, p.8) represented a large group of prominent economists when he remarked that choosing an

> Appropriate exchange rate regime...for economies with access to international capital markets, increasingly means a move away from the middle ground of pegged but adjustable fixed exchange rates towards the two corner solutions of either flexible exchange rates or a fixed exchange rate supported, if necessary, by a commitment to give up altogether an independent monetary policy.

Regime choice cannot be divorced from the choice of monetary policy arrangements and indeed, that choice is subordinated to monetary policy. As long as the supply of money is government controlled, the conduct of monetary policy influences the market for foreign exchange irrespective of whether or not that policy directly targets the exchange rate. Similarly, monetary policy matters for the foreign exchange market irrespective of the role government might play by directly intervening in that market.

A currency tends to derive its value from its purchasing power relative to other currencies. Table 3.1 indicates that policies designed to maintain an exchange rate at levels deviating from domestic purchasing power for a prolonged period will be misguided. As Machlup (1972, p.93) concluded, any intermediate exchange rate regime such as a fixed, adjustable rate was unsustainable: 'The system of rigid rates pegged for years at wrong levels and supported by selective restriction and bureaucratic controls of trade, payments, and capital movements, is thoroughly discredited'. Furthermore, speculative capital movements are encouraged when exchange rates are maintained at untenable levels. Indeed, continued Machlup, speculation 'is rampant just before pegs are removed and again after pegs are reset at levels which the market judges to be wrong' (pp.92–3). To be sure, movements in market-determined exchange rates may deviate for some time from reflecting the international purchasing power of a currency; this may need to occur in order to correct persistent disequilibrium in the current account of a nation's balance of payments. Such a disequilibrium may have been forthcoming from a major supply shock. It is also possible that changes in market-determined rates do not immediately reflect inflation differentials between nations; they therefore may reflect inappropriate real exchange rates for reasons that are due to the foreign exchange market being an imperfect communication mechanism. Information flows are by no means perfect. The Hayek, Friedman, Johnson, Machlup and Haberler group generally held that decisionmakers in foreign exchange markets will systematically make corrections to past errors based on misinformation.

Notwithstanding shocks, information imperfections and decision-making errors, the trajectory of thought running from Graham to Friedman, Johnson, Hayek and others, turned on the importance of monetary conditions and associated price level movements in choosing the most appropriate exchange rate regime. Gottfried Haberler (1980, p.46) summarized the practical, real world implications deriving from the polar cases presented in Table 3.1, for the circumstances facing policymakers in the late 1970s and early 1980s. There was, in short, no possibility of a sustainable set of international exchange rate choices that constituted a mixing and matching of intermediate regimes. Thus, according to Machlup,

the ideal international monetary order would be a universal system of fixed exchange rates, provided it could operate without imposing excessive inflation in some countries, too much unemployment in others, or stifling controls in both. Unfortunately, the best system is impossible in a world of high inflation and a high degree of downward wage and price rigidity. In such a world we have to accept the second best – the widespread use of floating exchange rates.

In fact the choice between either fully fixed or floating rates would not be so problematic if all prices were perfectly flexible. In that happy situation either regime would produce the same outcome.[9] The only way a universal system of fixed rates could possibly be implemented is with governments agreeing to be disciplined by, and adjust their domestic policies in accordance with, a rule-bound and enforceable international agreement. In Haberler's view, shared by Friedman, Hayek and others, the exchange rate regime is more likely to be adjustable or continuously changeable, depending on the degree of independence a government chose to have over its domestic monetary policy. Markets were better, through not perfect, stabilizers of exchange rates than governments, all the more so if macroeconomic policies were not properly integrated between countries. Finally, governments can change laws and policies at will.

Limiting variability: Cases for intermediate regimes

One feature in the choice of exchange rate regimes during the period from the 1970s, is the wide division of opinion over intermediate regimes. The consensus, if there was one, seemed to be concentrated around the need for greater flexibility than obtained during the BW era, but not so much as would have been the case in a market-determined, floating rate system. As we have seen, governments can intervene in foreign exchange markets indirectly, even when a so-called market-determined exchange rate regime is chosen. Monetary policy is not divorced from determining the value of a national currency relative to others. The proponents of various intermediate regimes desired more direct government intervention in foreign exchange markets. Many

---

[9]If relative prices (internationally) adjusted instantaneously, monetary authorities 'could then stabilize their money stocks and let the foreign-exchange market determine nominal exchange rates, or could peg exchange rates, and let the market determine national money stocks' (Kenen 1988, p.20). If output prices are slow to adjust, nominal exchange rates affect real exchange rates and these have an important influence on the level, composition and location of production across national borders.

countries in fact chose intermediate regimes during the post-BW era. We shall discuss the arguments for three types of intermediate regime in what follows.

1. Flexible 'bands' or 'target zones'

With rising international capital mobility, continued use of the BW-type fixed, occasionally adjustable, exchange rate regime became impracticable. Speculative pressures were becoming too powerful (Williamson 1976, p.55). John Williamson believed that the volatility of pure market-determined exchange rates resulted in an 'anti-trade bias'; it was nevertheless a belief that could not easily be demonstrated empirically (p.57). Foreign exchange markets were generally not efficient in a macroeconomic sense. Richard Cooper (1984a) kept good company with Williamson in expressing serious doubts about the movements of market-determined exchange rates. The repercussions of prolonged misalignments in currency values would be visited upon the real economy, that is, upon the allocation of real resources, sometimes for instance, with deleterious effects particularly in the area of capital formation. Here exchange rate variability induces risk premia that can delay crucial investment decisions.

> Abrupt up and down movements in exchange rates are not, by themselves, likely to affect trade and production very much, since they should reasonably be expected to be reversed soon if they are not clearly linked to more fundamental economic developments. The difficulty with flexible exchange rates is that another influence is also at work, which can transmute the influence of noisy news into larger changes in exchange rates than otherwise would take place. It is the presence of crowd or bandwagon effects in the trading community. Few know how to interpret the news. Many use a movement in the exchange rate itself as a source of information about market sentiment. So as to avoid being left behind, they jump on the bandwagon, thus pushing the exchange rate further in the direction it tended to go initially (Cooper 1984a, p.27).

Like Cooper, a long line of commentators had, by the 1990s, reflected on the experience with floating exchange rates from the 1970s and they found that market determination often moved currency values out-of-line with fundamental economic conditions, producing 'bandwagon' effects and other market excesses (Aliber 1987; Mussa et al. 1994, pp.33, 34; also Cooper 1999, p.114).

In order to dampen volatility and misalignment, Williamson proposed that monetary authorities adopt a 'band' or 'zone', intervening in foreign exchange markets when their currency threatened to hit the margins on either side of the band (Williamson 1985b, 1986; Williamson and Miller 1987). Actual setting of an exchange rate band would require some clairvoyance; it would demand considerable technical expertise in finding a fundamental equilibrating band in which some balance of payments (on current account) target would also have to be distilled. These would not be easy tasks. A monetary authority would form an idea just where it wanted the exchange rate to be for example against a common basket of other currencies; it would also need to have a broad notion of what long-run exchange rate would be appropriate, because short-run bands must incorporate long-run trends in economic fundamentals. Richard Cooper (1984a) and Robert Roosa (1984) gave their support to the exchange rate band idea. While the proposed band (or target zone) regime would impose constraints on domestic monetary and fiscal policy, if widely adopted it would lead to more extensive international macroeconomic policy coordination since international pressure would be brought to bear to keep exchange rates within the chosen bands. Thus 'nations would agree on some set of soft currency target zones and each nation would intervene in foreign exchange markets...and agree to international monetary cooperation in varying degrees, depending on their different circumstances, so as to minimize the cost of domestic adjustment to international disequilibria' (Salvatore 1995b, p.513). Furthermore, the IMF would play a role in multilateral surveillance of band-keeping activities. By far the most important merit of the proposal was that it would anchor exchange rate expectations in foreign exchange markets and thereby stabilize otherwise volatile currency movements. Paul Krugman (1989a, 1989b and 1991a) offered mild support for Williamson's approach, demonstrating that if a credible band could be specified, currency speculation would be a potentially stabilizing factor; expectations of future exchange rate changes would be rendered constant rather than variable by the band-anchoring technique. The commitment (and longer-term time consistency) of monetary authorities and their monetary policies was crucial to band maintenance.

As long as the option is kept open to change the band, this 'flexible band' exchange rate regime carried with it all the vagaries of the BW, fixed-adjustable regime and it would remain vulnerable to speculative attack. This weakness applies to any fixed regime including the 'basket peg' approach that fixes exchange rates in terms of several or many foreign currencies in a trade-weighted basket structure. Incidentally, Williamson (1999) continued to favour fixed exchange rate regimes (rather than a band) for East Asian economies following the Asian financial crisis in the 1990s. In the 1980s Rudiger Dornbusch (1987, p.16) added a degree of scepticism toward fixing exchange rates in the manner of setting zones or bands. His position was representative of a contrasting thought trajectory on this subject that was developing momentum at the time:

> The case for fixing exchange rates whatever the source of the disturbance is advanced by those favouring target zones. Their position is that exchange rates do not necessarily reflect fundamentals but rather irrationality, bandwagons, and eccentricity. The large movements in exchange rates interfere with macroeconomic stability, but they can and should be avoided by a firm commitment to exchange rate targets. On the surface it is difficult to see any difficulty with this prescription, but on further inspection...it is certainly not an established fact that exchange rates move irrationally and without links to fundamentals. Or, if they do move in this way, it is not clear that they do so more than stock prices or long-term bond prices. Why single out one price for fixing if it may mean that the other prices have to move even further away from their fundamental equilibrium values?

2.   Managed floating (with or without sterilized intervention)

Other than pure, free market exchange rate determination, episodic management or smoothing techniques were also popular during the post-BW era. The group of economists developing this trajectory of thought realized that floating rates could be helpful shock absorbers for external economic disturbances; such rates do not, as a consequence, encourage countries to adopt more trade policy protection or undergo severe deflation or inflation as means toward adjusting their external imbalances in the aftermath of such shocks.

The doctrinal basis of the managed floating regime was that foreign exchange markets do not work efficiently all of the time. Economists could remain altogether agnostic on this subject given that the strength of arguments for the efficiency of foreign exchange markets depended on the circumstances in which they were applied. Notable economists in this group, who we may say developed an eclectic view in this regard, included Peter Kenen (1988, pp.24–30) at Princeton, Max Corden (1983, p.63) at Johns Hopkins, and Rudiger Dornbusch (1980,

1987) at MIT. These economists were attuned to not only particular branches of exchange rate theory; they also kept open minds on the empirical evidence being provided on the determination of exchange rates and on the effects of intervention in exchange rate markets. A pragmatic view developed in favour of using monetary policy combined with exchange market intervention, systematically to stabilize floating exchange rates.

It was initially thought that intervention policies should be coordinated in major world economies in connection, at least, with the major currencies at the time (the yen, US dollar and mark). For example, in the most elementary case, the process would operate as follows: if a monetary authority intervened in the foreign exchange market and buys (supports) the domestic currency, it would then 'sterilize' these purchases by open market, monetary operations. The authority would sell that many fewer government bonds to the public so that the domestic money supply would be the same as it would have been before the exchange market intervention. This policy is tantamount to sending a signal that the monetary authority will intervene to smooth-out what it deems an unnecessary downward fluctuation in the international value of the national currency, without altering the domestic money supply. In this case the signal is intended to cause currency speculators to expect a possible increase in the international price of the national currency in the future. Accordingly, speculators begin buying that currency and bring about the necessary stabilization desired by the monetary authority without the necessity for further, and larger, exchange market interventions.

Rudiger Dornbusch (1980, p.182) warned that weak signals of the foregoing kind would not always be sufficient and 'large-scale sterilized interventions' would often be required to dampen exchange rate fluctuations. Certainly this interdiction would apply to some currencies in which there was significant depth and private market trading; small country currencies could also be subject to destabilization from large capital movements that could easily overwhelm relatively modest attempts to intervene in currency markets, let alone sterilize those interventions. While Dornbusch generally gave praise to pragmatic attempts by major industrial nations to smooth-out floating exchange rates, empirical research began to bolster the cause for interventions (if at all) without sterilization. In the 1980s, research initiated by the Jurgenson Report (1983) commissioned by the G-7 Economic Summit in 1982, was not all that supportive (Henderson and Sampson 1983; Rogoff 1984). Later, conflicting evidence was offered by Dominiguez and Frankel (1993). Overall the evidence was inconclusive; it all depended on the case, on the episode in currency fluctuation that a monetary authority was attempting to affect. In any case, the long-term benefits of sterilizing interventions were suspect and were not yet resolved. The short explanation for this conclusion turns on the very fact of ongoing international financial market integration in the post-BW era, and in this instance on bond market integration. If bond (or other financial asset) substitution was high and becoming more complete across national boundaries, then sterilized interventions working through bond market manipulation would not have much impact. As Peter Kenen (1988, p.40) summarized the problem:

> When foreign and domestic assets are very close substitutes, sterilized intervention is ineffective, a central-bank transaction in foreign currencies cannot have different exchange-rate effects from a central-bank transaction in domestic bonds, so one will cancel the other.

The more financial markets become integrated internationally, the more it was likely that foreign exchange markets would become good predictors of future spot exchange rates regardless of attempts by monetary authorities to manage current floating rates. Nevertheless this argument was not sufficient to deny the cogency of arguments for some form of managed floating that rested on the negative short-term resource-allocative effects of considerable exchange rate variations.

By the early 1990s an influential group of IMF economists were becoming more (though not completely) certain about the 'right' choice of exchange rate regime. They returned to a concern originally raised by Dornbusch – will the intermittent exchange market interventions be large enough to matter, given rising international capital flows?

> Sterilized exchange market intervention may be useful for helping to calm disorderly markets, and even, on occasion, for sending signals to the markets about policy intentions and exchange rate objectives. However, it is simply not potent enough in today's world of enormous and agile private international capital flows to manage exchange rates on its own when the markets have a concerted and determined view that a prevailing exchange rate is not sustainable (Mussa et al. 1994, p.3).

Direct exchange rate smoothing schemes may have a minor short-term impact on a currency but that is all. Indeed, by the 1990s even the 'managed floating' advocates were swinging back toward the Graham-

Friedman-Johnson-Hayek thought trajectory. Definitely, floating exchange rates would show less volatility under stable policy conditions. The IMF policy outlook, widely shared by a growing number of economists in the 1990s, promoted the use of monetary policy to target price level stability (rather than exchange rate stability in the first instance). A discernible shift in intellectual attitude took place in the late 1980s and 1990s. In this view fiscal discipline must be maintained and internal structural adjustment policies should be adopted to produce more efficient labour and product markets. As they related to choice of exchange rate regime, these policies applied just as much to any choice of regime. If countries with poor records of price stability chose to fix their currencies in some manner, monetary policy targeting price level stability would be easier to implement given that the exchange rate acted as a nominal anchor. In countries that largely allowed their currencies to float, monetary, fiscal, and structural adjustment policies could be designed to assist in minimizing currency fluctuations caused by internal economic conditions. Of course this IMF policy line was not divorced from a desire to provide an underlying rationale for the continuing relevance of the IMF. In this connection, it was the practice of IMF surveillance that should focus on getting the domestic economic fundamentals in order irrespective of the exchange rate regime. The IMF economists had been persuaded that there was not much advantage in seeking new devices directly to manage floating exchange rates (Mussa et al. 1994).

3.   Other arguments for fixed exchange rates and currency boards

In the face of a professional consensus moving toward market-determined exchange rates and currency unions, several prominent economists maintained a trajectory of thought opposed to the prevailing intellectual shift. That group may loosely be aligned with ideas originally but not wholly due to John Maynard Keynes. Against the consensus, represented by surveys and overviews on exchange rate regime choices by Martin Feldstein (1993) and Stanley Fischer (2001), James Tobin only gave qualified and grudging support for flexible exchange rates. Unilateral solutions to exchange rate choice, for example either: (i) choosing a market-determined exchange rate regime to gain national monetary policy independence, or (ii) choosing a managed floating regime with loose international policy coordination, could engender international financial instability. By the 1990s, unlike his position in the 1970s, Tobin agreed that the world had to accept widespread adoption of market-determined exchange rates (Eichengreen et al. 1995, p.162). More than before in Tobin's (1987) view, floating exchange rate regimes had to be buttressed by formal international policy coordination. Even for the world's largest economically dominant nations, complete monetary policy independence was a mirage in an increasingly integrated global economy. In this, Tobin drew support from others who favored macroeconomic policy cooperation if not formal coordination (Kenen 1988 Chapter 6; Bryant 1995; Goldstein 1994). Tobin remained adamant that a system of floating exchange rates without formal international policy coordination would lead to international financial anarchy. Reminiscent of Keynes in the 1930s and 1940s, Tobin (1982, p.126) suspected that much foreign exchange market activity was driven by animal spirits, by 'speculation on future speculation'. Policy coordination was imperative; it needed to manage this kind of activity and generate institutional arrangements and 'innovations...to reduce exchange rate instability and assure a modicum of national monetary autonomy' (Eichengreen et al. 1995, p.171).

Other important contributions to the exchange rate choice debate, all of which proposed some form of fixed rate, should also be mentioned here. First place should be accorded to Robert Mundell who made a major contribution to the study of the international financial architecture in the BW era (Endres 2005, pp.188–203). In the post-BW era he did not produce a formal plan that could be regarded as a complete blueprint for exchange rate regime choice. However he was convinced that exchange rates needed an anchor and should be fixed to that anchor. In some respects his approach to the issue would have been similar (as we shall see in Chapter 7 below on currency unions) to Richard Cooper's (1984b) plan that extended the idea of a 'single currency' to the world as a whole. Mundell's (1993) preference was that the IMF create and manage an international currency (such as the existing IMF-managed SDR) so that it may eventually 'evolve into a genuine international currency' (See also Mundell 1994, p.80). Mundell (1993) alluded to two other possibilities both of which anchored currencies to a commodity stock: (i) the creation of a commodity reserve for anchoring currencies, established according to an internationally agreed basket of durable commodities and (ii) anchoring (on an experimental basis) national currencies to a single commodity, notably gold.

A second group of economists developed a position that was essentially Keynesian in spirit – here the leading thinkers were Paul Krugman (1989b, 1992) at MIT, Paul Davidson (1992–93, 2000) University of Tennessee and Lance Taylor (1991, 1993 and also Taylor and Eatwell 2000) New School For Social Research, New York. All three began with the presupposition that speculative activity on foreign exchange markets was inherently destabilizing and that instability is transferred across national borders and to the real economy; it was not, in short, a purely contained, financial market phenomenon. The impacts of currency instability were profound – they reverberated on employment, specific industries and large scale, long-term investment decisions. As we shall see in Chapter 5 below, periodic financial and foreign exchange market instabilities and crises that punctuated the post-BW era gave some support to this view. In fact, during the post-BW era the term financial 'contagion' entered the discourse of economics as a summary description for the transference of exchange market volatility.

In the Krugman-Davidson-Taylor view, foreign exchange markets are not like any other commodity market; they trade financial capital and securities across national borders. In addition, those markets are only effective when allocating short-term capital because they operate on a short-term time horizon, despite the fact that quite sophisticated instruments for currency trading in the present and future had evolved along with floating exchange rates. Completely free market-based currency markets increase the extent to which short-term capital movements are accommodated at the expense of more productive long-term cross-border capital flows. Krugman (1989b, p.71) proposed a reversion to a BW-style, fixed, adjustable system but with a much deeper and explicit set of commitments by all major industrial nations to defend parities come-what-may. However, in the final analysis he was not completely sure such a system was workable in practice:

> My position is...interventionist. I have argued that the old-fashioned view that exchange markets are prone to destabilizing speculation is nearer the truth than the Friedman view...This means that the same argument used to justify the Bretton Woods system remains valid today...What is needed is a system in which the commitment to try to defend parities is explicit...[and] it can work for the world as a whole – maybe (p.71).

Lance Taylor always kept the problems of less developed countries and transition economies in view; he seemed to come close to advocating a scheme in which direct intervention to manage exchange rates between the world's major currencies (the US dollar, yen and (pending) euro) in tight exchange rate bands would enable other smaller and developing nations to peg their exchange rates to one or other of this trio. Paul Davidson (1997) chimed in with a similar message though he understood the pressing need not merely for binding monetary policy coordination to defend parities; he also argued cogently for controls on international capital flows because the defence of fixed exchange rates necessitated control over disruptive short-term capital movements. (We shall consider the arguments for capital controls in more detail in Chapter 4 below).

Lastly, in the category of fixed exchange rate regimes and associated doctrine, is the 'currency board' arrangement. This approach to regime choice was developed less as a coherent doctrine and more as a practical exigency – an operational response to finding a solid, nominal anchor for a nation's currency. More often than not, such nations had a poor record with inflation control. The currency board approach enshrines the nominal exchange rate peg in a law binding the monetary authority to issue new national currency (new monetary liabilities) through purchases of foreign currency assets at a given, fixed exchange rate. Thus each domestic currency amount is backed by an equivalent amount of foreign reserves. The result is quite direct in its impact on balance of payments adjustments; a current account deficit immediately contracts the domestic money supply and vice versa. Many small nations, emerging market economies and developing countries chose this approach in the post-BW era either because they previously had low monetary policy credibility or because they were in the process of transitioning from a planned economy to a more market-based system. In these cases a low level of financial market development also hampered a quick move to a fully market-determined exchange rate system. Essentially, the choice of the currency board option is based on the idea of importing monetary policy credibility and monetary policy time-consistency. One principal advantage was that if credibility and consistency could be demonstrated for long enough under the currency board structure, foreign investment would be encouraged. The historical experience during the post-BW era with the currency board option produced mixed results (Ghosh et al. 2000).

As with all fixed exchange rate regimes the rule of law is critical for the currency board option to operate; a domestic financial system that is sufficiently supportive is also a prerequisite. Both must function to avoid abuse of the currency board regime – abuse that might take the form of the wilful adoption of parallel currencies, evasion of currency board regulations, spontaneous public adoption of foreign currencies for many domestic and international transactions, and so on. As Frankel (1999, p.16) maintained, the mere pronouncement of the adoption of a currency board scheme does not guarantee its durability if 'laws are not heeded or changed at will'. Furthermore, the currency board

required a counsel of perfection, that is, 'solid fundamentals of adequate reserves, fiscal discipline and a strong and well-supervised financial
system' (Frankel 1999, p.16).

Ronald McKinnon's grand currency reform scheme

For most of the post-BW era Ronald McKinnon at Stanford University
worked tirelessly to formulate a complete reform scheme for the IFS,
which would replace existing national exchange rate regimes. He took
the view that the operation of contemporary foreign exchange markets
imposed significant costs on production and employment. His first
important contribution on this subject (McKinnon 1974) viewed completely market-determined exchange rates with scepticism. Increasingly as
the end of the century beckoned more nations were choosing market-
determined, unanchored exchange rates, imitating those of leading industrial nations (Emminger 1984, p.207). Yet in McKinnon's mind foreign
exchange markets were fundamentally inefficient in respect of their impact
on the real economy.

McKinnon argued that persistent current account deficits or surpluses
were likely a reflection of inappropriate governmental finances, including the conduct of fiscal policy. This argument had Keynesian connotations. Exchange rate changes in these circumstances would have little
impact on the current account imbalance and only tend to 'generate
serious financial instability' in the domestic economy (McKinnon 1981,
p.555). By contrast, the contemporary monetary interpretation of the
balance of payments and of exchange rate determination closely associated with flexible exchange rate advocates (especially, though not exclusively at the University of Chicago e.g. Frenkel and Johnson 1976 and
Johnson 1977), simply explained exchange rate volatility by pointing to
inappropriate monetary policies. Indeed, the monetary approach linked
sharp upward or downward movement in currency values to excess
supplies or demands of those national currencies (Rabin and Yeager 1982).
The focus on monetary forces alone had a substantial, implicit policy
implication: governments should stabilize domestic monetary conditions
first; exchange rate stability follows automatically. McKinnon (1981,
p.555) rejected this doctrine:

> The monetarists' advocacy of floating, combined with unchanging
> growth in some domestic monetary aggregate, implicitly presumes
> that the demand for each national money is stable and not much
> influenced by events in the foreign exchange market. If, from time

to time, national monetary systems are buffeted by individuals and firms, switching from one convertible currency to another – for reasons that may or may not be justified – then official action to stabilize the (nominal) exchange rate is warranted.

The matter became more complex when, in fact, the US dollar (or perhaps a small collection of major currencies) had to retain some semblance of stability given that it was the main international currency. In this case the US dollar would become a *de facto* anchor for the entire IFS. Yet the anchor was inherently flawed inasmuch as it was not tied to a binding international agreement or to a commodity such as gold (as in the BW era). What transpired in the post-BW era was essentially a system of currency regime choices imperfectly anchored to a floating rate US dollar standard (McKinnon 1996a, p.65). In this system interventionist currency smoothing methods were employed by major non-US monetary authorities without commitment to specific par values with the US dollar. The USA pursued monetary policies without too much regard for the floating rate value of the US dollar or the conduct of monetary policy and monetary conditions elsewhere. At the time, monetary policy was employed to determine interest rates which were, in turn, a variable used for countercyclical policy essentially formulated in a Keynesian manner. In short, the US monetary authorities were largely preoccupied with independently targeting domestic macroeconomic conditions including the US price level. There was no serious attempt made to anchor monetary policy to a common international price level (at least one common to major industrial nations).

Later in the post-BW era attempts were made by US monetary authorities to smooth US dollar fluctuations and episodically engineer specifically desired changes in the value of the US dollar in an accord with Germany and Japan. The accord had limited short-term success precisely because it relied on sterilized intervention in the face of large, unrestricted international capital flows (McKinnon 1996a, pp.65–73).

Likewise, McKinnon's plan was founded on the idea of formal international policy coordination at least among the US, Japan, Germany and perhaps other major European currency producers. These countries would formulate a plan for international monetary control to which other countries could choose to bind their exchange rate regimes. There would be a common monetary policy formulated for key industrial countries based on an agreed common standard for price-levels targeted, in turn, by monetary policies. As for exchange rates, these would essentially become stable if not fixed between the major economies. As Robert

Mundell (1993, p.611) had always argued, 'fixed exchange rates will not work in a vacuum'. McKinnon worked on finding an anchor for a relatively fixed exchange rate system and he found it in an international arrangement based on using monetary policy to stabilize a common price level. In the event, currency instability would be reduced and periodic bouts of high inflation followed by economic contraction would be avoided. McKinnon was sure that completely unexpected monetary disturbances cause currency fluctuations. These disturbances mostly arise from changes in international demands for money and associated cross-border currency substitution in investment portfolios. Those changes were a response to changes in expectations of inflation caused by a wide range of economic and political events in particular countries. An international agreement to target a common price level would, he believe, minimize the impact of such national events. And the shock-absorber role of highly flexible exchange rates would become redundant.

In practice, a cooperating monetary authority would need to relinquish its 'discretionary power to persistently inflate its price level at a rate differing from the common standard on which the coordinating group of major industrial nations had agreed' (McKinnon 1988, p.88). Finding that common standard presented practical difficulties, though not necessarily insurmountable problems. It should be calculated by estimating the purchasing power parity of wholesale prices. According to McKinnon (1988, p.92; 1996a, pp.78–80) monetary policies in different countries would aim to keep stable the common wholesale price index on internationally tradeable goods.[10] Whether measured in dollars, yen, marks (or later, euros), McKinnon's scheme for exchange rates assures, in principle, a nominal anchor for the entire system of key currency exchange rates. Aggregate monetary growth and the total growth of domestic credit could be targeted by monetary authorities as proximate objectives without the need for sterilizing interventions in foreign exchange markets. In summary, McKinnon was advocating a return to a fixed nominal exchange rate system between major currencies; it was a system

---

[10]Wholesale tradeable goods prices eliminate consumption taxes, retail mark-ups and generally exclude services. Actual consumer prices reflect all these. Therefore, there is room in McKinnon's scheme for real wage adjustments between nations because consumer prices would not be targeted by monetary policies. The scheme would not, however, have due regard for real wage flexibility induced by changes to labor productivity outside the major industrialized nations that were part of the proposed agreement. Here the emerging market economies and East Asian economies come to mind.

requiring careful, detailed monetary policy agreements between leading currency producers in the 1980s.

McKinnon's scheme was not adopted. Among other weaknesses, Dornbusch (1988a, p.111) underscored a crucial point: cooperation over monetary policy would not necessarily be enough to stabilize a common price level and thence exchange rates. Implicit in any case for fixed exchange rates was the need to coordinate fiscal policies as well: 'if fiscal coordination cannot be taken for granted, one cannot simply go ahead and announce the desirability of fixed exchange rates with monetary rules'. Dornbusch illustrated his argument with the case of US fiscal expansion driven by purely domestic considerations that would lead to increasing domestic credit growth and contraction elsewhere. (This is because interest rates would rise internationally). Japan, Germany and other major US trading partners would experience an economic downturn. Dornbusch added two other important criticisms of McKinnon's scheme. First, and quite presciently, newly industrializing countries in East Asia and South America would soon become major contributors to world trade and require, if not force, significant relative price and wage adjustments internationally. Removing exchange rate variability between the US, Japan and Germany – countries in which wages in particular were relatively inflexible by comparison with Asia and South America – would shift much of the burden of international adjustment to payments imbalances on to labour markets and production in the major economies. If nominal exchange rates are fixed by agreement, real exchange rate adjustments require speedy changes in domestic consumer prices and wages; if these are slow to adjust then the costs of nominal exchange rate fixing can be high in terms of lost output and employment. So Dornbusch concludes: nominal exchange rate change and variability is not always undesirable. Flexible exchange rates would, by contrast, allow major relative cost differences between nations to be reflected quickly across all markets.

Secondly, Dornbusch questions the feasibility of formal, detailed international monetary policy agreements given differences in 'economic philosophy'. Thus Germany, and to a lesser extent Japan, were notoriously more inclined to reduce inflation at any cost (e.g. more willing to engineer a recession) presumably for the long-term benefits that would be realized as a consequence, such as a more stable mark or yen respectively. Historically, policy preferences in the United States were patently different. McKinnon's plan was 'flawed from the outset' (Dornbusch 1988a, p.111) because it subordinated national interests and rankings of key economic policy goals to an international agreement. One or other nation would have to change the order of those goals to make the plan work.

McKinnon's answer would probably have been that the alternative was unilateral central bank action to influence exchange rate movements in an *ad hoc* manner (from an international standpoint) as the unique ranking of national policy goals demanded. In the event, this alternative was the obvious default option for policy in a world of high exchange rate flexibility, given divergent national policy-goal rankings. By the late 1980s evidence began to appear more frequently that called into question the so-called instability of floating exchange rates, suggesting that those rates were less volatile than many other asset prices in markets where government intervention was non-existent (Frankel and Goldstein 1989). Be that as it may, economists' opinions on the most appropriate exchange rate regimes, even for the leading world currencies, were not static during the post-BW era. Those opinions were like trajectories of thought – as we established in Chapter 1 – ever moving on the margins at least, in response to analysis of economic events, policy successes and failures, changes in the sophistication of financial markets and financial market institutions, and political realities. Nevertheless, distinguishable core trajectories remained on recognizable, divergent paths.

Conclusion

In the post-BW era, the problem of choosing an exchange regime produced some important doctrinal divisions in the literature of economics. Paul Krugman (1989b, p.71) was right to observe that the exchange rate debate during this period

> is full of strange bed-fellows; advocates of flexible rates may be traditional monetarists who want freedom to target their favourite aggregate or Keynesians who want to be able to pursue active stabilization policy; advocates of fixed exchange rates may be either global monetarists who want a monetary anchor or interventionist-minded economists who distrust financial markets.

While exchange rate policy prescriptions among prominent economists in the field occasionally changed in the period, they did not change so much as to obscure or radically alter underlying doctrinal beliefs on the role of currency valuation mechanisms and variations in currency exchange rates in the international economy.

The non-interventionist minded economists with whom we began this chapter held a consistent line of argument throughout the period under review such that, even with a vast amount of empirical evidence on exchange rate determination and experience with different exchange rate regimes, the bases of their argument remained essentially intact. Their argument may still be reduced to the list of advantages of market-determined exchange rates originally espoused in Graham's, Freidman's and Johnson's work during the BW era. Their post-BW followers may not have believed that foreign-exchange markets operate smoothly and completely efficiently, but the intervention of monetary authorities would, in their view, come with few benefits and make those markets less efficient. Hayek initially favoured fixed rates because of the monetary anchor requirement that Krugman refers to in the foregoing passage. Hayek then switched to supporting floating rates given the widespread free choice of currencies in the increasing market-based integration of global financial markets observed in the 1980s.

Here we should note the views of several economists emerging to prominence in the 1990s who contributed significantly to debates over the design of the international financial architecture and choice of exchange rate regime in particular. The open economy international macroeconomic ideas of Maurice Obstfeld and Kenneth Rogoff come to the fore in their article 'The Mirage of Fixed Exchange Rates' (1995) and also more comprehensively in Obstfeld and Rogoff (1996). Their 1995 exchange rates article for the most part reiterates the market-oriented position outlined earlier in this Chapter. In addition, they bring to bear more empirical evidence than was adduced by Graham, Friedman and Johnson, and they draw similar conclusions. They begin with the proposition that foreign exchange markets in the 1990s are broadly efficient. Their doctrine may be summarized as follows:

1. Changing regime choices from floating exchange rates to some form of fixed rates (other than a currency and monetary union) was not only infeasible; it was undesirable because the costs of any accompanying capital controls to make par values sustainable would be too high and the degree of international macro policy coordination would involve intolerable sacrifice of national policy objectives.
2. Economic fundamentals are broadly responsible for exchange rates; deterioration in those fundamentals increases vulnerability to sudden speculative currency attacks on currencies that are market-determined or fixed in some way (Obstfeld 1994a). Speculative attacks can occur regardless of the exchange rate regime.
3. Enduring changes in exchange rates are ultimately associated with patterns of relative price changes across national borders that reflect underlying cross-border costs of production. This is the case even

when domestic input and product markets do not adjust as quickly as do currency values.

4. Monetary policy stability is the key to exchange rate stability and not vice-versa. Therefore monetary policy institutions need reform; central banks must become independent of day-to-day politics and should concentrate on achieving national price level stability.

5. Sterilized intervention measures to manage floating exchange rates have limited usefulness and impact.

6. Policymakers' commitments either to a fixed adjustable exchange rate regime or some other kind of fixed rate such as a target band will be continuously tested by 'today's giant capital markets [that] magnify any weaknesses in a country's commitment...and leave little room to manoeuvre' (Obstfeld and Rogoff 1995, p.94).

7. Reduction in exchange rate volatility in the floating rate regime can be achieved by the 'safe' expansion of hedging and financial derivatives that reduce exchange rate risk. Safety might be assured by greater international surveillance and cooperation over the appropriate development and expansion of such facilities.

Proposition 6 in the above list was the focus of great controversy in the post-BW era. Those who were agnostic about the operation of foreign exchange markets (i.e. on whether they were beneficent or economically damaging) generally accepted the proposition. Here we would include the ideas of Dornbusch, Eichengreen, Tobin, Wyplosz and IMF economists. James Meade was unique in favouring market-determined exchange rates but he would have objected to proposition 4· monetary policy, fiscal policy and incomes policy should be free to attain internal, domestic economic balance; incomes policy would be used in tandem with monetary policy to keep inflation low.

Policy views were substantially different on the potential for creating more representative or correct exchange rate movements within flexible exchange rate regimes. That is, the exchange rate in any nation could react appropriately to targeted exchange market interventions (in the short term) aimed at managing sharp fluctuations in a currency's value. Of course, this approach denies the import of proposition 7. More sustained exchange market interventions across countries would require significant international collaboration – something that only proved rare, brief, and episodic in the post-BW era. Exchange rate management would not be so fragile if sterilized intervention was possible on a long-term basis. For some countries such intervention may be viable; it would act as an indirect control on monetary policy.

Max Corden and Stanley Fischer remained equivocal on the subject. They could see the short-term, practical usefulness of sterilized interventions, but at the same time were mindful of unstoppable private capital flows. A more eclectic view is encapsulated in Jeffrey Frankel's (1999) title 'No Single Currency Regime is Right for All Countries or at All Times'. Thus different regimes can work tolerably well for particular countries at different stages of economic and financial market development. Transitioning to an independent, free floating regime may take years, perhaps decades. The same point applies in transitioning to the other polar regime – full currency union. Finally, in this agnostic group who did not take a strong position either on the efficiency or otherwise of foreign exchange market operations or on the wisdom of exchange market interventions, Robert Mundell was unique in insisting on anchoring fiat currencies either to a commodity (or commodity basket) or to an internationally agreed, synthetic unit of account.

Of those who believed that foreign exchange markets were inherently inefficient and always likely to destabilize the real economy, we saw that McKinnon would accept nothing less than wholesale reform beginning with a key currency scheme designed essentially on fixed exchange rate principles. Williamson and many supporters of exchange rate bands, argued for fixed adjustable exchange rates but allowed for greater flexibility than under the older BW IFS. This view was not accompanied by strong arguments for controls on international capital movements. Therein, perhaps, resides a practical weakness. Krugman generally shared this view. By contrast, other economists including Davidson and Taylor, proposed some form of fixed adjustable exchange rate regime or managed exchange rate band, strongly supported by policies to control capital flows. Furthermore, in this view, the case for fixing exchange rates directly need not be an argument for appreciably constraining the freedom and independence of domestic macroeconomic policy especially if an international policy coordination blueprint could be formulated. Incomes policies were also an additional instrument in the armoury of policy-makers who accepted the Davidson-Taylor line. In the limit of course, excepting the capital controls requirement, this trajectory of thought is not far from the case for full currency union – a topic discussed in Chapter 7 below. The next chapter considers in more depth competing doctrines on international capital movements.

4
Choice of Capital Account Regime: When to Liberalize?

International liquidity and creditworthiness issues

At the end of the BW era there was much scepticism among economists about free market-determined international capital movements which paralleled their scepticism over the efficacy of market-determined exchange rates. That scepticism is scarcely surprising. Most of what were considered to be viable reforms of the IFS in the 1960s included some degree of exchange rate fixity and some accompanying degree of control over cross-border capital flows in order to support exchange rate commitments. Otherwise the reserves of monetary authorities could easily be depleted by speculative, cross-border capital-moving activity.

First, some broad definitional statements are in order. When capital flows freely across national borders it is constituted by a myriad of all types of investment portfolio transactions, borrowing, lending, foreign exchange trading, various financial, bond and equity claims, as well as direct investment in both productive equipment and services. It is rare to find complete freedom of all these capital movements. There are usually in existence many restrictions on all capital flows even if foreign exchange trading is completely free. As Cooper (1999a, p.90) explained it: 'capital account convertibility...falls far short of freedom for international capital movements, just as current account convertibility falls far short of ensuring free trade in goods and services'. If a nation experienced a net capital inflow over a specific period of time, this would be equivalent to saying that its international indebtedness has increased, or alternatively, that net foreign claims on domestic assets has increased. The increase in this case will be recorded in the capital account of the nation's balance of payments which will have a surplus – a net inflow of capital for the time period in question. There are many different dimensions and aspects of capital account liberalization only some of which may in fact be 'liberal-ized' in practice (Haggard and Maxfield 1996, pp.37–9). When a govern-ment chooses to 'liberalize' its capital account regime, it allows freer (though rarely completely free) capital convertibility of all capital flows in or out of its national domain. In terms of the inward movement of capital, a government may liberalize capital flows by changing regula-tions applying to: direct investment, foreign investment in domestic equities and real estate, foreign borrowing by domestic firms, trading of domestic financial securities by foreign residents, the international operations of domestic banks, the entry of foreign banks and non-bank financial intermediaries. In terms of the outward movement of capital, a government may liberalize regulations on: the repatriation of capital including profits and dividends by foreign resident companies and individuals, the trading of foreign financial securities and portfolio investments by domestic residents, and the cross-border operations of domestic banks and financial intermediaries.

The choice of exchange rate regime is not unconnected to the choice of capital account regime. Under an intermediate exchange rate regime in which exchange rates are pegged, the direct management of a nation's capital account in some way was considered vital. A central bank's reserve of foreign assets was used for this purpose. In the BW era this became the official 'liquidity' problem – the need for monetary authorities to keep a reserve of liquid foreign assets to support a fixed, adjustable exchange rate regime. When major industrial nations abandoned fixed exchange rates in the 1970s, this raised questions about the functions of official liquidity given the opportunity costs of maintaining it. Were official foreign reserves necessary under a floating exchange rate regime? Perhaps this is so, but only to shore-up monetary policy credibility that was then free to target domestic policy objectives. In any case, there was some uncertainty among economists on the necessity for foreign reserves in the 1970s (Williamson 1973). In principle, fully market-determined exchange rates go hand-in-hand with full capital account convertibility, so that there would be no need for central banks to hold significant reserves directly to support the exchange rate regime. Furthermore, the BW liquidity problem was no longer relevant, at least in theory.

Once again, in principle, market-determined exchange rates and international capital mobility are complementary. Capital would flow across national borders for several reasons including:

1. efficiency considerations: to obtain a favorable rate of return on investment on both fixed interest investments and money market securities of various kinds, and fixed, direct investment in industry;

2. institutional considerations: to take advantage of favorable monetary policy conditions, the international net debt/credit position, the quality and sophistication of financial intermediation services, and fiscal policy regimes such as taxation advantages.

Of course, in a liberalized capital account regime capital flows could easily be reversed, especially short-term capital, if either of the two considerations above, or some combination of them, became unfavourable. These conditions were becoming increasingly and periodically apparent during the post-BW era. John Williamson (1994, p.61) perceived that major changes had occurred in thinking about capital account convertibility. The international liquidity issue had been transformed into a creditworthiness problem: 'under conditions of high capital mobility the external constraint on a country comes from its *creditworthiness* rather than from its *liquidity*' (emphasis in original). Williamson added that no formal theory of the implications arising from this important change had been developed in advance of the phenomenon emerging. Earlier however, he came close to identifying the long-run implications of the post-BW creditworthiness problem – namely that a nation's long-run international indebtedness and debt sustainability would be pivotal in determining the nature, scope and stability of international capital inflows and outflows if capital accounts were liberalized (Williamson 1985b). By contrast, the main ideas that underwrote many early post-BW discussions on international financial reform were still captive of the increasingly irrelevant 'liquidity' problem (e.g. IMF 1972, 1974). In his 1994 retrospective Williamson had the advantage of viewing the development of ideas on capital flows over a period of more than 20 years in which the phenomenon of creditworthiness had emerged. Indeed, private credit rating agencies had also begun to flourish in this period. None of this gave Williamson any comfort; it was still possible to conceive of a new IFS, a more 'structured' one, 'than the one the world had endured for the last twenty years, but it does require that reform proposals be consistent with the fact of high international capital mobility among leading countries' (p.63). In the post-BW era, with flexible exchange rates among leading-country currencies, the capital account convertibility problem 'becomes an empty box' (Mundell 1994, p.79). To work efficaciously, highly flexible, market-determined exchange rates required full capital mobility. In the 1970s, economists did not generally appreciate the issue as an 'empty box' partly because the majority of nations had not by then chosen flexible, let alone, market-determined, exchange rate regimes or free capital account convertibility. This perhaps explains why, much later, Rudiger Dornbusch (1998, p.20) was moved to remark that the 'issue of capital-account liberalization has been coming on for 20 years. It is now as urgent a concern as is the question of the right exchange-rate system in a world of intense capital mobility'.

In the 1970s and early 1980s most leading economists retained a place in their thinking for the 'problem' of capital account convertibility even though the choice of floating exchange rates rendered the problem largely redundant. There did not appear to be a consensus at that time forming around the view that the mutual gains nations enjoyed from freeing-up capital flows outweighed the costs. At the level of trade in goods and services (as opposed capital) a consensus doctrine had by then emerged in favour of trade policy liberalization because it was generally thought that the net gains from trade were positive. In other words, while economists accepted arguments for freer (if not free) trade registered on the current account of the balance of payments, their positions on trade in capital, registered on the capital account of the balance of payments, diverged quite significantly. In the prevailing view, capital did not necessarily offer net gains from trade – from its movement across national borders – it was only lent and could be withdrawn or repatriated. Needless to say, this view became highly controversial later in the post-BW era. In addition, given that labour was not completely free to move across national borders the broader macroeconomic effects of freer capital movements were made more complex because they had implications for the employment of labour within national borders.

Why liberalize capital accounts? The sceptical view

The progressive internationalization of global financial activities was well underway by the mid 1980s (Bryant 1987). Notwithstanding the move among major industrial countries to market-determined exchange rates, the case for directing or containing international capital flows was still dominant in the literature of economics during the 1970s and 1980s. We will now consider some views along this thought trajectory.

Nobel laureate James Tobin (1978, 1982, 1989) was quite far-sighted in accepting the inevitability of more mobile international capital and significant capital flows relative to those that occurred in the BW era. He also appreciated technological advances in financial markets that would enhance capital movements and was realistic about competition between nation-states for scarce world capital. Later in the post-

BW era he accepted the role of flexible exchange rates if not fully market-determined rates (Tobin 1996, p.xii; Eichengreen et al. 1995).

The essence of Tobin (1974, 1978) was the argument for an international uniform tax on currency transactions that would act as 'sand in the wheels of our excessively efficient international money markets'. The doctrinal basis of this proposal, while not clearly spelt out, was the proposition that international financial markets did not operate in a genuinely efficient manner; they are driven by short time horizons despite the availability of more sophisticated financial instruments that take account of future requirements and imperatives. Capital should not be free to move without hindrance in response to volatile expected returns and short-term perceptions of national policy credibility. Short-term capital flows in particular introduce unwanted variability in exchange rates. A Tobin tax would slow down these flows (sometimes called 'hot money' flows) though it would, as originally proposed, also affect decisions to allocate long-term capital. While in the new post-BW IFS international capital provided the necessary means for financing current account deficits, the composition of capital flows was potentially destabilizing especially when it was dominated by short-term capital. And there were broader macroeconomic effects that had to be taken into account. Regardless of the chosen exchange rate regime,

> national governments are not capable of adjusting to massive movements of funds across the foreign exchanges, without real hardship and without significant sacrifice of the objectives of national economic policy with respect to employment, output and inflation (Tobin 1978, p.3).

In short, foreign exchange markets can impose severe real costs on an economy. The magnitude of these costs in terms of employment, output and inflation were not easily estimable in advance; it depended on the case. Empirical techniques were not sufficiently advanced at the time to find robust evidence to support or refute Tobin's claim. Whether or not the Tobin tax was the right policy instrument or indeed a workable instrument, Tobin was successful in focusing economists' attention on the costs of free capital flows. These costs were taken seriously and all the more so by those economists closer, in an intellectual sense, to New Haven (Yale) than to Chicago.

One of those economists close to New Haven, on principle, was Rudiger Dornbusch (Whitman 1980, p.186). Dornbusch (1980, 1986) understood the real costs of 'hot money', concluding that 'a more severe control of international capital flows may be unavoidable'. He referred in this connection to 'foot loose' capital that moves internationally in response to the incentive of tax shelters or even tax evasion and did not involve 'socially productive resource transfers' (1986, p.224). The problem in practice was to identify such capital and distinguish it from more productive transfers. In expanding on what he thought were major faults in Tobin's tax scheme, Dornbusch opted for broader, more indirect macroeconomic containment of capital flows. His comprehensive argument may be summarized as follows (Dornbusch 1980, pp.182–5).

1. The channel through which a Tobin tax would affect exchange rate movements is unclear. The excessive exchange rate volatility supposedly caused by capital flows could ultimately and more permanently be stopped if monetary policy was free to target domestic interest rates and, indirectly thereby, lessen current account imbalances (that would not then have required so much foreign financing in the first place). Yet even here there was still a problem: would a monetary authority need to take a view on what the 'right' exchange rate may be? 'Correct' real exchange rate changes are needed to adjust current account imbalances.
2. With market-determined exchange rates, a short-term current account deficit would be more difficult to finance with a Tobin tax; monetary policy would have to be tightened to raise interest rates so as to attract foreign capital and those rates would need to be higher than otherwise given the existence of the tax impost on inflows. There would therefore be a cost to 'throwing sand in the wheels' of international finance.
3. Domestic residents' investment portfolios, already insufficiently diversified by the home bias problem, would be additionally skewed toward domestic securities, given the discouragement to capital outflows represented by the tax.
4. Dornbusch alternative (i): some short-term sterilization of exchange rate changes might work better than a Tobin tax, thus reducing the domestic costs of high exchange rate variability.
5. Dornbusch alternative (ii): conduct domestic 'monetary policy deliberately to induce stabilizing capital flows' (p.185). Here monetary policy would directly target 'excessive real exchange rate movements' by influencing interest rates (Cf. 2 above), and thence the level of domestic income and expenditure.

6. Dornbusch alternative (iii): create an overall macropolicy environment that is predictable and prudent thus reducing the risks of large,
unanticipated movements in a nation's current account on the
balance of payments. As well, capital account liberalization is not
compatible with fiscal policies that result in persistent, large internal
budget deficits. At least, capital flows which responded to policy
shocks could be eliminated. Note that for Dornbusch, 4, 5 and
6 above were not mutually exclusive. That such policies would
ideally need to be fully harmonized across national borders especially among major economies was implicit in his recommendations
(Dornbusch 1986, p.225).

Tobin and Dornbusch emerged again as sceptics on capital account
liberalization in the late 1980s and 1990s following the experience of
various financial crises during that period. These crises reignited the
capital account convertibility debate. Dornbusch (1986 and 1987)
offered one new option for countries choosing a fixed exchange rate
regime, especially those wanting to take advantage of freer private international capital flows but wanting carefully to regulate them beyond
placing mere 'sand-in-the-wheels' – by slowing them down as per Tobin's
approach. His operational suggestion for policymakers was

> to combine the stability of inflation and real activity that comes
> from fixed rates with a dual exchange rate system for capital account
> transactions. If capital markets are irrational and primarily specu-
> lative it might be as well to detach them altogether from an influence
> on real activity. Rather than use scarce macroeconomic tools to adapt
> the real sector to the idiosyncrasy of financial markets, a separate
> exchange rate would detach the capital account and deprive it from
> distorting influences on trade and inflation (1987, p.17).

While creative, this suggestion for dual exchange rates, one for current
account transactions 'in a separate market at a fixed rate' and another
market for capital account transactions 'at a flexible rate' (Dornbusch
1986, p.224), with the latter being more uncertain and therefore prohibitive, did not find much favour among policymakers. It would have
entailed high administrative costs to minimize evasion and conceivably difficult implementation problems (Dornbusch 1988b, pp.37–8).
Doubtless the dual rate would have a negative impact on longer-term
direct foreign investment when its intention all along would be to affect
short-term speculative capital flows and isolate asset market fluctuations.

On the other hand, those costs would have to be compared with the high real costs of exchange rate volatility on goods and services trade. Most importantly in such a system, monetary policy would be freed to concentrate on domestic policy objectives. The 'dual' system was not a panacea for the choice of fundamental exchange rate regime; that choice always carried major costs. Therefore, in weighing up the costs and benefits of choosing a capital account regime there were costs implied for choices related to the associated, preferred exchange rate regime. The preference for a dual exchange rate system chosen to deal with capital account issues meant that all the standard 'problems of a fixed current account exchange rate regime remain: there is a need for enough flexibility to adjust to persistent real changes and also allow for divergent inflation trends' between countries (p.38).

Also during this time the IMF was considering momentous changes to its formal 'Articles of Agreement' (or mandate), so that it may actively promote rather than passively accept unrestricted capital flows (Fischer 1998). Tobin repeated his 1978 case for a global currency transaction tax: 'the costs of the status quo are high if macroeconomic policy is hamstrung and if it is diverted from more fundamental targets by exchange rate swings' brought on by unfettered capital flows (Eichengreen et al. 1995, p.164). Exchange rate stability must, in this view, be delivered without sacrifice of national monetary autonomy and without turning back the technological innovations and communication efficiencies realized in the modern operation of international finance. By comparison with the 1970s, international financial markets had become 'super-efficient...vehicles' (p.164) for allocating financial capital, but the vehicles were not suited to the many national economies that could not adjust quickly to large capital flows. Intervention was required at the national level through an internationally agreed tax policy. Moreover, even in the larger industrialized economies with developed financial centres and with market-determined exchanges rates, monetary authorities 'cannot always create exchange rate expectations consistent with the domestic interest rates they desire' to control inflation over the medium term (p.164). Monetary policy in this scenario becomes less independent, because it cannot be conducted with indifference to exchange rate changes, especially a persistent real exchange rate change that could threaten national macroeconomic stability. The vagaries of international capital movements need to be contained to protect output, employment, and inflation targets. Tobin, Wyplosz and Eichengreen repeated this message again at the end of the century following a further financial crisis experience in the late 1990s, this time in Asia. Capital account liberalization was not a panacea; it was suspected of fuelling crises rather than enabling nations quickly to adjust to them (Eichengreen and Wyplosz 1996; Eichengreen 2000). For Tobin (2000, p.1101) 'financial globalization' as it was then becoming known, was in fact 'unavoidable'. He agreed that the

> economic rationale for internationalization of asset markets is that it can assist the movement of productive capital from wealthy developed economies to poorer developing countries. But what matters are the net inflows of capital, not the gross volume of transactions. The emerging economies of East Asia, as well as some in Latin America and Eastern Europe, are beneficiaries of foreign business investments. But much of their capital inflows have taken the form of short-term loans of hard currencies from banks in financial centers.... The periods of increasing loans were also periods of increasing growth and investment in the countries receiving the loans; however, they were also, necessarily, accompanied by increasing overvaluation of national currencies and growing deficits on current account. Crises came when the lenders, viewing the growing deficits, became distrustful and refused to renew the loans (p.1101).

Slowing down (by taxing) capital inflows in particular, would reduce the risk of such crises, affect the time horizons of lenders, and enable greater monetary policy independence. Making currency conversion, thus capital convertibility, more expensive and perhaps targeting the proposed tax toward short-term capital flows, would encourage rather than deter direct foreign investment. Tobin was realistic: market-determined exchange rates, a tax to slow down capital flows and greater monetary policy autonomy, would not eliminate crises; it would only make them 'less frequent' and 'less costly' (p.1104).

In a second-best world, international financial integration required guidance and containment (Dornbusch 1997, 1998). While superficially desirable, Tobin tax proposals of various kinds merely lengthen the horizons of those moving their capital, and only slightly at that. Rocks rather than sand may be needed to slow capital movements in a more dramatic manner. In addition, in capital markets where financial intermediation and banking facilities were not modernized and as liquid, those moving capital face greater transaction costs. Thus in effect, in a large number of emerging market economies in particular, a Tobin tax (of sorts) is already in existence (Dornbusch 1998, p.21). By the late 1990s, instead of proposing an *ad hoc* (and difficult to implement) transaction tax,

Dornbusch was moving in the same direction as Eichengreen (1999a, p.91) in recommending 'a system of preventative capital controls' that limited short-term capital inflows 'or, at least, structures their maturities' (Dornbusch 1998, p.23). These controls could be designed on a country-by-country basis to discourage short-term capital flows; they would also not be easy to evade. Significant costs of allowing capital account liberalization arise when a country owes a large amount of short-term, unhedged debt. In the event, exchange rate movements add to national solvency risks. Unlike Tobin and others, Dornbusch was not able to suppress or deny the main efficiency argument for freer capital mobility even in the face of market imperfections. Provided accurate information is provided about national monetary and fiscal policy, as well as national accounts (both internal and external), capital markets operate both to support stable macroeconomic policy which ensures a low rate and variability of inflation and to punish excessive reliance on short-term, unhedged foreign debt. And, crucially, stable macroeconomic policy of this kind will not encourage capital outflows by residents and non-residents alike. On Dornbusch's reading of events later in the post-BW era, capital market participants paid close attention to information provided by debt rating agencies and in doing so were often mislead. Those agencies employed 'absurdly outdated' risk analysis techniques to assess such matters as governmental creditworthiness and 'country risk'. The focus of rating agency analysis had to be shifted from excessive reliance on current account risks in which debt-to-export ratios featured prominently, toward 'balance-sheet' risks in which short-term debt burdens were crucial (Dornbusch 1998, p.24). Only then would creditworthiness be assessed more accurately and responsibly.

Tobin and Dornbusch concentrated on the macroeconomic consequences of capital account liberalization. By comparison, Joseph Stiglitz, initially at Princeton and then at the World Bank, applied micro-economic reasoning to support his sceptical view of liberalization. In Stiglitz's view, markets for capital in general (and not only international capital) were not like ordinary commodity markets. There were ever-present information asymmetries in markets for financial capital so that liberalization had doubtful benefits. Indeed, speculative short-term financial market trading can often be destabilizing when information asymmetries are present; it can distort the allocation of scarce capital in both domestic and international financial markets, so much so that a tax policy might well be useful in curbing such trading (Stiglitz 1999). If domestic capital markets are not allocatively efficient because of the extent of short-term 'noise' rather than genuine information signals, then it would not be valid to extend the standard argument for freer trade in goods and services to freer trade in financial capital. Jagdish Bhagwati (1998) agreed – there was something fundamentally different in trading widgets as opposed trading financial capital. Regulatory frameworks need to be constructed to reduce information problems and associated risks, and ameliorate nations' exposure to speculative financial market trading. This is an especially important consideration for developing countries given the low scale and shallowness of their domestic financial markets (Hellman et al. 1996).

Not surprisingly, Stiglitz was adamantly opposed to the proposition that the IMF should promote full capital account convertibility regardless of national circumstances. There was some evidence later in the post-BW era that more pragmatic thinking at the IMF was becoming sympathetic to Stiglitz's view, or at least toward some restrictions on international financial trading on a country-by-country basis (Folkerts-Landau and Ito 1995). Nonetheless it was difficult to escape the view that these IMF concessions to the sceptics were based on the underlying IMF view that restrictions on some international financial transactions were only a temporary expedient.

Stiglitz (2000, p.1079) extended his argument against wholesale liberalization:

The central function of capital and financial markets is information-gathering – in particular, assessing which projects and firms are most likely to yield the highest return, and monitoring to ensure that the funds are used in the appropriate way. Moreover, markets for information are fundamentally different from 'ordinary' markets...For instance, whenever information is imperfect, markets are essentially...efficient – in marked contrast to standard results for competitive markets with perfect information.... Thus, [that] the...argument for capital liberalization is exactly the same as the argument for trade liberalization, is simply false.

When information is imperfect as it often is across all markets, the problem is compounded when markets are incomplete. Market incompleteness was a significant imperfection in some countries, thereby compounding the information problems (Greenwald and Stiglitz 1986). Developing countries in particular did not often provide full-market hedging facilities for financial market participants. In such circumstances the costs imposed on society as a whole of major capital flows such as a capital outflow, are considerable. On Stiglitz's version of the

Asian financial crisis in the late 1990s, financial market incompleteness in countries such as Indonesia made the crisis more consequential for domestic residents.[11] While Stiglitz agreed that more open capital markets will lead to more disciplined macroeconomic policy and ensure generally sounder policies, international capital market participants were fair-weather friends in this regard. In short, repeating a view long associated with John Maynard Keynes, Stiglitz (2000, p.1079) insisted that without some government management, international capital flows are 'markedly procyclical, exacerbating economic fluctuations'. The country-specific evidence was abundant: intervention, especially to curb short-term financial capital flows need not at the same time have deleterious effects on foreign direct investment. The task ahead was to design effective intervention (pp.1076, 1079, 1082–4). To believe that intervention in itself 'might reduce the flow of capital is as misguided as the worry that discouraging air pollution might discourage the production of steel' (Stiglitz 1999, p.1512).

Dani Rodrik (Harvard University) contributed a line of thinking running in close parallel with the ideas of Stiglitz. Rodrik's work was informed by empirical research relating to the impact of capital account liberalization on economic growth especially in less developed and emerging market economies. In several provocative contributions Rodrik (1997, 1998) and Rodrik and Velasco (1999), demonstrated that the links between international capital flows and growth were quite tenuous. Certainly, Rodrik argued, there was no proven case for the IMF Articles of Agreement to be altered in favour either of actively promoting capital account liberalization, or for expediting the liberalization process thereby increasing international financial integration. It was possible that existing capital controls in some countries were not the answer to reducing volatility in capital flows and exchange rates. Yet the benefits of removing those controls had not been demonstrated. Rodrik is relentless in communicating the message that liberalizing cross-border capital movements was not an end in itself; it would leave most less developed nations hostage to the imperfect evaluations of international credit rating agencies, 'to the whims and fancies of two dozen or so thirty-something country analysts in London, Frankfurt and New York' (Rodrik 1998, p.65). As a consequence, real economic development objectives unique to particular nations would be relegated to agendas set by

---

[11]Oustide the period under review, Stiglitz (2002a) contributed a major survey article analysing the risks and (low) rewards forthcoming from capital account liberalization. See also Henry (2007).

credit rating agencies. This outcome was tantamount to allowing 'blind faith in the efficiency and rationality of international capital markets' and to believing 'that the goals of foreign investors and of economic development will regularly coincide' (p.65). Here Rodrik expressed an emphatic rejection of the post-BW emergence of the creditworthiness criterion as a solution to the older BW liquidity problem. Something more than private capital was required and clearly, that 'something more' had to be provided by intergovernmental sovereign lending, and by various IFIs including the IMF and World Bank.

More strident polemical arguments against capital account liberalization were also forthcoming in the post-BW era from Robert Wade (1998–9, University of London), and John Eatwell and Lance Taylor (2000, University of Cambridge and New School for Social Research New York, respectively). Wade was adamant that cronyism was endemic in the operation of private capital markets in the Asian financial crisis during the late 1990s. Eatwell and Taylor stressed the need for global governance structures formally to regulate international capital flows.[12] Along a similar thought trajectory, Paul Davidson (University of Tennessee) implored policymakers to develop full social control of foreign exchange markets and international capital movements. He used a dramatic analogy:

> Reasonable people do not think it is a violation of civil liberties to prohibit people from boarding an airplane with a gun. Moreover, no one would think we are impinging on individual rights, if the society prohibits anyone from entering a theatre with a Molotov cocktail in one hand and a box of matches in the other – even if the person indicates no desire to burn down the theatre. Yet, in the name of free markets, we permit...one or more fund managers [to] anticipate the possibility of an exploding Molotov cocktail and therefore yell 'fire' in the crowded international financial markets any time the 'image' of a possible profitable fire moves them (Davidson 1997, p.672).

This passage takes Keynes's remarks about 'fair-weather friends' in financial markets to a new level – for Davidson they become destructive, fear-driven vandals with the potential to impose high real economic costs on

---

[12]Later, outside the period under review, Eatwell and Taylor (2002) make a case for a World Financial Authority to govern cross-border capital flows. See also Taylor (2002), Ocampo (2002) and Nayyar (2002) along the same lines.

the international economy. While Tobin's tax idea may be useful to hold back small-time destabilizing speculation, large 'boulders' rather than 'sand' is more likely needed to curb large capital flows. Indeed sand is more likely to be 'swept away in whirlpools of speculation' (p.685). A tax is not usually a sufficient disincentive; direct controls over short-term capital flows are more powerful and should be implemented (Davidson 1998). Consistent with Davidson's recommendation for exchange rate regime choice, major controls on capital movements would be imposed in tandem with a fixed, adjustable exchange rate system (Davidson 2000).

Sequencing capital account liberalization in a planned reform process

By the mid 1980s a new doctrine began to emerge that did not deny the usefulness of free capital mobility or the net efficiency benefits of capital account liberalization. The benefits could not, however, be realized unless macroeconomic fundamentals were appropriate and financial market institutions were sufficiently developed. In highly developed financial markets information and transaction costs are lower. Liberalization in capital markets only yields net benefits if other policy reforms are instituted in the first place and had time to work. Beginning with a largely inconvertible capital account, a nation could conceivably take decades to transition toward an open capital account regime.

The seminal work of Ronald McKinnon (1973) on the vital relationship between finance and economic development is a landmark in this field. It initiates a trajectory of thought that turns on placing financial capital and capital structure at the heart of long-run economic growth (Cf. also Levine 1997). It is only a short step from McKinnon's work on finance and internal economic development to propositions that maintain a strong relationship between international finance and internal, domestic economic growth. Later in the post-BW era, McKinnon (1993) and McKinnon and Pill (1996, 1997) turn their attention to the role of international finance and capital account liberalization in the economic development process. Their review of available empirical research indicated mixed results: some countries, even while they liberalized international capital flows, did not attract enough capital; some attracted too much external finance leading to a boom and bust economic cycle; and others were prone to excessive foreign borrowing, subsequent moral hazard and debt repayment problems.

McKinnon (1982, 1993) established a new doctrine founded on the 'order of economic liberalization' that applied to developing countries, transition economies, emerging market economies and developed countries moving to a more liberal, market-oriented economic structure. All too often in these instances large exchange rate movements and real exchange rate appreciations during periods of strong capital inflows tended to produce asset inflation, a less competitive export sector and an inevitable deterioration in the current account. The result was usually a widening deficit on current account and an economic crisis brought on by policies designed to rein in the deficit and by sudden capital outflows. Therefore, according to McKinnon's doctrine, capital account liberalization should be sequenced near the end of the liberal, market-oriented reform process. Moreover, capital account liberalization should be pursuant to opening the current account (liberal trade policy reforms). Prior to allowing freer capital inflows and outflows, the domestic finance and banking sectors of those liberalizing economies should be considerably strengthened, modernized, and properly supervised by a sophisticated regulatory regime, preferably through the central bank. Rather than be developed at the same time in a complementary manner with the external sector, internal financial reforms should be attempted first. In this way, short-term international capital flows, once they were liberalized, would more easily be identified and, if necessary, managed. As well, foreign debt could be appropriately hedged to reduce a nation's financial vulnerability. In the meantime, foreign direct investment could still be actively encouraged – the capital account could remain provisionally open to direct investment flows while the domestic financial sector was being modernized. Normally, foreign direct investment is well-managed and is accompanied by beneficial knowledge and technology transfers.

Paul Krugman (2000) reinforced McKinnon's approach. Credible, durable capital account liberalization must not be subject to the 'over borrowing syndrome'. Krugman's endorsement came with a warning: 'fire sale' foreign direct investment incentivized by a crisis situation may be detrimental to capital importing countries. It may not be enough to hold-off short-term portfolio capital which can often exacerbate a crisis. When foreign investment was aimed at exploiting opportunities to acquire temporarily cheap assets it may assist in limiting the depth of a crisis and slowing the rate of further asset deflation. Krugman warned that even an open capital account for foreign direct investment only, could lead to the replacement of otherwise efficient management of domestic assets for less efficient and exploitative foreign management intent on short-term asset stripping and temporary gain. Of course, this scenario becomes even more real if the initial crisis situation was caused by a capital account regime that was prematurely liberalized in the first place, leading to unhedged over-borrowing and a subsequent liquidity crisis.

Sebastian Edwards (UCLA) provided sound evidence and argument in favour of McKinnon's 'sequencing' approach. In concert with McKinnon's early work he identified a thought trajectory forming around the sequencing idea : '[m]ost analysts...agree that the liberalization of the capital account should only take place once trade liberalization has been implemented' (Edwards 1999, p.138). Edwards (1992) gave much more emphasis than McKinnon to labour market reforms and to specific financial sector reforms. Labour market regulations needed reform before the capital account was liberalized in order to allow greater flexibility in wage-setting and working conditions and to encourage labour mobility within and between industries. Financial sector reforms must take place in tandem with capital account liberalization, and he included details on the way forward with bank supervisory and regulatory reforms. There were three central ideas in his analysis:

> First, in a newly liberalized environment poorly regulated banks will tend to finance questionable projects, creating potential for financial meltdown. Moreover, with poor bank regulation – serious moral hazard issues will arise. Second, labor market flexibility will facilitate the reallocation of resources that follows major relative price change. And third, real exchange rate appreciations induced by major capital flows may frustrate a trade liberalization reform by reducing the export sector's ability to compete internationally (Edwards 1999, p.139).

Similarly Eichengreen et al. (1999, pp.10–12) also supported capital account liberalization only after major domestic financial market reforms but they avoided the question of the place of current account liberalization. Eichengreen (2000, p.1108) was adamant that more liberal capital account reforms 'should not precede recapitalization of the banking sector' in countries undergoing major financial disturbances or crises. There was always the risk in such sequencing that, in the meantime, 'maintaining barriers to capital flows and foreign financial competition will diminish the pressure for restructuring'. When capital account liberalization is attempted, foreign direct investment should be encouraged in the first instance by specifically targeted liberal policies. For these economists, capital controls may have an important role to play in altering the composition of capital flows, tilting them toward longer maturities and thereby protecting economies from significant real economic disturbances consequent upon capital flow reversals. An additional risk of controls is the higher cost of capital and subsequently lower economic growth (Edwards 1998 and Gregorio et al. 2000).

At the macroeconomic level, McKinnon's sequencing doctrine accepted the post-BW trend toward greater exchange rate flexibility; it was also founded on the prior implementation of fiscal and monetary policies that addressed persistent internal imbalances. External trade policy would not be radically liberalized; it would largely remain intact to assist in keeping down current account deficits and in maintaining domestic expenditure and employment. An initial deterioration in the current account deficit brought on by premature tariff reductions and removal of other trade barriers could precipitate an economic crisis. McKinnon was emphatic that the choice of a credible capital account regime could not be made in the midst of a crisis or an impending crisis, or in the immediate aftermath of a crisis when bank and corporate balance sheets were laden with debt, much of it probably unhedged foreign debt. To be sure, capital controls were rarely very effective and were no substitute for sound macroeconomic policies, a fully developed regime of bank supervision, and a financial market regulatory system that increases disclosure, promotes accountability, reduces moral hazard, evasion and corruption. The sequencing argument did not openly embrace any specific exchange rate regime and certainly not either a fully fixed or fully market-determined regime. This probably reflects caution not only about the credibility of all policy reforms made prior to liberalizing the capital account. The fact that smaller open economies and emerging market economies would not be able to develop sophisticated financial markets on a par with those existing in the world's major financial centers is also a matter of concern. Herein resides a weakness in the sequencing approach.

The national context mattered. As long as small domestic financial markets were not developed on a sufficiently large scale, the level of financial market development will rarely approach that of larger financial centers. Did this mean that capital account liberalization would not be possible? Richard Cooper (1998, 1999a) tirelessly repeated the point that many countries may reasonably and indefinitely 'choose to preserve the right to control at least certain kinds of capital movements into and out of their jurisdiction' (1998, p.19). It was simply not acceptable to repeat the old shibboleths and parables about getting economic fundamentals right, or establishing sound macroeconomic policies, and only then moving to maximizing the efficiency of financial markets and capital allocation by liberalizing capital accounts. Capital movements may well need continuous 'guidance or constraint' in many national contexts (Cooper 1999a, p.105). Running strongly against the consensus view in the post-BW era, Cooper (1998, p.18) opined that freer capital flows and market-determined exchange rates can be 'basically incompatible' especially for most countries other than those that are 'large and diversified with well-developed and sophisticated financial markets' (Cooper 1999a, pp.123–4). Countries that have chosen a floating exchange rate regime while at the same time presenting with imperfectly developed financial systems relative to those that are 'large and diversified', rely on the exchange rate as a key asset price. Yet that exchange rate, which is often a strong influence on prices for goods and services in the economy as a whole (if it is a relatively open economy), can be disrupted by fluctuations in capital flows. The result is unpalatable: major adjustment problems transmitted through a highly variable exchange rate. There are, in short, asymmetries between countries in the costs of choosing a liberal capital account regime, particularly macroeconomic costs. It would therefore not be possible for an optimal sequencing program ever to reach the supposed nirvana of an open capital account with freer trade and a market-determined exchange rate. To aim for such an outcome would be to commit a major policy error for many countries and result in financial crises. Liberalization of capital flows was a 'good idea' only in the right conditions. For Cooper (1999a, p.124) the right conditions are difficult to meet:

> The right conditions involve low barriers to international trade; a well-developed, well-diversified, and well-regulated domestic financial market; and a tax regime for capital that does not differ markedly from world norms. Until these conditions are met, serious misallocation could occur if capital movements are fully liberalized, and considering vulnerability is created for economies whose exchange rates are strongly influenced by changes in sentiment by [capital] owners – residents as well as non residents – of liquid assets. Countries in this condition...[either] must tie their currencies strongly to a major currency...or they must maintain restrictions on capital movements, particularly those movements that are subject to rapid changes in sentiment and are easily reversible.

Universal capital account liberalization is therefore not a good idea and nations should not be encouraged (or badgered by the IMF) into making such a choice as part of the process of 'sequencing' liberal policy reforms (Cooper 1998, p.12).

In a different vein, Rudiger Dornbusch (1998, pp.21–2) was disconcerted by the McKinnon case for sequencing reform in the current account, specifically trade policy liberalization, before liberalizing the capital account. Thus both trade liberalization and financial market liberalization involve some form of accompanying industrial restructuring – in the former case of goods and services production and in the latter case of the financial sector. Dornbusch could find no good reason why one sector 'should wait or which should come first' in the reform process (p.22). He added that since 'protectionism wastes resources' then trade policy may well be reformed sooner. He was concerned that sequencing could 'be hijacked by political pressures adverse to the best use of resources' so that the reform process should proceed 'full steam ahead' without account for sequencing. The denial of the value of sequencing is taken further by another trajectory of thought favouring immediate opening of nations' capital accounts at the same time as the liberalization of trade policy. We shall discuss this approach in the following section. Suffice it to remark at this point that Dornbusch's sympathy with the views of the sequencing approach only went so far as agreeing that there were high costs of free capital account convertibility. He agreed that certain conditions must be met before capital accounts were liberalized. Put simply, those conditions were microeconomic. The balance sheets of financial institutions had to be sound in the first place and those institutions required the support of a full official system of regulation and supervision as a prerequisite for capital account liberalization. His message was that

> financial opening must not occur in an environment where the [domestic] banking and financial systems are badly regulated and badly supervised. This is an argument not so much for delaying financial opening as for hastening the cleanup of financial repression, bad regulation and inferior financial supervision (p.23).

Putting off reforms in all the above senses just to satisfy a gradualist approach set out in a formal sequencing program 'is an invitation to a mega crisis' (p.20).

Choosing a freer capital account regime

In the orthodox neoclassical view of capital formation, capital (on the margin) moves to its place of highest return. The view that capital has a crucial role to play in the economic growth process if it is allowed to move freely is, of course, an idea that can be traced back to the founding classical economist, Adam Smith. For Smith, liberal trade in goods and services generated net gains, and the services of financial capital were included. The classical case for free trade extended to fixed and circulating capital. In the post-BW era, University of Chicago Nobel Laureate Robert Lucas refashioned and rehabilitated the original Smithian doctrine that capital accumulation was vital in the growth and economic development process. The difference in Lucas's approach is that he placed little emphasis on fixed capital *per se* and great stress on the importance of human capital. Economists overrate the place of financial capital in the growth process (Lucas 1990). Nonetheless, given that labour is relatively immobile internationally, the importance of foreign direct investment and financial capital mobility in general, is magnified. In this context, Lucas repeatedly argued that all capital investment flows should be liberalized, even more so in developing countries. Therefore any barrier to the movement of fixed capital for instance, would slow growth in the long run, simply because fixed capital is used by labour and can contribute to the augmentation of human capital.

Within national borders financial market liberalization serves generally to promote resource-allocative efficiency and thence higher long-term growth rates. We have it from Ross Levine's (1997, p.691) thorough survey of the literature, mostly of work completed in the post-BW era, that a well-functioning financial system enables:

(i)   hedging and risk-pooling;
(ii) scarce savings to be mobilized and allocated;
(iii) the distribution of media of exchange to facilitate efficient exchange of goods and services;
(iv) monitoring and control mechanisms to be formed to assess the use of finance; and
(v)   facilitation of capital formation and associated technological innovation.

Why, we might ask, would these factors not also apply equally to the functions of international finance – finance that crosses national borders? In the first decade following the collapse of BW, this question was not widely addressed. Either it was taken for granted that international finance functioned in exactly the same way as domestic finance, regarded as a minor addendum to the broader problem of growth and economic development, or treated with suspicion because it issued from 'foreign' sources. Many economists were suspicious of international finance variously because of its fair-weather, foot-loose, exploitative or pro-cyclical nature. That domestic private capital flows were also generally pro-cyclical within national borders seemed to escape the critics of external capital account liberalization. Notably there was scant discussion of the role of international finance in causing economic crises; it was not until the mid-1980s that this issue came to prominence in the literature of economics.

By the 1990s a doctrine had become fully articulated that was consistent in many respects with the classical view of capital and its role in economic development. In this trajectory of thought, to paraphrase the title of Maurice Obstfeld's (1998) article, the global capital market was a benefactor (much more than a menace) to all parties as far as long-term world economic growth was concerned. Capital exporting nations diversify risks. Savings constrained, capital importing nations are able to finance current account deficits and fund investment for growth. Here the focus is on long-run growth effects of capital flow liberalization more than on either the possible effects of temporary real exchange rate appreciations or loss of control over domestic monetary conditions (in the very small open economy case). A common complaint was that this classical thought trajectory ignored macroeconomic asymmetries between countries as regards the costs of choosing a liberal capital account regime. However, as Calvo et al. (1994, p.64; 1996, pp.134–5) argue, sterilized exchange market intervention can be used intermittently to deal with problematic capital flows. In any case, most of the costs of choosing a liberal capital account were thought to fall on poorer, less developed nations that were savings-constrained and thence persistently dependent on capital imports. Concern for such costs was understandable on distributional grounds. That open capital accounts might eventually facilitate vast capital exports from relatively poorer countries and emerging market economies to rich, high consumption countries (a remarkable occurrence in the early twenty-first century) was not seriously considered.

Maurice Obstfeld and Kenneth Rogoff (1996) produced a widely acclaimed graduate textbook on open economy macroeconomics in which, among many other things, they demonstrated in principle the advantages of liberal international trade in financial capital (also Obstfeld 1994b). Furthermore, Obstfeld (1995) studied international capital mobility in the late BW era. His evidence was completely opposed to Dani Rodrik's results on the impact of freer capital mobility. Obstfeld could also have turned to Quinn (1997), which in many respects contradicted the empirical results in Rodrik's work, and produced strong support for the view that just like domestically sourced finance, international finance enhanced growth and development. As always, empirical evidence can be inconclusive and unconvincing depending on the point of view one begins with – as economists have found (since Adam Smith) when trying to determine the precise relationship between open trade or liberalized current accounts and domestic economic development. What matters here is not a recapitulation of the data sets, empirical methods, beginning and end dates for various studies; it is the underlying doctrines that are of interest – for these seem to persist over time and draw on empirical evidence that suits cases made ultimately on principle. It is not just the shortage of relevant empirical data that is responsible for disagreements among economists.[13]

Obstfeld (1998) made a comprehensive case for liberalizing capital account regimes and for removing capital controls (also Obstfeld and Taylor 1998). In making this case he claimed 'that in confronting the global capital market there is no reason to depart from the conventional economic wisdom' (p.10). Studying more than a century of experience with capital flows from a classical perspective, including periods in which international capital mobility was severely restricted, Obstfeld developed a doctrine in favour of continuing liberalization. He repeats some of the standard advantages of liberalization common to liberalizing domestic capital markets and international capital markets and he takes for granted that these domestic markets are already liberalized or are being reformed along liberal lines. He adds that freer international capital flows enable greater geographical diversification of risk; mobilize international savings; smooth consumption patterns by allowing foreign borrowing when incomes temporarily decline (and vice versa), and contribute to macroeconomic policy discipline (because unsound policies would be punished by capital outflows and result in higher domestic interest rates). Measuring all these benefits is admittedly problematic.

---

[13]See Furman and Stiglitz (1998, p.102n139). The doctrinal perspective being advanced here clashes with those treatments that believe all problems and controversies on international financial integration can be resolved by appropriately designed and executed empirical work. For instance, in connection with capital controls and their effectiveness, Dooley (1996) argues that the matter is empirical and not one of principle or doctrine. This is correct only superficially. The reasons for maintaining or introducing capital controls and for removing them at any time, rest fundamentally on matters of principle as much if not more than on selected accounts of recent experience. As political scientists might say, interests and ideology play a significant role in economic policy decisions.

Broader consequences of choosing a more liberal capital account regime may be summarized as follows, paraphrasing the key points in Obstfeld (1998).

1. Increasing global exchange rate flexibility in the last quarter of the twentieth century enabled countries to choose freer capital accounts and more independent monetary policies to target domestic economic objectives.
2. Some fiscal policy constraints arise from choosing freer capital flows. It is especially difficult to tax disruptive short-term capital movements. Some international tax competition occurs insofar as capital tends to move to low tax jurisdictions.
3. Following point 2 above, and acknowledging Rodrik's (1997) scepticism, Obstfeld concedes that government fiscal outlays and social programs can be compromised by choosing a liberal capital account regime; higher taxes on labour and lower taxes on capital may be implied; social and political unrest, and unfavourable distributional outcomes may all be unintended consequences of liberalization.
4. Financial crises are experienced in open capital markets though they have also been evident when global capital markets have been highly regulated.

Obstfeld's (1998, p.21) far from satisfactory answer to points 2 and 3 relies on the pursuit of 'formal international tax coordination' so as to harmonize the cross-border tax treatment of capital. His more plausible response to point 4 is that financial crises are not unique to periods when global capital markets have been highly integrated along market-based lines and when exchange rate regimes have been highly flexible. Indeed, many crises have been propagated by choosing pegged exchange rate regimes in conjunction with extensive foreign exchange-market intervention and capital controls. For Obstfeld, a modernized, regulated and prudentially managed domestic financial system is a prerequisite for opening national capital markets to foreign capital flows. As well, the IMF's growing role in the post-BW era as an international lender of last resort can assist in alleviating crises. The IMF can promote more open international capital markets and 'stand ready with backstop finance should private capital flows prove troublesome' (p.27).

Altogether, Obstfeld represents a trajectory of thought on capital account convertibility with a long pedigree, and one that seemed to be supported at the IMF. He cites the liberalizing orientation of IMF thinking in the 1990s:

> the Fund is clearly right, it seems to me, to advocate an orderly process of progressive integration into world capital markets. Convertibility for current account transactions seemed risky as well in the 1940s, but it proved an unprecedented engine for global growth. International finance likewise can be an engine for growth, as it has been in the past...The Fund's official espousal of financial openness represents a break with the attitudes of its founders, but one that seems entirely realistic after a half-century of financial market recovery (p.27).

IMF economists were aware of the risks associated with choosing a more liberalized capital account regime yet they were generally convinced that the net outcome was positive in terms of long-run economic development (e.g. Citrin and Fischer 2000, p.1137).

How could nations deal with the seemingly intractable issue of choosing a capital account regime, especially given the possible macroeconomic disturbances purportedly experienced by capital importing countries in particular? The liberal, classical view is certainly not favourable to adding Tobin-type taxes – 'sand in the wheels' – to international finance. Three main policy approaches following the spirit of Tobin's ideas were proposed to slow down foreign exchange market trading in the 1990s:

1. margin deposits yielding no interest for every net position;
2. a tax on gross transactions; and
3. further prudential capital requirements for banks holding foreign exchange positions.

Peter Garber and Mark Taylor (1995, pp.173–4) assume that the three policy proposals above will be:

> aimed at foreign exchange transactions and positions which are somehow identifiable as such and not at cross-border credit in general. Since foreign exchange transactions comprise deliveries of bank deposits in two separate currencies, national efforts to stem such transactions will drive the foreign exchange component of these bank deposit transfers offshore; and the transactions will appear on domestic bank balance sheets only as a domestic

currency item. Moreover, even if explicit foreign exchange transactions can be controlled globally, other separate transactions,
though not explicitly foreign exchange, can be combined to mimic a
foreign exchange transaction. Hence it will be difficult to control
gross transactions.

Thus, in this view, 'a policy of throwing sand in the wheels of international finance would very likely amount to little more than a futile,
Canutian attempt to command the tides of international capital flows'
(p.180). Sophisticated financial markets allocate capital – and large
quantities of capital – in a forward-looking and timely manner. Such
markets embody innovation, that is, products, services and techniques
that change with advances in trading technologies and in response to
regulation. Furthermore, modern financial markets can disguise capital
account transactions as current account transactions by changing the
way trade-related transactions are invoiced. Finally, concerted rather
than *ad hoc* attempts to regulate and impose taxes of some kind on
financial services activity, including foreign exchange-market trading,
have to be comprehensive and if possible harmonized across borders in
order fully to be effective. The speed with which financial markets
move and innovate may not allow policymakers time either to put an
effective international capital control regime in place or maintain it for
very long.

At Harvard, Martin Feldstein (1999) opposed capital controls, instead
recommending that monetary authorities build foreign exchange reserves
as a type of insurance against periodic macroeconomic disturbances. At
the time, opposing doctrines focused on impending or actual financial
crises especially in less developed countries and particular geographic
regions, and they referred to the fact that such countries did not often
have the savings capacity to accumulate reserves. Those countries, mostly
small in economic terms, would soon find their paltry reserves depleted.
In principle Feldstein's recommendation still stands. Early twenty-first
century experience illustrates the principle that even less developed
nations can accumulate reserves and become capital exporters. At the
same time, even larger industrialized economies have not been able
to harness sufficient domestic savings, accumulate reserves (both internal
and external) and have become major capital importers.[14] Feldstein's

---

[14]For a modern discussion of this point and related capital account liberalization
issues see Prasad and Rajan (2008).

reserve accumulation idea is also complemented by the sterilization option. Monetary authorities need not simply provide their own currency in exchange for foreign capital because that would increase the domestic money supply. If domestic financial markets were sufficiently developed, bond sales can sterilize at least modest financial inflows. Monetary policy would have a modicum of control over domestic monetary conditions at least in principle. (The practice suggests that large capital flows are not so easy to sterilize all the more so if reserves are insufficient, Edwards 2000, p.10).

In summary, the more open capital account option so strongly supported by a group of prominent economists adhering essentially to the principles of classical economics, survived relatively unscathed in the post-BW era. The option and its underlying principles survived despite various episodes of financial crises in the last quarter of the twentieth century – episodes giving opponents of liberalization more ammunition to stop or at least delay the choice to make international capital movements easier. In the classical doctrine, if capital flows were freer, they would become more stable. The message seemed too simple, indeed deceptively so: policymakers in any particular capital receiving nation 'must muster a high degree of credibility and support clear, simple, market-oriented policies' (Calvo et al. 1994, p.65). A robust, credible policy regime could take decades to build successfully. Only then might the risks of macroeconomic disturbances, supposedly caused by capital account liberalization, be mitigated. That the creation of credibility in this regard could not be realized unless a freer capital account regime was in fact chosen (rather than indefinitely delayed) was something those who advanced other doctrines could not easily accept. To be sure, the long-run benefits of liberalization could not be quantified along a single dimension (such as positively connecting a more open capital account to GDP growth). The benefits of choosing a liberalized regime were dispersed and integrated with other cognate reforms and institutional developments – hence the obvious measurement difficulties. The liberal trajectory of thought emphasizes internal, domestic reform in banking and financial systems; the importation of more sophisticated and highly efficacious financial sector governance; greater facilitation of venture capital and entrepreneurial activity and improving private business operating performance. All these factors are enhanced by opening economies to international capital flows. More competition between private providers of capital and less reliance on bureaucratic (and in some cases corrupt), politically dominated governmental sources of finance, are also regarded as beneficial outcomes of liberalizing capital account regimes.

Conclusion

In this chapter we have outlined and exposited several doctrines on the choice of capital account regime. The thought trajectories associated with these various doctrines are clear and do not seem to have been pushed off course or blurred either by events or the plethora of empirical studies brought to bear on the effects of capital controls. Moreover, the trajectories have remained on course in the face of extensive case analysis and empirical work on the costs and benefits of capital account liberalization and on the relationship between capital account liberalization and economic growth. Just as with choice of exchange rate regime, pragmatic and eclectic economists focused on short-term circumstantial choice problems over capital account convertibility; for them, there were a myriad of intermediate regime choices. Different regimes were suitable in different contexts at different times. Various intermediate regimes involved some degree of impediment to free capital movements, some degree of indirect management through monetary and fiscal policies that influenced capital account transactions and changed the composition and time horizons of capital flows. Even so, the focus of many pragmatic economists on short-term capital movements and on the mechanics and operational viability of various capital controls belied underlying advocacy (and therefore doctrines) about longer-term choice options.

No doctrine discussed in this chapter was implacably opposed to foreign capital inflows that were definitely destined to direct investment in productive activities. Capital in these instances ended up in highly structured agricultural, industrial or service-sector capital. The various trajectories of thought may be delineated as follows:

1. More liberal capital account regimes were not generally a good idea, except perhaps for major industrialized economies. Some regulation of capital flows was desirable (e.g. Stiglitz, Tobin, Rodrik).
2. Liberalization was never a good idea and international capital flows require strong management at the local and international level. Sudden, cross-border capital reversals are destructive of both output and employment (e.g. Davidson, Wade, Taylor).
3. There were often net benefits deriving from the choice of a more liberal capital account regime but these could be realized only under special, quite demanding, conditions. Therefore it is best to enquire from the outset: when and where should more liberalization of the capital account be appropriate? (e.g. McKinnon, Cooper, Dornbusch).

4. Another identifiable doctrine surveyed in this chapter maintained that more open capital accounts are generally desirable; it did not seriously contemplate the question – how should capital flows be regulated? This view turned on making a case for the long-run benefits of choosing freer capital flows, that is: how soon can a nation choose freer capital account convertibility? The answer provided was 'the sooner the better' (e.g. Obstfeld, Rogoff, Feldstein, Fischer).

The first two thought trajectories emphasized the asymmetries between countries as regards to costs of liberalization, especially liberalization of short-term capital flows. Here the high real exchange rate consequences under flexible exchange rate regimes loomed large. As well, the costs incurred in financially fragile small open economies and developing countries were especially important. Those thought trajectories insisted that such costs were not inconsequential to the ultimate choice of capital account regime. Different regulatory approaches were then considered in order directly to manage international capital markets and to manage the scope of capital account liberalization. The third group of economists favoured indirect management of international capital in which critical prerequisites – sequenced, structural policy reforms – were necessary before freer capital accounts are chosen (if at all in Cooper's case). Freer capital movements were therefore only beneficial in net terms at higher levels of economic development. Preeminent considerations when choosing a capital account regime are therefore the level of development and policy reform credibility.

The fourth, classical, free capital market group accepted the reality of occasional financial crises – crises that may be more frequent with more open capital account regimes. No regime choice was costless. Crises notwithstanding, freer capital flows, cognate policy reforms and policy reform-credibility were mutually interdependent; the former must deliberately be chosen from the outset as part of a commitment to market processes and the latter conducted and built in tandem over time. Ideally, according to this last group, a genuine capital account regime choice may be possible. In many cases, however, the opportunity of being able to choose may be removed by the actions of market participants.

In the following chapter we shall see how doctrines pertaining to the choice of capital account regime were complemented by parallel arguments on preventing economic crises, and policies aimed at responding to crises. In the post-BW era, crises were often attributed to significantly fluctuating currency values and volatile international capital movements.

5
International Financial Crises: Ideas and Policies

Early post-Bretton Woods discussion: The Minsky-Kindleberger framework

In the early years of the post-BW era, especially during the 1970s, it is surprisingly hard to find economists discussing international 'crises' – either economic crises or more specific financial crises. In the pre-BW era, the work of Ragnar Nurkse (1944) became the point of reference for international currency crises, and his work influenced the formulation of the formal BW agreement (Endres 2005, p.14). In the BW era, significant balance of payments imbalances were considered to have caused broader adjustment, confidence and liquidity problems (Bordo 1993) – the term 'international financial crisis' was rarely used. Paul Krugman's (1979) article modelled balance of payments crises; he was one of the first economists to use the term 'crisis' frequently in the post-BW era. However, priority and authority on the subject in this period must go to Charles Kindleberger's *Manias, Panics and Crashes: A History of Financial Crises* (1978). This book has been reprinted and revised over six editions with the last edition appearing in 2010. Furthermore, it is very rare to find prominent economists in the 1990s referring to research specifically on crises (or subjects with equivalent substantive content) before the 1980s. For example, Lawrence Summers' 'International Financial Crises: Causes, Prevention and Cures' (2000) does not cite any literature on the subject earlier than 1983. We are driven to conclude that a certain confluence of events post-1980 gave rise to increasing attention, by economists, to the subject of international crises. Indeed, it may confidently be asserted that increasing use of the term 'international financial crisis' was a creature of ongoing, market-oriented international economic integration, and was one of the pervasive consequences of integration in the post-BW era.

As already indicated, in terms of precedence Kindleberger's (1978) historical treatment of crises sets the scene for all other contributions in the post-BW era. Like all accomplished economic historians Kindleberger was aware that economic experiences across vastly different contexts and time periods were not directly comparable. Yet he was sure that the post-BW era had ushered in more frequent financial crises though none as prolonged or severe as the 1930's Depression. For Kindleberger, periods of high volatility in prices, currencies, asset values and episodes of widespread bank failures all combined in one way or another, sometimes in different permutations, to make crises a 'hardy perennial' (1978 and 2005, p.1).

The most general, comprehensive definition of a financial crisis, the species of crisis prevalent in the post-BW era that often spread internationally and led to a broader economic crisis, was stated by Barry Eichengreen and Richard Portes (1989, p.1):

> A financial crisis is a disturbance to financial markets, associated typically with falling asset prices and insolvency among debtors and intermediaries which spreads through the financial system, disrupting the market's capacity to allocate capital... [This] definition implies a distinction between generalized financial crises on the one hand and isolated bank failures, debt defaults, and foreign exchange market disturbances on the other.

What often follows in a 'generalized' financial crisis is a cross-border financial and economic crisis – a sharp deterioration in all major international macroeconomic indices both financial (money prices, asset values, interest rates, equity prices, bankruptcies) and real indices (consumption, investment, GDP, employment). The latter will indicate the degree of generalized economic crisis pursuant to the financial crisis.

The central theme in all the editions of Kindleberger's *Manias, Panics and Crashes* is the insuperable problem of rationally managing financial markets in a capitalist economy. In his anatomy of the typical crisis he used the still much neglected work of Hyman Minsky (1975, 1982) at the University of Washington. Minsky (1975) had developed an approach to financial crises that stemmed from a unique interpretation of Keynes's *General Theory of Employment, Interest and Money* (1936) and especially Keynes (1937) in which Keynes responded to criticisms of his *General Theory*. Minsky combined his interpretation of Keynes with ideas from Irving Fisher's (1933) 'debt-deflation' theory of great depressions and with a thorough understanding of the workings of financial institutions. Two of Minsky's articles – one on 'Financial Stability Revisited: The Economics of Disaster' (1972) and the 'Potential for Financial Crisis' (1984) were highly portentous in describing some of the basic monetary forces likely to produce international crises in the post-BW era. (See also Minsky 1980a, 1980b). Here we shall restrict the exposition to a general, elementary statement of the Minsky 'financial instability hypothesis'. Minsky's hypothesis was that pro-cyclical credit expansion and contraction create financial crashes in major industrialized economies. Instability in the supply of credit was central to financial crises, and international crises as well, once the IFS became more integrated in the 1990s and cross-border capital flows increased. In Minsky's model, speculative capital can only move if it is accommodated by monetary policy.

Minsky-type crises involve a general genus which encompasses a range of crisis species: general financial, banking, real estate, currency, stock market, regional, industry, government fiscal and international varieties. The general contours of any crisis involve: speculation, monetary expansion, significant price changes in real assets, followed by an eventual sharp exit of market participants into liquid assets and a deflationary trend in asset and securities prices. Large exogenous shocks such as industrial innovations could often trigger an exuberant attitude and expectation of higher profits in certain favorably affected sectors of an economy. Credit is then generously extended, increasingly toward those profitable sectors, creating a speculative boom. Imprudent bank lending is not often controllable or managed wisely by monetary authorities, or, if it is, it is usually too late. Innovation in financial markets and financial institutions usually run ahead of the ability of monetary authorities to monitor and regulate them. The international transmission of exuberance and the subsequent wave of pessimism are easily transmitted through:

1. Changes in commodity and industrial input prices.
2. Currency movements.
3. Interest rate movements.
4. Capital flows.
5. Cross-border changes in prices of assets such as widely traded equities and financial securities.

In the transition to a slump or crash that follows a boom, financial distress among individuals, banks, and corporate entities increases as they find themselves less able to service debt. Household, corporate and bank balance sheets then require a long period of reconstruction, thereby slowing any subsequent recovery.

Minsky (1986, 1991) offered some important clarifications to his earlier work as well as outlining policy implications with national and international ramifications. Without entering into the technicalities of his approach here, Minsky's thinking focused on the 'complex, sophisticated, and ever-evolving financial institutions' characterizing the capitalist economy that contributed to its inherent financial instability. He investigated the relationship between financial flows, investment and changing asset pricing. In developing his ideas he unashamedly adopts what we may label an inside-out perspective, that is, a 'Wall Street view of the world: the principal players are profit-seeking bankers and businessmen' (1991, p.158). His 'instability hypothesis' has its origins in periods of successful economic performance. In those successful periods, owners of businesses increasingly feel assured about their existing and future 'cash flows from operations' and accompanying profits. In response, they hold a lower level of liquid assets than otherwise and often borrow more on the basis of expected, growing cash flows and profits. They are especially assisted by pro-cyclical credit creation and ongoing innovations in the financial services industry. Eventually the various patterns of financing that businesses rely on prove to be unsustainable (pp.159–62). The result is a financial crisis leading in many (but not all) cases to a broader real economy crisis in which profits continue falling, bad debts increase in the banking sector, investment and employment decline.

In 1991 Minsky was persuaded that a major depression-like financial crisis had not occurred in the post-BW era because central banks had acted effectively as lenders-of-last resort in the incipient crisis phase, boosting liquidity when required, and this kind of action has helped avoid a long debt-deflation cycle. As well, fiscal policy, that is, larger government deficits, have been used to counter aggregate income reductions. In summary, argued Minsky, big 'government and a central bank that is willing and able to intervene' explain why a major, lasting financial crisis had not occurred (p.164). However, he was persuaded that an international financial crisis could still be possible if there was a major financial disruption in a large economy such as the USA. If a crisis was triggered in the United States, for example, when at the same time it was running historically high domestic and external deficits, then the ability (not the willingness) of government to stave-off a broader, enduring crisis would be minimal. The accumulation of a large 'U.S. deficit on trade account is a drain on domestic profits. Furthermore, the accumulated deficits have led to large foreign holdings of U.S. financial assets'. For policymakers, ensuring stability from that starting point using fiscal policy is not an easy task.

The [fiscal] deficit that is needed to sustain profits in the aftermath of even an aborted financial crisis may well be enormous. In [this] environment...the interventions needed to sustain the economy... may well be beyond the combined efforts of the Federal Reserve and the Treasury (p.164).

Therefore, national policy responses may be insufficient and coordinated international policy action would be necessary. In the event, Minsky predicted that high-saving, capital exporting countries with open current accounts may have to implement policies that oriented their economies toward greater domestic consumption (p.164).

Overall, Minsky's outlook is highly pessimistic. Each crisis that is successfully contained only leads to further development of financial market innovations that continue to make capitalist economies 'prone to crisis'. As one commentator on Minsky's work remarked:

for Minsky, financial crisis was only the most extreme case of an ever-present problem that faces any financially dependent economy, the problem of refinance given the shifting balance between cash commitments and cash flows. From this point of view, Minsky's work is best understood as a contribution to the general theory of money. Indeed, it must be said that his work represents the most significant American contribution of his generation to the...tradition of monetary thought that sees money arising as the natural by product of business finance (Mehrling 1999, p.150).

In a modern monetary economy driven by the imperatives of business financing and refinancing, crisis containment is, at best, a 'transitory phenomenon' (Minsky 1991, p.165). Containment only prevents the complete collapse of corporate and bank profits. As crises became deeper and more protracted, big government, higher taxes and higher government spending are required to protect the key cash flow and profit-generating engines of the economy. For Minsky these were predictive, not prescriptive, lessons from his analysis. In addition, government fiscal easing as a containment mechanism can be fragile; government debts, in the limit, may become unmarketable. Here Minsky mentions the case of Argentina's government debt problem in the 1980s as an example. And there 'is nothing in principle nor in the facts of an economy with debts that says that the United States cannot become [another] Argentina' (p.166). These are dramatic, pessimistic conclusions, though mainly focused on the United States. It is not clear that a crisis caused by financial instability in one nation or region of the world economy cannot be counter-balanced by developing engines for growth and prosperity elsewhere. Is it inevitable that a crisis must be systemic in a global sense or be transmitted with equal force, impact and consequences to other nations? Perhaps, though only if the crisis originates in one of the world's largest economies such as the United States. However, it is not necessarily the case that other nations must also be facing the same combination of deficits on internal government budgets and external accounts (as in Minsky's USA example). The only positive aspect of Minsky's work is the recommendation he makes for economic restructuring in other more open, capital exporting nations not experiencing a contemporaneous crisis.

Kindleberger had considerable sympathy for Minsky's approach although he did not share the same pessimistic conclusions. He approved of the debt-deflation mechanism inherent in Minsky's system. Kindleberger's policy response scenario to impending financial crises included a role for national policies, international macroeconomic policy coordination and active responses by IFI's especially the IMF. He saw the IMF as an emergency lender in dampening the impact of financial crises (Kindleberger 1978, Chapter 2 and 1991, pp.129, 132). The IMF would act as a recycler of savings from capital rich nations running current account surpluses (such as the surpluses of Middle East oil exporting countries in the late 1970s). We will have further occasion to examine the case for the IMF as an international lender-of-last resort (ILLR) in the next chapter.

Paul Krugman's characterization of international financial crises

1. Crisis taxonomy

Of all the prominent economists' ideas reviewed in this chapter, Paul Krugman's would appear to be the most fertile. Krugman was a prolific contributor to the discussion of international crises, both in formal academic articles and more accessible surveys of the issues in the popular media. Krugman drew heavily on historical experiences and heavily peppered his analysis with examples. He was generally in favour of unfashionable solutions and policy responses to crises. Certainly he did not spare much space for orthodox, IMF-led bailouts and IMF policy prescriptions.

Krugman (1991b, p.87) paid tribute to the Kindleberger-Minsky approach because it offers a 'single crisis story' in terms of the underlying, generic aspects of all crises in the post-BW era. Thus Kindleberger and Minsky

> argue that there is a standard crisis story, in which naive investors get pulled into an asset market by the belief that they can benefit from rising prices, thereby reinforcing that very rise; then they stampede together for the door when the price finally stabilizes or begins to decline, precipitating a price crash. The price crash then, through a variety of channels, destabilizes the macro economy (p.87).

From what we have exposited of Minsky's approach in particular, this is a very loose and incomplete description of the forces he thought were involved in causing crises. In Minsky's analysis there was no plurality in the 'channels' of a crisis transmission to the macroeconomy; the channel was singular and ran through the process of business asset financing and refinancing rather than the banking and financial system in general.

In distinguishing his approach from the Kindleberger-Minsky line of thought, Krugman provides an informative taxonomy of financial crises motivated by events in the post-BW era. His rationale for the taxonomy is as follows:

> First, the way a crisis plays out depends on the actors in the market; and these actors are very different when the focus is on foreign exchange markets and the balance of payments than when the focus is on stock markets. Second, the real effects of a financial crisis that begins with a run on the U.S. dollar will not look the same as one that begins with a run on the Japanese stock market (p.87).

Accordingly, Krugman distinguishes two main types: (i) currency crises and (ii) contagion crises. A crisis propagated from a currency problem may not be international – it may be restricted to a nation or region. A sudden loss of confidence in asset values (in real estate or stocks for instance) can lead to a severe decline in values that spreads well beyond national borders. Hence 'contagion crises' are more likely to be international in scope than more geographically specific, currency crises. The word 'contagion' came into vogue as a descriptor of crises in the 1980s and 1990s. Up until the 1990s, currency crises were widely discussed in the economics literature; contagion crises were rarely mentioned. Krugman's crisis-types can both have real economic effects (in due course) if they are permitted to continue for an extended period.

Krugman (1991b, p.88) argues that currency crises 'inevitably involve ... acts of commission or at least omission on the part of central banks'. By comparison, contagion crises usually have little to do with monetary or fiscal mismanagement, at least in the origination stage. The contrast extends further into matters of individual rationality: while a currency crisis is often the result of rational reactions by market participants to substandard monetary policies or mismanagement of an exchange rate regime, it is difficult to analyse contagion crises assuming anything like rationality on the part of individual decisionmakers. Indeed, as a result of a crisis in a distant market, asset price crashes can occur without warning in a national jurisdiction with stable economic fundamentals and sound macroeconomic policies. For example, Krugman (1998a, p.24) explains:

> For some reason – perhaps an economic crisis on the other side of the world – investors become jittery and start pulling their money out [of financial asset markets] *en masse*. Suddenly the country is in trouble, its stock market plunging, its interest rates soaring...The crash in asset values may cause previously sound banks to collapse; an economic slump plus high interest rates may cause sound companies to go bankrupt; and at worst, economic distress may cause policy instability.

The accompanying collapse of economic confidence becomes self ratifying or self fulfilling to market participants. Here Krugman is especially focused on 'smaller countries, with a shorter record of success' in operating sound economic policies; these countries are 'always at risk' of a contagion crisis. Economic policy in such countries can often be preoccupied with avoiding losses of market confidence. Even if policies are fundamentally sound prior to a crisis, policy afterwards must 'cater to the perceptions, prejudices and whims of the market' (Krugman 1999, p.113). Often these perceptions tend to be oriented toward the short term. Moreover, in these circumstances, policymakers must assume the role of amateur psychologists, all-the-while second guessing the reactions of markets to particular policy stances. In fact international economic policy 'ends up having very little to do with economics'. Somewhat perversely, policymakers' desire to act in bolstering market confidence can lead to trade-offs with otherwise desirable policy objectives concerned with long-run sustainable growth and employment (Krugman 1998a, pp.24–5).

2. Currency crises and speculative attacks

Krugman (1979) followed by Maurice Obstfeld (1994a, 1996a) among others, introduced the idea that currency crises may be precipitated by unsustainable exchange rate regimes given economic fundamentals or at least given expectations of changes in those fundamentals. These economists later adduce several examples in the post-BW era in different places where unsustainable fixed or pegged exchange rates prevailed – the ERM crisis; the Mexican currency crisis and the Asian currency collapses – all in the 1990s. If capital movements are largely unrestricted, a currency regime of the above kind can be attacked by speculators who will hasten that change in exchange rate or overall exchange rate regime by exhausting central bank reserves used to honor the fixed rate. There was nothing new in this phenomenon as it had been noticed in the pre-BW era by Frank Graham (Endres 2008). One new point in the discussion of the subject in the post-BW era, especially in the 1980s and 1990s, was that speculative attacks were explicitly acknowledged as completely rational responses to bad exchange rate policy. Such attacks were not always driven by what Kindleberger (1978) called 'manias and panics'. Therefore, currency crises were, in a sense, also rational and obviously avoidable if the appropriate exchange rate regime is chosen along with supportive macroeconomic policies. Be that as it may, it is equally possible that speculative attacks quite unnecessarily blur the outlook for, and unwarrantedly destroy the credibility of, an exchange rate regime. In such circumstances, speculation becomes destabilizing; it creates exchange rate changes that 'at best exaggerate the swings in underlying fundamentals and at worst generate completely pointless variability' (Krugman 1991b, p.95). This view has a long pedigree in the history of international economics, at least going back to Nurkse (1944) who considered free foreign exchange market activity destabilizing. Speculation, in this view, propagates currency crises without necessarily any real prior deterioration in economic fundamentals. There is only a short logical leap from this position to prescribing some sort of vigorously defended fixed or fixed adjustable exchange rate regime, or a target zone regime.

That previously sustainable, pegged exchange rates could be attacked by speculation and then made unsustainable is one of Obsfeld's (1996a) main conclusions. In such a case, financial market participants may be operating on false expectations fed by misinformation. Here the foreign exchange markets, in particular, are considered very imperfect communication mechanisms. The outcome of misinformation and false expectations becomes self-fulfilling. If, for example, a government is defending a pegged exchange rate that markets initially perceive to be fairly valued or sustainable, it may attempt to bolster that perception by keeping monetary conditions tighter than normal. Market participants could read particular macroeconomic indices – such as rising unemployment consequent upon tighter monetary policy – as a signal of impending action by monetary authorities to ease monetary policy and perhaps even make a discrete change in the exchange rate peg. Such a scenario may precipitate a speculative currency attack in which foreign reserves held at the central bank are depleted and thereby reinforcing the expected exchange rate depreciation. Without strong controls on capital account convertibility (from demands to move capital out of the country by both domestic and foreign residents) a scenario like the above illustration could quite easily develop. Instead of borrowing more foreign capital to shore-up reserves and defend a pegged exchange rate, the central bank in the above case may reset the pegged rate. Market expectations of this change have been fulfilled. Self-fulfilment may have lent a helping hand only, according to an alternative view, since it may well have been the case that the country in question was vulnerable from the beginning though not certain to face a crisis. Economic fundamentals may have been too fragile from the outset to offer sufficient resistance against speculative attack. As we saw in the previous chapter, as long as capital can move relatively freely across national borders, it is always likely, but not certain, that a fixed exchange rate regime of some kind will break down. In short, any kind of fixed regime is incompatible in the long run with an open, convertible capital account and therefore also an invitation to a currency crisis.

If a country finds itself in a position where its exchange rate regime becomes unsustainable, a common response in the post-BW era was to move to a more flexible and often market-determined regime. A currency crisis often preceded such a policy change and the change was accompanied in many cases by initially tighter monetary and fiscal policies. Usually, in the short run, the subsequent effects were historically higher real interest rates (as an antidote to expected inflation), falling GDP, and for a time an overvalued real exchange rate as short-term capital inflows took advantage of higher domestic interest rates. As a consequence, especially in small open economies, export competitiveness declined and current account deficits expanded (Krugman

1991b, pp.97–9). Again Krugman underscores a perverse need on the part of macroeconomic policymakers to pander to investor confidence in a nation's financial markets. The link between domestic interest rates and the market-determined value of a national currency is so strong that to ease domestic monetary policy and cut interest rates would inevitably trigger another, perhaps more devastating, currency crisis (Krugman 1998b).

While the economic theory of currency crises advanced in a technical sense in the 1980s and 1990s, the precise timing of currency collapses eluded prediction even though deteriorating underlying economic fundamentals could be seen *ex post* as acting like a trigger for a crisis. Those fundamentals – some would say proximate crises causes (other than the exchange rate regime itself) – could be listed as follows though not weighted in an index pinning down the timing of a crisis:

1. high, persistent and accelerating inflation;
2. high, persistent and rising unemployment;
3. growing accumulation of foreign external debt due mostly to high, prolonged current account deficits as a percentage of GDP;
4. rising government debt with implications for government solvency and creditworthiness;
5. political instability.

It is always possible that a confluence of the above circumstances in one country could cause a currency crisis and a broader economic crisis nationally and internationally (Krugman 1991b, pp.100–3). The crisis may start by the 'herd mentality' or 'bandwagon effects' in currency markets. Moreover, according to Krugman (1996, p.347), it is 'very difficult to distinguish between crises that need not have happened and those that were made inevitable by concerns about future viability that seemed reasonable at the time'. By contrast, it was not difficult to set out the expected effects of currency crises. Krugman (1991b, p.108) concludes in a similar manner to Minsky, with a dire prediction: 'if there is a type of financial crisis to worry about, it is probably a currency crisis – [caused by] the United States as a giant Latin-style debtor – rather than a replay of 1929'.

Is any type of pegged exchange rate regime sustainable under conditions of capital mobility? Krugman disapproves of this question being posed at all, for two broad reasons. First, the question implies that any type of pegged exchange rate will raise the risk of currency crises. Furthermore, a negative response to the question narrows down a nation's choice of exchange rate regime to one of two extreme possibilities – a market-determined exchange rate or some form of fixed rate embodied in a formal monetary and currency union. Given the difficulties involved in arranging the latter, this narrows the policymaker's choice to freely floating, market-determined exchange rates. As we saw in the previous chapter, Krugman was vehemently opposed to making this regime the only choice for most countries – there seemed to be no middle ground on exchange rate policy. Indeed, the 'no middle ground' view seemed to become the conventional wisdom in the aftermath of the 1990s Asian crisis. The consensus was that relatively fixed exchange rates had previously diminished the external competitiveness of some Asian economies. Their attempts of maintain pegged nominal exchange rates were not consistent with the freer international capital flows widely permitted in the region (notable exceptions being China, India and Malaysia). Thus, following this conventional view, minimizing the risk of crises and containing them would be enhanced by choosing market-determined exchange rates rather than curtailing capital flows. Jeffrey Frankel (1999, p.7n6) offered a perspective very similar to Krugman's; he rejected the conventional wisdom:

> What would have happened if the emerging-market currencies of East Asia had floated freely throughout the 1990s? They would probably have appreciated strongly through 1996, producing even larger current-account deficits than actually occurred. The crisis, when it came, would have taken a different form – a burst bubble – but might arguably have been even worse than it was if larger international debts had been run up in the meantime.

Furthermore, while the problem of 'sovereign liquidity', as it was called by the Group of Ten (1996), was usually linked to the inability of monetary authorities to defend pegged exchange rates (as occurred regularly in the BW IFS), countries that in fact may have chosen floating exchange rates in the post-BW period could equally find themselves with sovereign liquidity problems – as described in the foregoing passage from Frankel. In the event, national creditworthiness would be severely downgraded; organized bailouts through the IMF or from inter-governmental sources would inevitably be called for.

The second reason why it was inappropriate to claim that any type of fixed exchange rate raised the risk of a currency crisis relates to economic fundamentals. Most countries, in Krugman's view, earn a currency crisis not by choosing a particular exchange rate regime *per se*, but by allowing

economic fundamentals to deteriorate sufficiently to 'cause' a crisis. Therefore, the credibility of economic policy is central. Currency crises are, in a
very general way, expected if not predictable. If they occur, as they did in
Mexico and Asia in the 1990s for example, Krugman was quick to call for
the use of radical policies that broke the link between domestic interest
rates and exchange rates. Here policies containing international capital
inflows were important. Policies that did not permit interest rates to rise
so much as to attract capital and keep a floor under a pegged exchange
rate regime were also important. Krugman also kept offering the highly
unfashionable option of exchange controls, that is, greater restrictions on
capital account convertibility (e.g. Krugman 1998b).

3. Contagion crises

As an international species of financial crisis, a contagion starts with a
country or regional problem; it occurs when a major financial market
disturbance in one or more countries causes financial problems in one
or all of the various asset and securities markets, including currency
markets. As well, bank failures could be a feature of a contagion crisis
within and between countries. These can be manifested by temporary,
exaggerated price changes that are not necessarily the result of irra-
tional actions by market participants. Information transmission across
markets, assisted by advances in communications technology, can signal
changes in the behaviour of major, usually well-informed investors.
Such changes might include sudden, dramatic alterations in investment
portfolios that are quickly imitated by less sophisticated investors who
'follow-the-leader' as the case may be. Stock market contagions seem
to follow this pattern. After an initial crisis has occurred in one market,
country or region, real trade links in commodities, goods, and services
are affected, thereby transmitting the crisis to other countries. If currency changes are involved in the transmission process, these can in turn
change the degree of international competitiveness between countries
and dramatically impact export earnings in countries not directly experiencing a financial crisis. There is no presumption in Krugman's description of contagion crises that currency crises are always independent; twin
crises may occur in sequence. A contagion may supervene on a currency
crisis. And a combination of the two may produce a global economic
crisis underpinned by systemic risk. Concerted national and international
policy action would then be required to reduce its impact. The difficulty
for policymakers is to remove systemic risk which occurs when the allocation of capital cannot adequately be diversified efficiently to reduce risk
of losses. Systemic risk is endemic to contagion crises; it leads to highly

conservative investing, low risk-taking and falling economic growth. The world's supply of savings is not used efficiently or indeed accumulated and actively invested anywhere in a manner that serves as a foundation for long-run international economic progress. A prolonged, secular, international economic stagnation would then be in prospect. If a twin crisis took hold – currency crisis followed by a contagion crisis – this would necessitate a 'Return of Depression Economics' (Krugman 1999) on a world scale.

Joseph Stiglitz on crises causes and policy responses

Examining the underlying and specific sources of contagion crises and associated policy implications was a task Joseph Stiglitz (at the World Bank) set himself during the 1990s. He was working broadly in the spirit of the Keynesian tradition, adding insights from institutional research and the economics of information as applied to financial markets. He exhibited a distrust of arguments in favour of allowing market forces to play a major role in correcting crises, let along assisting in crisis prevention. In this endeavour his view consistently developed against the background of a general doctrinal attitude to the role of government in economic affairs. Thus, he rejected the proposition that well-functioning markets are only possible if governments reduce their activity in the economy (Stiglitz 1989).

The East Asian economic crisis and subsequent contagion crisis in the Asian region in the 1990s acted as stimulus for a thorough assessment of crises (Furman and Stiglitz 1998; Stiglitz 1999). During that period Stiglitz developed a deep appreciation of the East Asian economies (e.g. Stiglitz 1996; Stiglitz and Uy 1996). Generalizing across the Asian region, it was possible and perfectly reasonable to list proximate crises causes such as: mismanaged exchange rate regimes, wasteful investment, opaque corporate and government agency accounting practices, and high current account deficits. While in some way these factors were causes, they were not central. Furman and Stiglitz (1998, p.6) explain:

> While a variety of factors may contribute to a crisis, it is important to identify the central factors; in a statistical sense, these are the factors that would be given the highest weight in a statistical model explaining the probability or severity of a crisis. And in interpreting the causes of a crisis, one should use Occam's razor: rather than listing every factor that might have contributed to the crisis, one

should identify those factors that, by themselves, are large enough to have caused (in a stochastic model, to have high probability of) the crisis.

One of those central factors, indeed a major explanatory variable, was the ratio of short-term national debt to official reserves used to support various Asian currency pegs. Much of the debt was unhedged, partly because financial markets in the region were not well-developed and lacked scale. In the 1990s there 'was a sudden change in the markets' perception of risk. Although such changes can sometimes be related to events within a country or to a country's policies, often shocks are almost entirely external' (Furman and Stiglitz 1998, p.6). This brief passage describes what Krugman had called a 'contagion crisis'. The rapid liberalization of financial markets and capital accounts across the East Asian region are identified as events making the Asian economies vulnerable to external shocks. The East Asian region in particular had made itself open to the risk of crises by premature financial market liberalization (pp.15–17).

The liberalization of international capital flows into and out of the East Asian economies had made it especially difficult for monetary authorities to manage monetary conditions and exchange rates. Much international capital was allocated to private investment projects that should have yielded sufficient returns to more than pay for debt-servicing costs given an existing exchange rate peg. However, a discrepancy emerged 'between private and social risk in decisions about accumulating...short-term foreign-currency-denominated debt' (p.20). As Stiglitz (1999, p.1512) explained it:

> the experience of East Asia has confirmed lessons from experiences elsewhere: there are large systemic risks imposed on the economy by financial sector weaknesses and the surges of capital flows associated with capital account liberalization. The costs of these disruptions are felt not only by borrowers and lenders who engage in the transactions, but also by workers, small business[es], and others throughout the economy.

So economy-wide ('social') risk was ignored; much foreign investment was left unhedged. When a crisis supervened, a major capital market failure eventuated, shifting costs onto society as a whole. An additional dimension to capital market failure was the moral hazard outcome in which banking institutions and financial intermediaries deemed too big to fail, were presenting to governments and IFIs for financial bailouts. If bailouts occur the likelihood increases that the recipients will take less responsible financial actions in future (because they expect further bailouts). As long as there is potential for bailouts, moral hazard entails a misuse of resources as borrowers become less circumspect in managing capital.

In addition to the costs of private market decisions to borrow funds internationally on a short-term basis, government policies were also responsible for the Asian financial crisis. Thus capital account liberalization was not consistent with the various exchange rate policies in the region. Given the predominant choice of pegged exchange rates, domestic monetary policies had to remain tighter than they might have been under a market-determined exchange rate regime. Interest rates were kept higher than otherwise, encouraging both domestic residents to keep their savings at home and attracting foreign capital inflows. There was one more or less obvious effect of such policies: higher interest rates, while normally dampening the inducement to invest in domestic markets and projects, 'created additional incentives to [finance] investment through unhedged short-term borrowing'. More long-term investment for industrial development became relatively neglected in favour of domestic stock markets and commercial real estate (Furman and Stiglitz 1998, p.26). In the realm of microeconomic policy, the East Asian region had not developed a comprehensive, transparent set of internationally harmonized regulations in the finance and banking sectors. In this respect, risk-adjusted bank capital adequacy standards and debt risk-management provisions were not thoroughly instituted or consistently applied. Restrictions on the liability structures of firms to which the banking system lent funds and sectoral limits on lending (e.g. to the real estate sector) should have been implemented (pp.27–30).

Overall, Furman and Stiglitz argue that financial crises in the post-BW era were more often caused by a combination of poor economic policy formulation and human fallibility. Financial market policies were not robust; the external capital account regime should not have been so liberal and was not dovetailed with other macroeconomic policies (pp.31–2). The single most important crises-determining factor was capital account openness; it was especially harmful because it allowed short-term international debt accumulation and thereby imposed unnecessary constraints on government policies designed to achieve other economic objectives such as economic stability (using counter cyclical monetary and fiscal policies) and long-term growth. Hence Stiglitz (2000, p.1080) asks,

> does opening of the short-term capital account – making the country subject to short-run oscillations in sentiment – provide significant <u>extra</u> external discipline? On the negative side, the openness to capital flight makes countries especially sensitive, e.g., to corporate or capital tax rates or to interest rates. Thus, openness may impose costly <u>constraints</u> on the ability of government to pursue legitimate objectives. (His emphasis)

This view was, of course, connected to the views of 'post-Keynesian' economists who, as we have already seen, believed that governments had to keep interest rates at an extremely high level to prevent capital outflows. In having to endure higher than normal interest rates, monetary authorities in the East Asian region contributed to the subsequent crises: they raised the probability that financial intermediaries and highly leveraged domestic borrowers would default, thereby reducing business confidence in the region's economic outlook and further disturbing financial markets. As Jeffrey Sachs (1998) commented in discussion of Furman and Stiglitz's work, the way policymakers in fact responded to the incipient crisis badly affected the confidence of financial market participants in the region. Stiglitz (1999, p.1519) believed that the conventional policy responses of monetary and fiscal austerity had been the main cause damaging confidence and raising domestic economic uncertainty in the East Asian economies. Capital outflows were a common outcome, further perpetuating the crisis. Other prominent economists offered complementary views and evidence turning on the effect of high real interest rates on currency values in the region. Real exchange rates appreciated significantly before the crisis occurred; while dampening inflation they tended to reduce export competitiveness and raise current account deficits (Edwards 1989a; Dornbusch et al. 1995). Persistently overvalued real exchange rates can precipitate a broader economic crisis with a lag – after the worst of a financial crisis had already passed. In practice, it is only possible to determine the size of a real exchange rate overvaluation in retrospect, after a currency crises has occurred (Furman and Stiglitz 1998, pp.38–48).

Stiglitz was addressing the conventional doctrine on crises in the 1990s; that doctrine had inconsistently advocated capital account liberalization on the basis that freer markets in capital lead to the efficient allocation of resources. As we saw in the previous chapter, Stiglitz demonstrated how, in less developed countries, imperfect information and incomplete markets combined to make financial markets persistently inefficient. In fact, 'capital account and financial market liberalization are systematically related'. A nation's vulnerability to economic crises was often raised by liberalizing financial markets prematurely in the economic development process and simultaneously allowing freer capital account convertibility. That vulnerability can reveal itself either by way of a currency crisis or by the relatively speedy, cross-border transmission of a contagion crisis (Stiglitz 1999, p.1509).

If a crisis was underway, a comprehensive stabilization program was recommended (Stiglitz 1999, pp.1513–15). 'Comprehensive' meant going beyond simply stabilizing volatile macroeconomic variables such as exchange rates and key financial market indices. Merely allowing interest rates to rise in order to dampen inflation rather than promote production would not do. Policy prescriptions turning on the liberalization of markets, reducing government deficits, tightening domestic credit, floating exchange rates and privatization of government assets were not desirable as a first step, if at all in Stiglitz's response program. His preferred strategy was as follows:

1. Remove policies that appear to encourage short-term cross-border capital flows.
2. Strengthen the balance sheets and operating structures of financial institutions, including banks.
3. Directly intervene to stabilize international capital flows that 'are not mediated through the banking system' (p.1513).

Stiglitz was realistic in proposing this program, noting how difficult these ideas were to implement even in highly developed-country financial markets. Minsky would no doubt have endorsed his conclusion; he would have seen it as an inevitability – the result of continuing innovation in financial markets in response to market regulation or the lack of regulation. Thus

> [i]t is important to recognize that the first two sets of measures, as important as they are, are both difficult – especially for less-developed countries – and are far from sufficient to inoculate countries against the kinds of instabilities that have been so prevalent in the last quarter of a century. Transparency in the form of mark-to-market accounting (requiring banks to record all assets at their current market

value), for instance, is resisted today in the United States...(which is in part attributed to poor regulation, including inadequately transparent information systems)...Even under the best of circumstances, obtaining the relevant data may be difficult – and is becoming increasingly so (p.1513).

Policy measure 3 is especially vital; it was lacking in the East Asian economies before the crisis. There was no point in prohibiting bank borrowing from international sources; such a policy would be ineffectual – it would 'be like putting your finger in a dike – it plugs up one hole, but the water will find a way around. If there are economic incentives (or misguided perceptions) that led to a desire to borrow abroad, companies that can and will do so, even if banks cannot do so on their behalf' (p.1514). However, banks needed to be supervised by regulatory authorities. Private foreign borrowing was problematic and should always be mediated through a well-regulated banking system. Stiglitz was aware that strategy 3 would vary depending on the country – one size did not fit all (a practice, as we shall see in the next chapter, he finds objectionable about IMF policies and crisis recovery programs).

As for the international policy implications issuing from Stiglitz's approach, the IFO needs to be formally redesigned to create harmonized rules and policies to control short-term capital flows. As an experienced World Bank economist, he insisted on some form of international collective action, though in the 1990s he is not clear precisely on the kinds of policies that should be established in some international blueprint.[15] International collaboration, research, consultation and policy formation through IFIs such as the World Bank and IMF were essential ingredients of any concerted world program to prevent and respond to financial crises. The priority in such a program, to repeat his message, was to deal with short-term capital flows that expose less developed countries in particular 'to significant risks without commensurate return' (Furman and Stiglitz 1998, p.102). There is a simple analogy to make the point even clearer: 'If a single car has an accident on a road, there is a presumption that the driver made an error; if there are repeated accidents at the same curve, then the presumption should be that the road is badly designed' (p.102). One obvious implication here is that temporary capital controls ought to be part of the armoury of policymakers in

---

[15]Though, outside the period under review, see Stiglitz (2008) for more details on his proposed reforms.

countries experiencing a crisis and perhaps even more permanent controls maintained thereafter. Such controls should be sanctioned by international agreement. As for sovereign debt problems resulting from a currency crisis or a contagion crisis, merely putting in place an ILLR such as the IMF would not be sufficient to protect the world economy from a severe economic downturn. The hallmark of an ILLR is that it makes funds available automatically to 'qualifying' member governments. However some governments can lose control of bank reserves very quickly because of a range of malpractices in financial markets, including the inappropriate use of hedging and derivatives. Whether such a country should be entitled to a bailout is debatable. In any case, Stiglitz was not satisfied that the rules for operating a genuine ILLR in a crisis were clear; yet the IMF seems to have assumed the ILLR role *de facto*. We shall discuss this matter further in the following chapter.

Much like Krugman, Stiglitz framed crisis response policies with specific reference to LDCs and emerging market economies. That all post-BW era crises were concentrated in LDCs such as Latin America and East Asia may have been broadly correct (though the ERM crisis in the early 1990s was an exception). Since that time, of course, the international financial crisis in the early twenty-first century had its origins in, and was propagated by, developed nations that already had in place sophisticated and (seemingly) well-regulated financial systems of the kind recommended by Krugman and Stiglitz in the 1990s. (Again, Minsky's approach seems to have more general explanatory power than either that of Stiglitz or Krugman). These developed nations were nonetheless open to international capital flows; and these flows were long term and heavily invested in major Treasury bond markets. Perhaps none of this should deny the value of concentrating crisis analysis and policy proposals on LDCs? Stiglitz's ideas were mostly propounded while serving at the World Bank. He was accordingly concerned with the impact of crises on poverty and international inequality. Crises can widen the differences in the rate of human development (such as child mortality rates) and general improvements in human well-being between rich and poor countries. These distributional impacts of crises within and between countries were naturally of concern to his World Bank economist-colleagues (e.g. Ferreira and Litchfield 1999).[16]

---

[16]For the latest discussion of these distributional consequences see the World Bank Development Research Group (2008).

Crises from the vantage point of eclectics and pragmatists

In this section a group of economists is distinguished according to their belief that there was a definite trade-off between economic liberalization including financial market liberalization and the depth and frequency of both national and international crises. This group includes Barry Eichengreen, Rudiger Dornbusch and Jeffrey Sachs. We have had occasion to mention these economists in previous chapters. Here we are interested in their positions on crises causes and policy responses.

The historically informed approach of Eichengreen should be considered first. His is the most thoroughgoing in the treatment of crises in this eclectic group. He considered a large number of financial crisis experiences over a long period of history (e.g. Eichengreen et al. 1995, 1996). No single factor seemed responsible for all crises yet some common general factors could be listed as playing a role depending on the case. For example, reduced international competitiveness in an open economy results in larger current account deficits, more unemployment, and growing internal, fiscal deficits – those factors often figure as standard pre-crisis events. Eichengreen did not rule out self-fulfilling elements as well. Eichengreen and Rose (1999, pp.30–1 and more generally from a long-run historical perspective Eichengreen 1996a), describe the transmission channels through which cross-border capital flows, coupled with foreign exchange market instability and speculative currency attacks, cause contagion crises. First, speculative attacks can strongly affect the current accounts of the countries concerned because they change the competitiveness of export industries. Trading relationships with other countries can change dramatically; the currency impacts of speculation are transmitted to international trade and show up in trading patterns over time. Secondly, common macroeconomic policies and conditions between countries can lead currency market traders to infer that currencies of other, immediately unaffected countries, with similar policies are also vulnerable. Thus, for instance,

> [d]ifficulties in one country pursuing a program of exchange-rate-based stabilization, for example, might lead currency traders to revise their assessment of the likelihood that other countries pursuing this macroeconomic strategy will carry it off. An attack on one currency and the issuing government's response to the pressure may thus provide new information relevant for expectations of how

other governments will respond if placed in a similar position (Eichengreen and Rose 1999, p.31).

To be sure, the link referred to in this passage is asserted; it is always difficult to ascertain conclusively whether or not a speculative attack has occurred. Moreover, it is difficult to determine the precise channel of transmission to other countries – to their currencies and economies. The transmission is rarely evident in a single link.

Eichengreen (1999a) focused on policies and reforms required for the whole IFS when crisis events seemed to be increasing. First, there is a good economic case in his view for international financial market liberalization, though national financial market reforms should be approached first and with great circumspection. As discussed in Chapter 4 above, sequencing liberal policies should begin with changes at the national level in the light of the fact that institutions vary between countries. Moreover,

> sequencing capital account liberalization is an important but complicated issue. Countries vary greatly: in their levels of economic and financial development, in their institutional structures, in their legal systems and business practices, and in their capacity to manage change in a host of areas relevant for financial liberalization (Eichengreen et al. 1999, p.10).

Therefore, there is 'no cook book recipe for the sequence of steps to follow and no general guideline for how long the process should take' (p.10). Indeed, external financial liberalization, that is freer capital account convertibility, may either be adopted after the domestic financial system is properly reformed, or liberalization may be attempted in parallel and contemporaneously across internal and external sectors. Though it sounded platitudinous, 'orderly' reform was the watchword – a position Eichengreen had in common with the Group of Seven (1998, p.7) on financial market liberalization. The precise sequencing of more liberal policies depends on the case. In some countries it is a mistake rapidly to liberalize if the domestic financial system is in disarray because of a crisis of some kind and when the finance industry is experiencing liquidity or solvency problems (as in East Asia during the 1990s). Similarly, extensive 'orderly' liberalization may take a decade or more. The infrastructure for the domestic financial system in LDCs, for instance, is often weak or non-existent (as in Eastern European emerging market economies in the early 1990s). Sachs (1995a, p.8) took a similar position to Eichengreen's: financial liberalization is generally desirable but it should be sequenced reasonably with other sectoral reforms and it should be implemented gradually.

It was a common refrain among eclectics and pragmatists to maintain that freer capital account convertibility should not proceed 'before banks have upgraded their risk-management practices, supervisors have strengthened their oversight of the financial institutions and governments have corrected their macroeconomic policies' (Eichengreen 1999a, p.2). What is adequate in respect of risk management and financial market regulatory supervision is thrown into question when larger, advanced industrialized countries with sophisticated and regulated financial systems undergo upheavals and crises. It is a feature of economists' discussions of the causes and cures of financial crises in the 1980s and 1990s that regulatory reform in advanced (Western) financial markets is not the focus of attention. Eichengreen is no exception. The reform agenda he proposes, 'post-Asia' in the 1990s, is exclusively referenced to financial markets in LDCs. Eichengreen (1999a, pp.4–6) rejected utopian, 'pie-in-the-sky schemes'; such schemes would completely restructure and renegotiate the IFO in the face of financial crises occurring in the 1990s. He insisted on the political realities affecting international economic policymaking and therefore concentrated on incremental operational reforms of the existing IFS. Thus,

> economic policy is framed in a politicized environment. It cannot be assumed that regulators and other economic policymakers will carry out their tasks without allowing themselves to be influenced by political considerations. To the contrary, lobbying and pressure politics inevitably shape the policies that are pursued. Realistic policy advice requires acknowledging these pressures and not assuming, for analytical convenience, that policymaking institutions...can be made to follow rigid apolitical rules. Moreover national governments are jealous of their prerogatives...realistic policy reform requires recognizing these uncomfortable facts (p.4).

Political realism often made some economists 'uncomfortable' because they had to acknowledge a trade-off between (an ideal of) full liberalization and crisis avoidance or stability. The optimal approach to reform was to make marginal changes to improve that supposed trade-off. When financial factors play a significant role in post-BW era crises, there is no way that the IFS can be reformed to immunize nations from contagion as long as trade and capital movements remain relatively open (compared with the BW-era). The pragmatic view, to paraphrase an old adage, is that a globally integrated world economy based on market processes without financial crises and without economic volatility, is like Catholicism without sin. In preparation for more crises, Eichengreen recommended that the IMF upgrade its position as an ILLR but not bind itself in the process to 'following rigid and political rules'. The IMF must become an active advocate of certain policies. Eichengreen's previous research reported in Chapter 4 above, favoured the IMF acting as at least a conditional advocate of capital inflow taxes for LDCs and for flexible exchange rates. In this, he accepted the reality of the existing IFS in which capital flows were becoming large in magnitude and more flexible exchange rates were being widely adopted to reduce the impact of speculative currency attacks.

Jeffrey Sachs (1995a) and Sachs et al. (1996a, 1996b) also remained focused on practical lessons derived from several post-BW era financial crises. Apart from covering issues and policies also canvassed by Eichengreen, Sachs gave special attention to sovereign debt crises that were especially common in the 1980s and 1990s (e.g. beginning with the Latin American debt crises in the early 1980s). When debt crises begin they are normally marked by fear that a government in a particular country will likely default on its loan commitments, causing market participants to abandon currency, bond and stock markets in the affected country. A financial collapse ensues. Sachs favoured immediate action by the IMF to offer emergency loans or organize inter-governmental lending packages to reduce the impact of financial crisis contagion in any particular region of the world economy. To deal with any resulting currency crises it was important, ideally as a crisis avoidance measure rather than a containment action, to regulate the banking system in such a way as to prevent widespread development of private, foreign-exchange denominated accounts in domestic banks. An international regulatory regime may be instituted to limit those developments in order or discourage residents within a national jurisdiction from quickly and easily choosing to switch out of domestic currency deposits into foreign currency accounts (Sachs 1995a, pp.6–7).

There are two notable features of the pragmatic treatments of crises outlined in this section so far: (i) their readiness to accept that crises will occur regularly and (ii) their policy prescriptions are historically specific. Both Eichengreen and Sachs refer to issues associated exclusively with contemporary crises in the post-BW era, without seeking to develop an over-arching theoretical framework or set of principles about generic crisis causes and remedies. Theirs' is an institutional approach. Similarly, while Rudiger Dornbusch regularly made technical and analytical contributions in international economics, his discussion of crises is comparatively informal (Dornbusch 1991, Dornbusch et al. 1995). On national crises, one of his joint studies considered the case of Mexico in which pro-market reforms were a contributory cause of both currency crises and relatively low rates of economic growth (Dornbusch and Werner 1994). General slumps in market confidence, in the Mexican case, were not easily rectified within markets left to their own devices. In both the national and international realms, Dornbusch (1991, p.123) considered financial market liberalization 'a really very potent source of financial instability' and eventual crisis. Here he meant by 'liberalization' complete and unfettered deregulation of financial markets rather than a reformation of market regulations. The key question was not when to liberalize financial markets but how to do so in order to create markets conducive to the productive alloca-tion of international capital, especially direct foreign investment. This view was intuitively plausible even before it was substantiated by Jeffrey Frankel and Andrew Rose (1998); they demonstrate how greater foreign direct investment, rather than short-term capital inflows, reduced the risk of crises.

The regulatory reforms Dornbusch recommended were not, as he understood them, always able to keep pace with the reality of actual financial market innovations. Indeed, ideally, financial 'regulation should be way ahead of the unlocking of very, very repressed financial markets' in LDCs. Yet in the enthusiasm to liberalize with impunity in emerging market economies in particular, investors and financial market traders were able to adopt practices not permitted in more advanced financial markets (Dornbusch 1991, pp.122–3). The weak linkages in the IFS created by inappropriate liberalization are a recipe for eventual market breakdown and financial crises. His conclusion was portentous, coming several years before the East Asian financial crisis. He enquired as to

> where the next crises are being generated. My impression is that financial deregulation in developing countries may be doing just that. There is great enthusiasm [for example,] underway to take Korea and give it a modern, healthy financial system, where the Korean savings can be taken to London to put into junk bonds (p.122).

A final strand in the eclectic, pragmatic line of thinking on crises was concerned with international economic and financial policy coordination

– especially the coordination of macroeconomic policies. The kinds of concerted international action required depended on the crisis in question, and the countries and regions affected. Nevertheless, as Jacob Frenkel (then at the IMF) (1991) argued, policy coordination among the largest industrial nations such as the European community, among the G7 or G20 and so forth, is essential from time-to-time for crisis prevention and crisis alleviation. If the crisis is propagated in one of these larger economies then policy coordination in response is essential. Frenkel favoured monetary policy coordination because fiscal policy was not as flexible and certainly varied markedly between countries. Just how coordination would be mediated is not clear, though the IMF might have a leading role. Otherwise, the scope for coordination and the scope of coordination, including the preferred range and depth of policies to be coordinated, the various methods and possible effects of coordination were all controversial (Frenkel et al. 1996, pp.19–25). While there are obviously different policy priorities across countries, there were key commonalities. For example, most countries used monetary policy actively to target inflation and could easily use policy to change monetary conditions in the face of a shared crisis. As well, the larger industrial countries could cooperate and perhaps formalize a common policy in a sovereign debt crisis (Group of Ten 1996).

Influenced by contemporary events in the post-BW era, all-too-often the pragmatic line of thought on crises neglected the prospect of crises propagated in larger industrialized nations. The intellectual concentration was on the vulnerability to crises in LDCs and emerging market economies. As we noticed earlier in this chapter, Minsky and Krugman warned of the prospect of a financial and subsequent general economic crisis issuing originally from a highly developed economy such as the United States. Nevertheless, the pragmatists possessed deep institutional knowledge of crises in the post-BW era. They agreed that markets generally operate in a rational and efficient manner (unlike Krugman and Stiglitz) yet always understood the potential for market participants to act in a destructive manner when their outlooks were biased toward the very short term. In the event, markets can operate inefficiently from the standpoint of the economy and society as a whole. The pragmatists viewed with equanimity high levels of international capital flows and financial market reforms tending in the direction of greater liberalization. Their doctrines doubted the orthodox, market-based idea that liberalized financial markets and freer capital account convertibility always acted beneficently to discipline the actions of economic policymakers. In their view, markets can overreact to garbled signals, more especially when financial markets are prematurely liberalized in LDCs, and are badly regulated. Furthermore, even when financial markets are ostensibly well-supervised and regulated such as in the EMS during the early 1990s, there is a degree of scepticism, for instance in Eichengreen's work, that markets can in fact be continuously consistent, disciplinary institutions for macroeconomic policy. If markets were sufficiently well-informed and operating in this disciplinary manner then it raises the question as to why they do not foresee impending crises and work to prevent their occurrence (Eichengreen et al. 1995). By contrast, the proposition that financial markets are a source of crises is well-established. In the spirit of the pragmatic, eclectic approach Thomas Willett (2000, p.31) remarked

> that is not wise at present to assume that international capital flows will provide either a reliable early warning system [of an impending crisis] or a source of continuous discipline for governments' macro-economic policies. Financial markets, like voters, have tended to sanction politicians for bad economic policies – although often only after much damage has been done. (Bracketed insert added)

For the pragmatic group of economists reviewed here, there is always a lack of certainty in the structural dimension of a crisis as opposed to its cyclical elements. Governments and market participants can assess these elements in a different way: the latter can then assess a set of policy responses as being unsustainable or likely to have little or no remedial effect. Governments will calibrate their crisis response policies by, for instance, considering output, employment and income targets as if the crisis was merely a transitory, cyclical event. By comparison, market participants could perceive matters differently and see the policy responses as lacking credibility because they may not address structural elements. This divergence of perspective on the reasons for a crisis is not easy to correct; it will reduce the effectiveness of government crisis management and recovery policies and any international coordination of those kinds of policies. For the pragmatic, eclectic economists taken as a group, 'the market' acts as a brake on what might otherwise be efficacious crises response policies.

Pro-market approaches to crises and crises resolution

Markets can be considered as mere messengers before and after a crisis has begun, rather than direct causes of crises or as brakes on recovery policies. This theme is promoted in another economic thought trajectory in the post-BW era. Here we select the ideas and policy prescriptions of economists who, while as with other groups of economists they were not monolithic, accepted the proposition that markets would generally work well in the absence of serious macroeconomic policy errors. Further, they considered markets as providing a disciplinary force on economic policies, nudging them in the direction of increasing liberalization and inducing policy adjustments that, if timely, could counteract crisis tendencies. By contrast with the eclectics and pragmatists, they generally denied the trade-off between economic and financial market liberalization and the frequency or severity of crises.

Let us start with a benchmark position along this thought trajectory – the work of Anna Schwartz at the National Bureau of Economic Research. Early in her career Schwartz made a celebrated contribution with Milton Friedman that included reflections on the monetary causes of the Great Depression (Friedman and Schwartz 1963). In this work, sharp reductions in the quantity of money held by the public accompanying a banking crisis seemed to be a prime cause of subsequent widespread economic depression. In many cases of economic crises, poor monetary policy decisions did not help avert banking problems and in many cases exacerbated them. The accepted source of a real economic crisis for Friedman and Schwartz was a policy failure – the inappropriate contraction of the money supply. In these circumstances, the attempts by individuals to increase their cash holdings made banks more vulnerable to collapse and certainly more conservative in their lending practices.

Schwartz made several important contributions to the subject of international financial arrangements and crises (Schwartz 1986, 1987, 1998). In the light of early research with Friedman, Schwartz (1986) deemed that genuine financial crises (that on her terms must have significant real economic consequences) were not observable in the post-BW era. There were no crises on a par with what occurred in the world economy in 1931–33 or in the United Kingdom in 1866. On her understanding of crises, sharp declines in asset prices, commodity prices or currency collapses, financial industry problems and sovereign debt problems were 'pseudo' crises. In reflecting on the East Asian crisis in the 1990s Schwartz (1998, pp.251–2) identified 'two myths' attached to orthodox commentaries on this event:

1. Loss of creditworthiness by one country arbitrarily tarnishes other (often neighbouring) countries without credit problems, thereby producing a contagion crisis.

2. Bailouts of the country that has lost creditworthiness are essential to avoid contagion.

Schwartz proceeded to puncture these 'myths'. In the typical post-BW currency crisis an inappropriate exchange rate policy, namely some form of pegged currency (fixed against the US dollar or against a basket of currencies) invited or repelled capital flows. As we saw in Chapter 3 above, pegged exchange rates were often attacked because they acted as a nominal anchor, keeping down the rate of domestic inflation, further attracting capital inflows (for a while). An appreciating real exchange rate usually followed and, correspondingly, export competitiveness declined (in the common, open economy case). As well, capital imports were not often used productively, were usually unhedged, and eventually resulted in growing non-performing loans or bad debts in the banking system. Lastly, countries facing currency crises usually held insufficient foreign currency reserves to defend the pegged exchange rate. National creditworthiness would suffer accordingly. Domestic monetary policy would likely have to be tightened, but to go too far down that route would compromise domestic policy objectives such as growth and employment. Foreign exchange market participants would question the credibility of monetary policy, sell the currency more heavily and domestic asset market values would also decline markedly. A devaluation of the previously pegged currency would be expected by the markets. All these fundamental economic pressures confirm Krugman's view cited earlier that countries in fact earn their currency crises. Some other countries with similar, though not necessarily identical, fundamentals would naturally be drawn into the same kind of currency and domestic asset sell-off. Overall, it seemed 'ludicrous to believe that financial troubles in a Mexico or a Thailand can trigger a calamity of global proportions' (Schwartz 1998, p.254). Calamities on an international scale only occur if economic fundamentals deteriorate everywhere. As well, sound exchange rate and monetary policies in countries other than those immediately affected by 'financial troubles' stave-off contagion crises. This view of course contrasts starkly with Barry Eichengreen's (1999a, p.1) dramatic remark following the East Asian financial crisis that global policymakers were confronted with an 'urgent' issue – 'to contain and resolve the macroeconomic <u>and financial crisis threatening much of the world</u>'. (Emphasis added).

As for the 'bailout myth' Schwartz was convinced that some form of public, IFI-related bailout of private investors would be used to 'reward' inappropriate, unsustainable economic policies. She suspected that the main beneficiaries of international bailouts were wealthy investors, many of whom were residents of advanced industrial nations. Clearly the moral hazard problem loomed large in her mind (Schwartz 1998, pp.253–5). Instead of rescuing people in 'crisis', bailouts favour 'politically connected speculators' who will be able to recover their 'money-losing ventures' (p.225). No empirical evidence is used to substantiate this doctrine.

Overall, Schwartz's policy prescriptions were straightforward:

1. financial institutions would learn from the failure of previous lending and borrowing practices and upgrade their risk management;
2. monetary authorities in affected countries should provide more liquidity to prevent 'banking panics and forbearance, and under capitalized banks';
3. countries should adopt stable, predictable monetary and fiscal policies; and
4. all countries should seriously consider moving toward the adoption of market-determined exchange rates (pp.254–5).

Without being explicit, there is a strong implication in Schwartz's work in relation to point 4 above, about the place of exchange rate policy. In themselves, market-determined exchange rates are not sufficient to avoid 'crises' but they limit the risk and reduce their transmission. Changing degrees of creditworthiness will make some countries more or less vulnerable to internally generated crises. Foreign exchange reserves should be accumulated to avoid credit downgrades and the need to call on contingency credits from an IFI. Emergency financing situations only compound the creditworthiness problem.

Against the benchmark set by Anna Schwartz, other economists who we might impound in the pro-market thought trajectory on the analysis of financial crises (causes and responses) do not quite reach the same conclusions. Stanley Fischer at the IMF was broadly aligned with Schwartz's policy stance though he favoured last-resort, emergency lending to affected countries because the impact on the economy and social conditions was often too great to ignore. In addition, the cross-border, economic spillover effects of a financial crisis in one country or region on another should not be discounted. He was confident that IMF loan conditions could be used to encourage nations to adopt the broad policy regimes preferred by Schwartz. Fischer (1998) strongly supported the capital account amendments to the IMF Articles of Agreement. In the face of the East Asian financial crisis as it was then widely known, Fischer did not retract from actively advocating the full liberalization of nations' capital accounts 'over time' with due allowance for interim, transitional capital controls. Post-BW financial crises notwithstanding, the creation of an 'international environment of free international capital movements provides enormous opportunities for countries and the international monetary system' (pp.9–10). The clear implication is that ultimately, international financial markets and cross-border capital flows are not crisis causes, but mere messengers of underlying problems in both economic fundamentals and policy orientations.[17]

Additionally, the involvement of private capital in the resolution of financial crises should not be overlooked. Lending activities of official IFIs such as the IMF, WB and regional development banks following a crisis can encourage private owners of capital to participate because of the credibility that IFI involvement offers (IMF 1999).

> Involving the private sector is necessary not only to ensure that investors assume the risks implied by their loans, thereby helping to ensure that yields are correctly priced, but also because the official sector will not have sufficient financing available to do otherwise...[For example the] official sector has promoted modifications of contracts – for instance, by including collective action clauses in bond contracts – in a way that would make their restructuring easier under specified crisis circumstances (Citrin and Fischer 2000, p.1139).

To be sure, this last idea may be counterproductive, since 'lenders may have in place overall country exposure guidelines, which would imply that other emerging market credits could be withdrawn when the contingent lines are drawn down' (p. 1139). Certainly, this proposal and other ideas actively to involve (rather than force) the private sector to assist in crisis resolution were at initial stages of development in the 1990s. The important lesson from this pro-market trajectory of thought emanating from the IMF was that the market should not be sidelined when considering how to deal with financial or other crises, even if market critics had concluded that markets cause crises.

Lawrence Summers, sometime at Harvard, later an economist who worked for a period at the World Bank and then at the United States

---

[17]Later, outside the period under review, Fischer (2003b, pp.15–20) reiterates and further substantiates this pro-market view.

Treasury, made two important contributions to the crisis debate. His position on the policy responses to crises diverges from Schwartz's benchmark but nevertheless concluded with a pro-market prescription. He rejected the view that the costs of moral hazard were high relative to the benefits of supporting the real economy from financial disturbances (Summers 1991, pp.136–7). Taking bank failures as an example, these can create 'reputational externalities where one bank's failure affects the public perception of the health of other banks' (p.147). Instead of a generalized monetary policy accommodation of liquidity in financial markets (as recommended by Schwartz), Summers seemed sympathetic toward a targeted banking policy approach – providing loans to selected, fragile banking institutions that were 'too large to fail' (p.136). The 'too large' criterion would have important ramifications again in the twenty-first century. Large financial institutions would impose significant exter-nalities if they were permitted to fail. In addition, last-resort lending to major financial institutions would reduce the negative impacts on the real economy, on firms for example, that depended on the continuation of normal banking and financing arrangements. To the extent that the existing banking 'relationships represent a kind of capital, beneficially owned by both borrower and creditor, both will suffer losses when a bank fails' (p.147). If large banks fail, the macroeconomic ramifications would be serious: falling aggregate demand, reductions in the money supply (all other things remaining the same as far as monetary policy actions were concerned), and ultimately a general deflation. And Schwartz's solution, if such problems arose in the United States – amounting to reducing the Federal Funds rate and increasing the general provision of liquidity to the financial system – 'is not likely to be sufficient to stop prophecies that predict the failure of [many other] banks...from proving to be self-fulfilling' (p.150). Here the nature and scope of the governmental financial safety net was at issue more than the extent.

After having reflected on many post-BW era financial crises especially in the 1980s and 1990s, Summers (2000) envisaged more scope for reform of financial sector regulation in LDCs; he repeated the standard pro-market refrain about the need for stable monetary policy; and a desirable policy bias toward discouraging short-term cross-border capital flows and pegged exchange rate policies. He went further than Schwartz in attribut-ing short-term debt inflows and subsequent crises supposedly caused by such inflows, to inappropriate policy orientations, that is to

> the distortions that can result from restrictions on foreign direct investment, inward equity portfolio investment, or the access of

non-residents to long-term bond markets; or policy distortions and tax incentives that can lead to an excessive reliance on debt relative to equity finance. Of course, underdeveloped capital markets, where long-term forms of finance (i.e., equity, long-term bonds) are not widely available, will themselves create a bias in favour of short-term flows in the right environment (p.9).

He insisted on giving priority to the process of international capital market liberalization and against the introduction of new capital controls. More broadly, economic liberalization programs of various kinds (not restricted exclusively to financial markets), were 'proven strategies for productivity, economic efficiency and growth' (p.9). Any emergency loans extended by various IFIs to countries experiencing a crisis could be made highly conditional on the implementation of 'credible' adjustment policies (pp.10, 11). That way, the moral hazard effects would be minimized.

There follows in Summers survey a standard set of general policy recommendations some might regard as clichéd, or at least as a counsel of perfection. First, there is an exhortation to preserve national policy autonomy as much as possible on the grounds that national

[c]risis response, like crisis prevention, has two dimensions: national policies that can restore confidence and international efforts to finance a credible path out of crises. Of these, by far the most important is the response of national authorities in the countries concerned. If there is one lesson that has been brought home most forcefully by the events of recent years, it is that countries shape their own destinies – and the international community can never want sound policies or economic stability more than the government and people of the country itself (Summers 2000, p.10).

Second, there is a list of specific 'sound' policy orientations: providing confidence to markets by requiring greater 'transparency' and information flows from policymaking institutions; avoiding 'lax fiscal policy' so that fiscal 'tightening' could be a key element in restoring market confidence; setting the 'right' monetary policy, again to bolster confidence; supporting 'healthy' banks and financial institutions and intervening directly in 'unhealthy' ones; establishing 'strong and effective social safeguards' and using an ILLR in emergencies to bail out sovereign debtors with certain market-oriented policy reforms required as a condition (pp.11–14). One of the main problems for this line of

thought is that it exuded a degree of (some would say blind) optimism regarding the long-term growth prospects for all countries
that were fully integrated in an IFS based predominantly on market
processes. Critics would argue that such optimism was not matched by
the perennial experience of damaging financial crises.

Maurice Obstfeld, whose ideas we have had occasion to outline on
other subjects in previous chapters, also took a pro-market line of
thought on crises. He concurred with other economists impounded in
our pro-market group, in believing that pegged exchange rates were
always vulnerable to speculative anticipation of par value changes. He
conceded that there can be important practical situations in which currency pegs may be 'run [i.e. speculated against] even though they might
have survived indefinitely in the absence of a run' (1996b, p.394). Thus,
like Summers, but unlike Schwartz, he entertained the idea of a self-
fulfilling speculative currency attacks just as may occur when reputational externalities are damaged in a domestic banking system. In the
international case, one country's insolvency can affect market perceptions rightly or wrongly, about another neighboring country. The
latter may be perceived as being in a similar, or at least impending,
vulnerable position of insolvency, even though it may have sound
economic fundamentals (Obstfeld and Rogoff 1995, p.86). What is
crucial, for Obstfeld (1996b, p.395), is that fundamental economic forces
are involved in influencing whether or not a crisis occurs. Whatever
the actual state of those fundamentals, they do not make the onset of
a crisis inevitable or a unique outcome. Technical and analytical work
by economists cannot isolate a self-fulfilling element in any crisis.
Crises are not the inevitable result of, for example, a particular trend in
economic fundamentals. Obstfeld provides a more specific example:

> Countries can have patches of bad luck, and most, even those without
> badly trending fundamentals, do. The occasional cyclical downturn is
> a common form of largely temporary bad luck. In these circumstances,
> a country may become vulnerable to attack if it is pegging its exchange
> rate and if the authorities lack the political will to resist strong attack.
> Such attacks are not independent of what is happening to the funda-
> mentals in the economy – but they are not always necessary outcomes
> either (pp. 394–5).

At the very least, the exact characteristics and timing of a crisis can
never be predicted. Historical work, including econometric studies, can
only result in taxonomies of crisis characteristics and key variables

common to past experiences. Doubtless, the experience of crises and effective recovery measures vary considerably between countries.

What, then, are the policy implications of all this? First, more flexible, market-oriented exchange rates were necessary for nations that could not always keep their economic fundamentals on a sustainable trend (Obstfeld 1996b, p.402). Second, international capital market integration was desirable (Obstfeld 1998). Contagion crises often grow into a 'default crisis as in Mexico and Asia' where domestic capital market liquidity problems and international access to capital markets is interrupted. Then emergency financial support is required from IFIs and friendly sovereign lenders. Debt relief in these circumstances is one thing; enforcing loan conditions quite another, more intractable problem. Obstfeld did not appear as confident as Fischer and Summers in believing that pro-market reform conditions (for loans) would easily be met. In any case, domestic capital market liberalization was essential. The ERM crisis in the early 1990s did not lead to major disruption to capital markets in the region probably because there were deep, sophisticated financial markets operating there. Like the more pragmatic economists surveyed earlier in this chapter, Obstfeld called for improvements in the regulation of financial systems in LDCs though he was aware of an 'inherent problem facing all countries, industrial and developing alike'. That problem turned on the 'difficulty of supervising financial institutions' operating outside national jurisdictions, beyond the reach of their respective monetary authorities (Obstfeld 1998, p.25n13). It was the lack of harmonization of financial market regulatory regimes that could then cause crises. Moreover, ill-informed investors trying to diversify their savings portfolios may have insufficient infor mation, or find relevant information too costly to source; then they will inevitably do the job of international capital allocation inefficiently. Indeed, freer international financial markets 'may promote contagion by weakening incentives for gathering costly information and by strengthening incentives for imitating arbitrary market portfolios' (Calvo and Mendoza 2000a, p.72). In the absence of 'credible data on official foreign reserves, the maturity of foreign borrowing, and the quality of domestic investment' (Obstfeld 1998, p.26) this capital allocation problem might suggest a flaw in the pro-market program for international financial market liberalization. (See also Calvo and Mendoza 2000b). On the contrary, the best policy response was not to restrict international capital flows. As well, IMF policy surveillance and IMF – mandated requirements that member nations improve their economic data bases and data reporting would enhance the efficiency of international capital markets. Policymakers were growing in acceptance (as of 1998) of economic openness and market-based, international financial integration. Obstfeld was no exception in believing that 'despite periodic crises', liberalization 'holds significant benefits' (p.28). There were genuine 'hazards' in adopting this course; he was resigned to the fact that the benefits and hazards were 'inseparable in the real world of asymmetric information and imperfect contract enforcement' both in financial markets and in the provision of emergency finance from any ILLR. We shall now discuss the emerging ILLR role of the IMF in the post-BW era.

6

The IMF: Post-Bretton Woods Era Functions and Reform Issues

Introduction

International organizations, that is, supranational institutions such as those purposefully created in the 1930s and 1940s to deal with economic problems (e.g. the Bank for International Settlements (BIS), International Money Fund (IMF), United Nations and International Bank for Reconstruction and Development later renamed the World Bank), typically function to effect cooperation on international policy matters. Sometimes these organizations have set in motion regimes of international cooperation on given issues based on principles, norms, rules, modes of consultation and decisionmaking processes around which the views of member nations converge. The vast array of international organizations created in the twentieth century take for granted some degree of international interdependence and integration that is managed for the good of all members of the international community. Some policy coordination and policy integration is assumed; some international organizations have embodied a public goods aspect without strictly entailing international government. The creation of peace through international treaty organizations, or enhancing public health status and agricultural production through the WHO and FAO respectively; the establishment of international trade and payments systems, freedom of the seas and regimes for exploiting common resources are all examples of 'international public goods without international government' (Kindleberger 1986). Of course not all instances of cooperation through international organizations need to be successful or enduring. For example, full macroeconomic policy coordination promoted through the OECD or the IMF may be possible episodically, though conflicts between national and international obligations and imperatives may arise because of either divergent national economic cycles or differential political pressures.

In the twentieth century, IFIs such as the IMF emerged as agencies that could hasten the pace of international financial integration. The single most valuable, 'natural benchmark' available to economists for thinking about international interdependencies and cross-border interactions envisages a 'world in which markets for goods, services and factors of production are perfectly integrated' (Rodrik 2000, p.178). IFIs add another dimension, suggesting that integration requires some form of deliberate coordination to supplement, or even replace, markets in some contexts. Here some principles of international collective action apply and they entail significant international governmental functions for the purposes of increasing international policy harmonization. Some form of global market failure may provide the rationale for collective action through an IFI. For instance, we could refer in this connection to inter-governmental cooperation and financing for financial crisis management; finance for developing country infrastructure projects; policy harmonization on matters of financial system regulation, accounting standards, labour standards, migration, international currency regulation and monetary stabilization; multilateral economic surveillance; establishing cross-border rules for trade in goods and services and so forth. International cooperation through international organizations on many of these matters began in the pre-BW, interwar years (Endres and Fleming 2002). All these phenomena would not be the spontaneous outcome of untrammelled international market forces – in many instances IFIs modify or correct the perceived failings of such forces.

Imperfections in the operation of financial and currency markets in particular – both domestic and international – offered a strong basis for the continuing operation of the IMF in the post-BW era. The IMF became increasingly more active as a monitor of financial markets, as a technical advisor, as a lender for financial crisis prevention and amelioration. At the highest level of generality, the IMF was responsible for ensuring the effective operation of the IFS in a world of imperfect, and in some regions incomplete, financial markets.

Since its inception in the late 1940s, the IMF has always retained financial responsibilities in the international economy. Its mandate to circa 1972 was to assist in financing temporary balance of payments deficits among member countries in an international economic regime dominated by controls on capital mobility and fixed, adjustable exchange rates. Following the Bretton Woods meetings, the IMF articles of agreement established that some IMF financial assistance, policy monitoring and advice was required to avoid frequent currency changes and effect adjustment in short-run balance of payments imbalances (whereas 'fundamental' imbalances required more drastic policy changes at the national level – again assisted by IMF advice). Right at the end of the BW era the Board of Governors of the IMF contemplated options for the reform of the IFS (IMF 1972). Altogether, the ideas and options canvassed in that report did not address or foresee the main post-BW era controversies that were to erupt over the place of the IMF in a world of increasingly flexible exchange rate regimes, rising international capital mobility on a scale previously unimagined, frequent currency crises and contagion crises. By the 1990s, IMF research reported on the 'diversity, both of exchange rate arrangements and the functioning of financial markets'; the volatility of flexible exchange rates, the expansion of private capital markets, and the myriad of problems faced by some member countries in accessing capital from those markets (Mussa et al. 1994, pp.13–14). While the IMF has never been a monolithic organization in terms of economic ideas and suggested policy options, in the following section we shall review some of the principal ideational themes and policies, that is, trajectories of thought, that were developed and followed by IMF economists. Our focus will be on the ideas that related to the perceived, proposed or actual role of the IMF in the post-BW era. We will avoid discussion of the minutiae of actual IMF practices and programs and their evolution. For example we shall set aside the fine details of specific IMF financing schemes for balance of payments problems and adjustment, changes in loan conditionality, ongoing changes in the governance structure of the IMF and so forth.[18] As in previous chapters, the core ideas will be the centre of our attention – ideas, in this case, on the reasons for the existence and functions of the IMF in an increasingly integrated world economy.

Some models and ideas informing IMF functions

For the design and control of its various financing and functioning programs as an international lending intermediary – originally for balance of payments adjustment problems and crises – the IMF came into the post-BW era with an already developed 'model' or theoretical rationale for its lending activities. This model amounted to a coherent

---

[18]On these issues see James (1996), Pauly (1997) and Boughton (2001).

way of thinking about economies and economic adjustment problems especially under fixed and fixed-adjustable exchange rate regimes, or target-zone regimes. The model became widely known as the 'Polak model' after the pioneering work of IMF economist Jacques Polak in the 1950s. Polak provided an underlying doctrine, not just a purely logical structure, to inform IMF policies as applied to macroeconomic and monetary adjustment mostly in LDCs. In the post-BW era, the IMF was less involved with major lending programs to large, developed industrialized countries that could easily access burgeoning international capital markets; it became an institution devoted mostly to LDCs and emerging market economies where fixed exchange rates of some form were still common. The shortcomings of the Polak model would become more obvious with the advent of regular financial crises in the 1980s and 1990s but that did not, initially, deter its proponents.

IMF researchers articulated a model linking standard, available policy instruments in any nation to external economic balance, that is, to desired balance on the current account of the balance of international payments. Here we shall confine our attention to one of the Polak-type models developed expressly for short-run problems of the kind usually addressed by the IMF. The IMF used a simple model that provided the intellectual rationale for the Fund's lending programs and conditions attached to those programs. Naturally, the financial dimension of macroeconomic management seemed the best concentration for economists working in an organization charged with international monetary responsibilities. That the fundamental problems encountered by IMF officials in practice were monetary, rendered less useful more popular Keynesian tools of macroeconomic analysis (in the 1970s) which relied on output and income determination and an associated income-absorption conceptualization of the balance of payments (Rhomberg and Heller 1977, p.6). Since balance of payments 'adjustment' issues were at the forefront at IMF advisory activities in the 1970s and 1980s, these enjoyed a central position on the research agenda. For short-run analysis, the original IMF Articles of Agreement embodied an implicit conception of adjustment which meant realizing and maintaining a deficit (or surplus if possible) on current account that was financially sustainable over the medium term without the need for major exchange rate changes. That conception acted as a presupposition in the model sketched below.

Early IMF research on the monetary approach to the balance of payments was born out of pragmatism – specifically out of a need to simplify critical aggregate economic relationships so as to fit the structure of, and data availability in, developing economies generally subject to IMF-supported adjustment programs.[19] For the most part, data were restricted to financial flows rather than national income accounts. Jacques Polak and his research staff designed a simplified macroeconomic model through which to determine policies for alleviating balance of payments disequilibria. The model assumed that the level of domestic credit is the only potent policy variable available to monetary authorities given that the money supply is not controllable in a fixed exchange rate regime. In its simplest form, the model sets monetary equilibrium (in terms of monetary flows) under conditions of pre-determined real gross domestic product for a fully employed, small open economy with fixed exchange rates (Blejer and Frenkel 1987; Edwards 1989b). From this, the target level of international reserves (or the target balance of payments) is determined and the monetary authority in conjunction with IMF advisors could establish assumptions about money demand and the target rate of growth of domestic credit.

A capsule summary of the model is as follows. Let the money supply (M^S) be determined by the amount of high powered money (H) in the system, and the money multiplier (m):

$$M^S = m.H$$

The money multiplier is determined by asset holders (the currency deposit ratio, cu), and by behaviour in the banking system (the reserve deposit ratio, re, which is determined by market interest rates, the discount rate and the required level of reserves): thus, $m - (1 \mid cu)/(re \mid cu)$. The amount of high powered money is composed of two components representing financial assets held in the international and domestic spheres:

$$H = eR + D$$

Where eR is the amount of net foreign assets (the exchange rate e, and foreign assets R) and D is the amount of domestic credit.

---

[19]Key papers outlining theoretical underpinnings were first produced by Polak in the 1950s. Frenkel and Johnson (1976, p.31) later describe these papers as representing a 'short-lived burst of theoretical interest' in the monetary approach at the IMF. However, it should be stated that an 'oral tradition' existed among IMF researchers from about 1948 which incorporated many key insights later associated with the full-fledged monetary approach (IMF 1987, p.1; Polak 1996, p.220).

The demand for money in the model is determined by the level of national income on the assumption that the income velocity of circulation remains constant. Thus, over time the rate of change of money demand is relatively easy to determine if there is a well-founded set of expectations about the rate of growth of the economy. This view was later re-stated in an IMF (1997: 14) report in the following way: 'all that is needed is that the demand for money, or velocity, respond in a predictable way to variables such as real income, prices, interest rates and so forth and that it be independent of changes in domestic credit'.

Nominal money demand is written as $M^d = P.f(y)$ where P is the aggregate price level and y is the level of real income.

The balance of payments target can be determined by assuming that the money market is in equilibrium. Substituting from the relevant definitions above, the level of net foreign assets is a function of the price level, real income, the behavioural characteristics of asset holders and the banking system, and the amount of domestic credit.

$$eR = g(P,y,m,D)$$

The application of the Polak model and the design of a financial program by the IMF involved picking targets for the appropriate level of net foreign assets (see description of the process in Edwards 1989b). Following Dornbusch and Fischer (1994, pp.613–15) the assumptions of the model imply that policy decisions turn on the simple balance sheet identity expressed in first differences:

$$e\Delta R = \Delta H - \Delta D$$

Given a fixed exchange rate e, the IMF in conjunction with the domestic monetary authority will establish the planned change in net foreign assets, ΔR^*. The planned change in high powered money, ΔH^*, is then set with reference to the demand for money (presumably a predictable empirical regularity) and the value of the money multiplier ΔH^* must be sufficient to produce the correct change in the stock of money to offset changes in money demand. Now given ΔR^* *and* ΔH^*, the sustainable, planned level of central bank credit creation, ΔD^*, can be derived. As described by Edwards, the process above is an iterative one with several steps involving initial settings and recalibrations in order to achieve the desired balance of payments outcome.

The description above allows us to note several important insights of the Polak model that were to become a hallmark of the monetary approach to the balance of payments and IMF policy prescriptions. First, as long as ΔH^* offsets changes in money demand, changes in domestic credit only result in changes in international reserves. The money supply is endogenous: any attempts by the monetary authority to increase domestic credit through open market operations will be ineffective as the level of net foreign assets will change in a corresponding negative fashion. Second, at any point in time, to the extent that $\Delta D_1 < \Delta D^*$ then, at the same time, ΔR_1 will deviate positively from ΔR^*. If policymakers are required (by the IMF) to place high weight on negative deviations in net foreign assets when current account deficits appear unsustainable in the short run, ΔD^* is a ceiling on domestic credit expansion.

The short-run solution to balance of payments imbalances on current account countenanced by the model involved active use of credit ceilings as criteria for the assessment of IMF-supported, crisis adjustment programs. It is a simple rule-based policy framework, consistent with the long-run fixed, adjustable exchange rate rule, which severely limits the need for discretionary action by domestic policymakers. The rule would act automatically to secure adjustment. Policy analysis would involve monitoring changes in domestic credit and noting the corresponding targeted changes in international reserves. The basic empirical regularity relating the money supply to international reserves was 'tested' in the process. While, according to the model, credit changes are matched by equal changes in international reserves, that was a long-run outcome which did not act as an imperative in the IMF policy monitoring process; what mattered was whether the direction of change in the short run was consistent with the desired balance of payments outcome.

Given the model's fundamental proposition that the balance of payments was a monetary phenomenon, the two immediate policy implications were that (i) monetary policy had direct effects on the balance of payments and (ii) policies that exacerbate or neglect the monetary consequences of balance of payments surpluses or deficits will not be successful in bringing about 'adjustment' (before a full blown crisis occurred) in the sense already defined.

The IMF's model contained the view that the Keynesian apparatus as then understood was overly concerned with interrelationships between international adjustment and domestic employment. One principal advantage of the monetary approach to the balance of payments is that it leads directly to the determination of the overall current account balance (or imbalance) as the difference between changes in the demand for money and changes in net domestic assets with changes in domestic credit acting as the vehicle (or catalyst) for that difference. Innovative work undertaken at the IMF focused on the relevance of all this to less developed nations.[20] First, less developed economies lacked sufficient, good quality data on relevant (Keynesian) aggregates such as national income components and national product data. Therefore balance of payments determination conceived along income-absorption lines could not easily be established by IMF researchers. By contrast, monetary data were more readily available, this being the result of central bank supervision, and current account data were also available because records were usually well-kept by customs administrators. The model was less demanding of data sources. Second, the monetary approach permitted a meaningful approximate analysis of the relevant aggregates, such as the rate of change of domestic credit, with the help of a model of the transmission process underlying the adjustment of the balance of payments to any type of shock. Third, the elementary financial structures observed in LDCs, including thin asset markets and simple financial instruments, meant that alternatives for holding money were quite limited. Implications for the balance of payments of a difference between the creation of new money and credit and the additional money residents wished to use either to buy home-produced goods or hold in the form of domestic financial instruments, were clearer in these simple circumstances. Fourth, a monetary analysis of the effects on the balance of payments of a range of economic policies was especially appropriate in LDCs where control over domestic credit was relied upon as a principal instrument of demand management.

For IMF researchers it was considered unnecessary to identify the doctrinal basis of their practical, working model. In a retrospective during the late 1980s when the very same Polak-inspired monetary approach was used actively to design IMF adjustment programs, IMF economists still regarded rigid doctrinal biases as downright unpalatable in a policy analysis context; they wished 'to dispel the notion that these programs are all based on a particular view of the economy or on the conviction of a single school of economic thought' (IMF 1997, p.2). More precisely, the implicit intellectual linkages sometimes made between the IMF's monetary approach and 'monetarist' doctrine were quickly dismissed by IMF practitioners on the following grounds: (i) the model was a minimal, eclectic one which did not need to draw intellectual authority

---

[20]The remaining material in this paragraph relies heavily on Rhomberg and Heller (1977 , pp.7–9).

from contemporary monetarist theoreticians; (ii) the model was constructed for short-run macroeconomic management to ensure the best use of IMF finance over that period; (iii) monetary policy is not isolated in the model as the only remedy for balance of payments problems since the control of domestic credit may largely depend on the fiscal balance – there is also no presumption in the IMF approach that monetary policy is always to be preferred as a tool for effecting balance of payments adjustment. Altogether, the IMF's approach suggests only that 'monetary processes will bring about a cure of some kind' (Frenkel and Johnson 1976, p.24) in the balance of payments. This proposition hardly aligns the IMF with the monetary ideas being developed contemporaneously by monetary theorists in the University of Chicago. Furthermore, it was demonstrated by an IMF researcher that Polak's original model could be incorporated in a Keynesian structure with rigid nominal wages in the short run and with domestic output, inflation and interest rates all responding to monetary policy (Montiel 1985). Rather than a coherent economic doctrine, the IMF required an understanding of likely adjustment in a country's balance of payments as a result of a domestic credit ceiling imposed by conditions attached to its lending policy. While monetarists would not have been happy with all this, Keynesians would have been equally disappointed. A completely rigorous Keynesian explanation of output determination is missing from the IMF's rather eclectic, but definitely rule-based monetary approach. Indeed, real GDP is regarded as exogenous. The nominal income equation in the original Polak model is a variant on the quantity theory of money and that would not satisfy a Keynesian – though this did not matter much in practice for policymakers and policy formation in the context of short-run, IMF-led adjustment programs.

Theoretical work on the IMF's model was not regarded as an end it itself; it was done in the service of giving technical advice to member countries facing short-run external imbalances. The research agenda on international economic policy accompanying the original Polak model was designed in an atmosphere which underscored the need to have a practical motivation; identify some elementary, working empirical regularities that could be relied upon (and perhaps confirmed) in practice; required limited datasets; be innovative where circumstances allowed and attended to a country's institutional peculiarities which may alter time lags between policy changes dictated by the model and changes in relevant economic variables.

Doubtless, while IMF researchers distanced their work from leading contemporary doctrinal trends in economics practised as an academic discipline, their policy-oriented research had a clear normative bias: the financial programs designed under the guidance of their monetary approach to the balance of payment prescribed a set of correct policies – in fact propagating an economic policy orthodoxy in its own right which involved active use of credit ceilings. Restricting domestic borrowing from the banking system improves the balance of payments preferably before a currency crisis occurs; causality runs crisply from monetary restraint to less inflation and improved external balance. In the short run no scope is allowed for maintaining investment, operating near full capacity or income distribution considerations. The IMF thereby played a significant role in shaping the short-run balance of payments adjustment paths observed in some developing countries in the post-BW era (Gregorio et al. 1999, pp.26–7). IMF researchers gained experience in applying their model and seemed generally satisfied with its use in operational activities up until the 1980s. Subsequent developments in international macroeconomics incorporating time consistency considerations, expectational variations, complex intertemporal matters and the lessons from the analysis of speculative currency attacks and currency crises were not easily translated into specific policy implications and therefore took a long time to register in IMF thinking and operational activities (Goldstein 1989, p.75). Nonetheless, the IMF's critics as we shall see presently, focused on one major implication of the monetary approach.

When LDCs face a shortage of international reserves under some form of fixed exchange rate regime and then seek IMF assistance, 'the policy indicated to speed the national adjustment process is deliberate monetary contraction' (Johnson 1977, p.265). For one thing, contraction would reduce domestic costs and increase export competitiveness in relatively open economies and improve the current account outlook. Yet neither current account deficits that place pressure on reserves under fixed exchange rates are necessarily bad, nor are internal government deficits necessarily bad – it all depends on the case. Persistent current account deficits may indeed be a catalyst for a currency attack and currency crisis. However, loose monetary policy and fiscal profligacy may not be the root cause of such deficits as implied in the IMF model. By the late 1990s the model was considered 'archaic in a world where trade and debt service can be swamped by capital flows'. The IMF approach was underestimating the 'role of banking and finance' in propagating LDC currency and contagion crises (Gregorio et al. 1999, p.27).

Alternative policies to monetary contraction not directly implied by the Polak model included currency devaluation and import restrictions though these had inflationary consequences and imply the failure of monetary policy. Thus as Harry Johnson (1977, p.265) noted, the effects of alternatives to monetary contraction were 'transient' given the eventual inflationary impacts even though they imply 'less social strife and transitional unemployment'. The latter will only persist if one assumes a 'Keynesian' world of money illusion and economies that exhibit price and wage rigidities. Nonetheless, currency devaluation was traditionally recommended by the IMF in tandem with monetary (and fiscal) contraction as a way of thwarting speculative currency attacks.

Notwithstanding the efficaciousness of the underlying IMF doctrine, it might be argued that the IMF's monetary approach was applicable only in cases where quick results were required. Such cases may include the need for immediate monetary stabilization either to avoid or contain a crisis. The monetary approach was divorced from other IMF activities associated with broader capital account issues and currency regime changes that would contribute to economic growth over the medium term. 'Adjustment' from the IMF point of view in the 1970s and 1980s at least, was never meant to be confined to a single set of policies confined to financial or monetary conditions (combined with fiscal austerity as the case demanded). While the underlying Polak doctrine implied such a position, other structural adjustment policy packages that were growth-oriented were also part of the IMF's armoury. As Polak (1999, p.5) reported, one of the prime reasons for the perceived 'failure' or 'ineffectiveness' of IMF-supported adjustment programs in the 1980s was that 'few of the problem countries with which the Fund has been dealing took early adjustment action and then stuck to it consistently. In many countries, policymakers took the better part of a decade to adopt the full range of financial <u>and</u> structural policies that had to be implemented' (emphasis added). Later in this chapter we shall have cause to examine the ideas underwriting IMF-favoured 'structural adjustment' policies – ideas that went beyond what John Williamson (1990) labelled as the 'Washington consensus'.

In rationalizing the functions of the IMF in the light of developments in the IFS in the post-BW era, the position of influential IMF economists should be considered. Stanley Fischer (1998) sums up the overall attitude among IMF economists in the 1990s, not only in respect of the liberalization of capital accounts. He envisaged the IMF as an agent for the promotion of economic liberalization in general – including current account opening, and the wider use of market processes to enhance economic efficiency (rather than distributional objectives) within IMF imposed programs. The IMF would insist on regulatory standards for members' financial systems but would always be present to support countries facing unforeseen financial crises regardless of the existing regulatory regime. Usually such support would be contingent on greater capital account openness. Given the limits of IMF funding, openness to private international capital markets and favourable sovereign lenders would help forestall and contain crises (IMF 1999). Indeed, IMF funding involvement, while always limited, can add credibility in a crisis management situation and thereby 'bail in' private foreign capital if a country's capital account is open. As Citrin and Fischer (2000, p.1139) argue, one method favoured by the IMF for minimizing the moral hazard problem associated with 'bailouts' was

> to get existing investors to help provide net new financing or to share in the losses associated with crises – that is, to bail in the private sector by requiring them to provide some of the crises financing...Involving the private sector is necessary not only to ensure that investors assume the risks implied by their loans, thereby helping ensure yields are correctly priced, but also because the official sector will not have sufficient financing available to do otherwise.

Naturally a precondition would be quickly to restore the confidence of capital market participants – both domestic and foreign. This is a delicate balancing act in most cases, since policymakers often want to buy more time to make the necessary macroeconomic adjustments. By the end of the period under review (by 2000), the IMF was still experimenting with the phenomenon of private sector bail-in and the associated policy lines it was pursuing to encourage sovereigns 'to seek private contingent financing arrangements' (p.1139).

Jacques Polak (1998, p.53) maintained that the IMF could still actively use its broad traditional instruments – all of which had undergone considerable reshaping and extension during the post-BW era. These instruments, as elaborated by IMF economists, included economic policy and financial market reporting and 'surveillance' (Mussa 1977); 'conditionality' as it applied to IMF emergency financing and debt structuring schemes (Guitian 1981, 1995) and technical – economic advice in implementing IMF programs. In all these respects a decidedly neoliberal or market-oriented complexion pervaded the notion of the IMF using its 'instruments' to help improve the functioning of the IFS. Economic liberalization for IMF economists during this period had a specific scope. Rather than advocating the complete freedom of markets to operate as an ultimate objective, come-what-may, and rather than suggesting more or new types of restrictions on the operation of market processes, the IMF line of thought emphasized the need to remove 'unnecessary, ineffective, and counterproductive restrictions' on a wide range of economic activities (Polak 1998, p.53). Improving the economic performance of IMF member countries would ultimately take place by 'structural adjustment' policies pursuant to various loan conditions. Those policies would take time to implement, so that by comparison with IMF lending in the BW era, in the post-BW era lending was generally made over more extended periods than before (Polak 1991, pp.2–3). Overall, the IMF 'instruments', properly employed in the sense of enhancing economic liberalization, would ostensibly contribute to international economic integration.

By the 1990s, the IMF outlook moved somewhat toward acknowledging two relatively new features of the evolving IFS.

1. Contagion crises: 'the transmission and magnification of economic disturbances' (as it was called by IMF economists, Mussa et al. 1994, p.33). Here new forms of financing would be thought of, and new loan conditions established depending on the country and the nature and scope of a specific crisis. To generalize, however, despite changes in detail, there was little change in the neoliberal stance underpinning those conditions.
2. Market exuberance: a factor that may cause major exchange rate misalignments and economic volatility. Here economic reporting, consultation with member governments, and member collaboration through IMF facilitation would assist in dampening exuberance. For example, better coordination of monetary policies between major industrialized nations so as to reduce key currency misalignments among floating exchange rates regimes could be effective. Gradually, voluntary 'international monetary policy' coordination became an important IMF mantra in the post-BW era. The IMF admission that markets could produce economically damaging exchange rate changes (among market-determined exchange rate regimes) was a doctrinal qualification. It has been ignored by most critics and caricatures of ideas and policies developed at the IMF. The specific contribution of the IMF in cases of market-driven exuberance would be to underscore the crucial importance of harmonizing macroeconomic policies, especially monetary policies, and to apply moral suasion: the IMF would have the rather lame task of emphasizing 'the international implications and intentions of domestic policies and to direct attention and peer pressure against policies that are inappropriate from both a domestic and international perspective' (Mussa et al. 1994, p.33).

In addition to these two new challenges to thought and action at the IMF up to 2000, IMF thinking evolved to the point where loan conditionality could be said to have both primary and secondary objectives. Generally, the former involved adjustment to, or containment of crises including short-run balance of payments and currency problems, along with price level stabilization and long-run growth issues. It was presumed (with caveats) that the short-run and long-run primary objectives did not conflict. In the literature of academic economics this was (and still is) a controversial presumption. Rudiger Dornbusch (1990a) at MIT was a qualified supporter of the IMF presumption in believing that there was a natural sequence from restoring short-run stability that set the economic preconditions for subsequent longer-run growth. The 'secondary' objectives of IMF activities were articulated later in the 1980s, and they included poverty alleviation, social and physical environmental goals, restrictions on military expenditure in countries receiving IMF loans, and general 'political' considerations (Polak 1991, pp.24–32). We turn next to consider some prominent rationalizations that were fundamentally supportive of the IMF's liberalization agenda, with particular reference to its primary objectives. To repeat, those objectives were more strictly economic, being concerned with economic stabilization to avoid, respond and contain crises.

Further doctrinal support for IMF programs and policy

It is not normally possible to predict the onset of currency or contagion crises of the kind that occurred in the 1980s and 1990s. Ideas and policies formulated by the IMF on crises and how to treat them underwent changes during this period. As Stanley Fischer (1999a, pp.F571–5) at the IMF reported, the IMF continued to reform its operational activities in response to new demands – though not the underlying doctrinal position. Employing what seemed to be a range of platitudes, he urged member countries 'to pursue responsible policies and defend their economies in the face of adverse external developments before a crisis strikes' (p.F571). That such countries should be responsibly informed (in advance) by IMF surveillance activities so that irresponsible policies could be identified in advance of a crisis might well have assisted in crisis avoidance, despite political problems facing real world governments. In short, the IMF had some responsibilities of its own that some critics claimed were not being fulfilled, especially in the area of economic surveillance.

Of course, no one should have expected the IMF to have been more responsible for predicting crises or for designing full-proof policies that would prevent them. Furthermore, as we saw in the previous chapter, the advanced technical-analytical research by academic economists was not really up to the task of crisis prediction. Even narrow economic fundamentals did not in themselves indicate with any certainty whether or not a crisis would occur. Yet inability to predict did not obviate the necessity of the IMF to ease the burden of adjustment faced by countries in financial crises, irrespective of its causes (Fischer 1999a, p.F571).

With reference to the plethora of studies on the effectiveness and failings of IMF lending programs – a topic well-researched by IMF economist Manuel Guitian (1995) – it is easy to report that a large number of prominent economists in the post-BW era were broadly in favour of the IMF functioning as an emergency lender in crises, taking more responsibility for urging changes in monetary and exchange rate policies, and where possible facilitating international macroeconomic policy coordination (Goldstein 1995; Krueger 1998, pp.2011–12). Anne Krueger in particular was sympathetic to the complex problems facing the IMF acting as an international lending intermediary, advising on exchange rate policies and exchange rate misalignments and also often requiring, as a condition of lending, certain macroeconomic policy reforms. By the 1990s the IMF was predominantly lending to LDCs and emerging market economies. It was always likely in retrospect that loan conditions might (say) be too weak in some cases, or that because of the lack of enforceability, IMF programs might fail. However, this was not the central problem facing the IMF. The main dilemma was

> how, in a world of high private capital mobility, the Fund can continue its historic role with individual developing countries when they confront balance of payments difficulties or crises, without at the same time providing assurance to potential lenders that they will be 'bailed out' and can therefore lend safely without adequate regard to country risk (Krueger 1998, p.2006).

Thus, crisis management as it became known in the post-BW era, where large private capital flows are involved, created deep practical and philosophical problems concerning the importance of moral hazard. Allan Meltzer (1998, p.272) at Carnegie Mellon expressed the problem pointedly: '[s]ince 1971 the IMF has been looking for new things to do. It has solved the problem by creating moral hazard'. Be that as it may, moral hazard was surely regarded as a secondary problem when the IMF was required to respond to a catastrophic financial collapse and loss of confidence in a member country's currency, financial markets and economy.

Notwithstanding the important moral hazard issue (which we will discuss later on in this chapter), the IMF had to deal with conflicting demands if it wanted to meet its primary macroeconomic objectives as already outlined. The IMF's secondary objectives seemed superfluous when crisis management was at hand (Krueger 2000, pp.38, 42). Indeed, the World Bank functioned precisely to achieve poverty reduction, so there was a danger of overlapping and sometimes conflicting, objectives if the IMF took its secondary objectives too seriously (Krueger 1998). In Krueger's view, crises had to be managed without the distraction of secondary concerns such as poverty problems, geo-political or strategic considerations. Therefore, the IMF's core competency was the ability to create financial stabilization programs and it should concentrate exclusively on enhancing that competency. According to Krueger (2000, p.39), the IMF had recognized three general, prior characteristics of post-BW crises, necessitating changes in some degree or other depending on the case, in crisis management policies:

(i)   a fixed nominal exchange rate policy;
(ii) excessive growth of domestic credit; and
(iii) historically large current account and government deficits.

In general Krueger's diagnosis mirrored the IMF approach up to the 1990s. What was new about post-BW crises, and what the IMF had to contend with in designing lending programs, was the more complex duality of a balance of payments crisis and a financial (currency plus contagion) crisis. Here Krueger ignores the complications introduced by a contagion and splits the type of crisis into two distinct divisions:

> In the case of the balance-of-payments crisis, the traditional [IMF] remedy is for exchange-rate devaluation and a tightening of fiscal and monetary policy to reduce the excess of domestic expenditure over domestic income. In the case of the financial crisis, however, the traditional remedy is to expand the money supply and to lower interest rates. Reduced interest rates ease the burden of debtors and thus enable more of them to meet their (domestic) debt-servicing obligations (p.39).

If a currency devaluation is adopted according to the first 'traditional remedy' along with monetary and fiscal contraction, this inevitably raises the foreign debt servicing costs of banks and private domestic residents; it creates more havoc in the financial system as an unintended consequence. The financial system becomes weaker, not merely illiquid but in the extreme, completely insolvent. The doctrinal dilemma was clear: the IMF's financial programming, Polak model, applied a general monetary approach to balance of payments crises, yet that model 'worked' only to the extent that a financial crisis was not also in evidence. As for government fiscal policies, these were not always so bad when a crisis is at an incipient stage. Eventually, however, government accounts fall into a parlous state as well, since, assuming currency convertibility is permitted,

> expansion of domestic credit at fixed nominal exchange rates was equivalent to increases in the contingent liabilities of the government. At the onset of the crises...[there may not have] been significant fiscal deficits; but it makes little difference whether governments finance new airports, capitals, and information corridors by issuing debt themselves or by implicitly guaranteeing (as a fixed exchange rate does) the exchange rate and inducing foreign capital inflow (p.39).

In practice, the IMF had to read economic signals carefully to obtain sufficient intelligence to apply its core competencies in each country case; its activities recognized the trade-off between responding exclusively to a balance of payments-driven crisis and addressing a broader collapse in a nation's financial system. Jacques Polak was a highly experienced IMF economist. He was aware that the IMF was often criticized for applying its traditional monetary approach as if it were a universal recipe. In fact, there was no doubt in his mind that each country case had to be evaluated before some balance of the two 'traditional' remedies (as Krueger called them) were applied (Polak 1991, p.65). And the preexisting conditions had to be diagnosed properly, often without sufficient data. This inevitably led to some contestability of ideas and policies within the IMF itself, to the benefit of IMF policymaking. Thus, according to Polak, the

> differences of view prevalent within the staff with respect to major policy issues greatly reduce the risk that the Fund will impose standard recipes across countries and enhance the possibility of an outcome that reflects the requirements of the particular case (p.65).

Adding to policymaking complexity at the IMF, there was no objective, *ex ante* test enabling IMF economists to tell whether (a) a country in crisis faced a creditworthiness (liquidity) crisis, so that it would not be able to afford, through its current account, sufficient imports to sustain its economy or (b) a country had an insolvency problem in its financial and banking sector that could lead to a complete financial collapse. Some of the pre-existing problems could not easily be established with any degree of certainty. For example, what was the extent of the currency overvaluation? What was the magnitude of a country's unhedged foreign debt problem? What were the total debt-servicing obligations of individuals and government? Answers to such questions were crucial because the

> greater the prior degree of currency overvaluation and domestic debt, the greater is the relative attraction of relying on relatively more currency depreciation. The greater the prior domestic inflation rate and foreign debt, the greater is the attractiveness of using tighter monetary policy and less currency depreciation. Even the maturity structure of outstanding domestic obligations affects the trade-off between tighter money and greater currency depreciation. The conflict between the objectives of external and internal balance, when internal balance includes the health of the financial system, is evident. It is small wonder that critics of the IMF could be found on both sides of the argument (Krueger 2000, p.40).

The IMF dealt with the trade-off expressed by Krueger as the case demanded; it applied more 'radical' market-oriented policies, monetary contraction and fiscal austerity in some countries such as Poland, and 'more gradualist' policies given different pre-existing conditions, in countries such as Hungary (Polak 1991, p.65).

Endorsing the policy orientation of the IMF in the 1990s, Krueger favored more flexible exchange rate regimes; promoting liberal capital and current account policies, including the reduction of trade restrictions; more economic intelligence gathering and surveillance to reduce the risk of crises, and policies for strengthening the operation of financial markets in LDCs. These general policies accord with what Polak (1991, p.64) described as a 'convergence of ideas' by the 1980s on the appropriate, underlying economic liberalization goal. The pace of policy implementation in all these respects would vary depending on negotiations between the IMF and member governments but the pro-market neoliberal policy direction was abundantly clear. Obviously the policy direction was controversial, often had deleterious consequences in the short term for output, employment and general social conditions and sometimes conflicted with the World Bank's mission to reduce poverty. Krueger was sure that by concentrating on crisis management – prevention and amelioration – the IMF was thereby enhancing human well-being in LDCs.

Certain running repairs could be made to reduce trade-offs encountered by IMF policymakers. Balance of payments crises and financial crises could be 'delinked' (Krueger 2000, pp.40–1) if foreign currency denominated domestic debt obligations could not be legally enforced in the receiving country. That way, foreign capital suppliers would be more circumspect about lending; they would assess risk more carefully. Another option is for developed, industrialized nations to promulgate restrictions requiring their domestic financial institutions 'to accept liabilities' in less regulated foreign jurisdictions such as LDCs only in local currencies and/or requiring full hedging of currency risks associated with LDC lending. These regulatory changes, if they could be implemented with international agreement, were not especially controversial. They represented advances in thinking about international financial market risk management. Similar ideas were formulated by Kenneth Rogoff (1999, pp.37–8). For Rogoff, a 'deep pockets', collectively managed lender-of-last-resort would not be needed. The IMF would not have to take on such a role. Instead, with changes of the kind suggested by Krueger (and Rogoff), deep private capital markets could do the heavy lifting job of assisting LDCs in times of prosperity and impending economic crisis. These ideas were broadly consistent with the thought trajectory that had developed over the post-BW era at the IMF. The ultimate aim was to improve the composition – the quality and time horizons – of private international capital flows rather than directly control them (Fischer 1999).

In a similar vein to Polak, Fischer, Krueger and Rogoff, Maurice Obstfeld (1998, p.27) championed the IMF's break from 'the attitudes of its founders'. He meant, of course, the founders' scepticism toward international financial markets. Kenneth Rogoff (1999, p.36) chimed in with similar sentiments. He considered that LDCs would generally experience an immediate reduction in foreign lending from private capital markets if formal controls on capital movements are reintroduced in an attempt to resolve the dual problem of balance of payments crises and financial crises.

Main criticisms of IMF functions and the tarnished 'Washington Consensus'

From the mid-1970s concerted criticism of the IMF approach was mounted by several prominent economists. In this section we shall review the main ideas behind this criticism, parts of which brought into sharper focus the doctrinal bases of IMF thinking.

At the Institute for International Economics in Washington, John Williamson (1990) gave a catch-all label to a policy agenda common to IFIs and the US Treasury during the 1980s. That agenda was widely applied to the Latin American debt crisis and was dubbed the 'Washington consensus'. There were ten areas of policy reform commanding wide assent in this context, and which of course were also inherent in IMF programs and policies. They were as follows (Williamson 2003, p.1476).

1. Government fiscal discipline (Cf. IMF emphasis on fiscal austerity).
2. Reorienting government expenditure away from subsidies toward direct human capital development.
3. Tax reform with generally lower tax rates.
4. Financial market liberalization and removal of direct controls on interest rates.
5. Competitive exchange rates, though not market-determined and not rigidly fixed rates (Cf. IMF emphasis on 'flexible' exchange rates and preference for market-determined rates).
6. Current account liberalization – freer trade policy.
7. Foreign direct investment liberalization – not general, freer capital account convertibility (Cf. IMF emphasis on freer, more open capital account).
8. Privatization of government enterprises.
9. Reform of economic regulations in labor and product markets – not deregulation.
10. Expansion of private property rights.

We have noted the important differences between the Washington consensus and what Polak called the 'convergence of ideas' at the IMF (under policy agendas 1, 5 and 7). Otherwise the IMF approach was consistent with the consensus. Overall the IMF adopted a more pro-market stance than the consensus view in Washington. By comparison though, untrammelled market forces would have imposed more stringent and harsher outcomes if the IMF did not exist.

At the London School of Economics, Robert Wade (1998–9, p.44) was a strong critic of the IMF in the post-BW era and he highlighted a more extreme version of IMF policy reforms. The IMF surpassed the Washington consensus, which became much reviled and reinterpreted in the 1990s.[21] According to Wade, the IMF used its control of bailout money to obtain two kinds of policy changes from

> the crisis-affected countries. The first is to restrict domestic demand using higher interest rates, lower government spending, and stiffer taxes, the objective being to stabilize the currency and make it easier for countries to repay foreign debts. The second is to undertake liberalizing reforms in finance, corporate governance, and labor markets. In particular, the IMF has pressed the governments involved to keep making it easier for financial capital to move in and out of their countries (in other words, to liberalize their capital account), though in the wake of the crisis it has also emphasized a complementary strengthening of domestic financial regulation and supervision.

Wade's view is representative of the main criticisms of IMF policies. These critics often preferred to resurrect aspects of the old BW-system. BW placed the highest priority not on maximizing the flow of international private capital as an end in itself, and not by association, maximizing private investor confidence. On this interpretation, BW did not favour liberalization of capital accounts; it stressed economic stability and growth. The chief difficulty with Wade's account (and interpretation of BW), is that in fact, the IMF in the post-BW era was trying to secure short-run stability in the face of crises of various types so as to achieve long-run stability and growth. It was not that Wade and fellow critics confused correlation with causation – they did not blame the IMF for causing financial crises. The essence of their critique was that IMF interventions deepened financial difficulties and created more economic problems on the promise of a return to prosperity in the future so long as market-oriented structural changes and austerity policies were followed.

Another dimension of the Wade-type critique was the assertion that, in the process of liberalizing so as to adjust to crises, allowing freer international capital flows and freer trade increased international inequality. National economic policies were placed in an economic straight jacket, bound by the overriding need to keep international financial markets in a state of perpetual confidence about the domestic economy. That way, it was thought, national creditworthiness would

---

[21]See John Williamson (2008) for an assessment of all the interpretations and reinterpretations of the consensus.

be maintained. Furthermore, some force in the critics' argument derived from the reasonable supposition that much IMF lending during crises served as a watertight insurance policy encouraging irresponsible private foreign lending to LDCs. As we saw in Chapter 5, Paul Krugman, along with John Eatwell, Dani Rodrik and Lance Taylor, had made similar points. One of the main propositions of these economists was that the IMF should avoid the issue of structural economic reform altogether. At least, structural change issues should be kept separate from the more traditional IMF preoccupation with monetary, fiscal and exchange rate policies. In fact, structural change should not be an issue in conditions attached to emergency crisis lending and crisis management (Independent Task Force 1999, p.5, whose membership included Morris Goldstein and Paul Krugman). If that happened, the standard critical assaults on the IMF as a slavish follower of an extreme version of the Washington consensus might have been blunted.

There were at least two groups of economists who took a common position on the point that the IMF should not use financial crises as an opportunity to force structural changes and institutional reforms on some countries. On the one hand there were economists who strongly favoured capital account liberalization such as Martin Feldstein (1998a). Feldstein argued for opening, as much as possible, crisis-country capital accounts; the IMF's objectives in this connection must be 'to revive access to international funds' (p.32) so that the crisis country could be weaned-off IMF assistance. Requiring major structural and institutional reforms should only be necessary if they are essential to reviving access to private international capital markets. As well, according to Feldstein, major industrial powers such as the USA and Japan must not be permitted to use IMF programs and loan conditionality as a vehicle for the promotion or maintenance of their own trade and investment policies. In taking this view Feldstein seemed quite severely to circumscribe the place of the IMF in the world economy. Thus, overall the

> IMF should remember that the borrowers and the lending bankers or bondholders should bear primary responsibility for resolving the problems that arise when countries or their corporations cannot meet their international debt obligations. The IMF should provide technical assistance on how the debtors can improve their current account balances and increase their foreign exchange. It should act as a monitor of the success that the country is making in moving to self-sustainable liquidity, providing its own funds as

an indication of its confidence in the country's progress rather than as a bailout of international lenders and domestic borrowers (pp.32–3).

Barry Eichengreen (1999b, pp.209, 225) took a similar view. He was especially concerned to reduce the extreme 'politicization' of the IMF. He was not, however, as positive as Feldstein on the need to open LDCs to the vagaries of world capital markets. On the matter of structural reforms at the microeconomic level in crisis economies, Eichengreen equivocated: IMF macropolicy reforms do not work so well if not accompanied by consistent structural policy changes. Yet structural reforms can be intrusive and resented by domestic residents and therefore be politically destabilizing. In that situation, IMF involvement loses legitimacy (Gregorio et al. 1999, pp.48–50).

A second group of critics who did not like the extension of IMF loan conditionality into issues of structural economic change include Krugman, Wade and Taylor. Their position turned on the view that IMF activities and loan conditions imposed a pro-cyclical bias on its loan recipients – a bias toward output reduction in the short-run, deflation, and government expenditure contraction when a country was in crisis – thereby only worsening the economic downturn. None of these critics appreciated the kinds of trade-offs identified by Anne Krueger (exposited earlier in this chapter) that were inherent in the IMF's role as crisis manager.

George Stiglitz (1999) reinterpreted the Washington consensus; he bundled together the types of policies favoured by the consensus and used them as a broad symbol of an underlying doctrine, a doctrine of 'market fundamentalism'. The IMF, it was argued, attempted to prosecute its programs and policies on the basis of an outmoded vision of a perfect, competitive market economy thereby minimizing the role of the nation state in crisis management. This theme is further developed in his work outside the period under review (e.g. Stiglitz 2002b, 2002c, 2008 and Basu 2003). Stiglitz (1998) called for a move toward a new, post-BW consensus policy agenda for the IMF, one that would include greater concern in all IFI programs for growth promotion, inequality and redistributional impacts. It is by no means clear from what we have exposited from the later writings of Jacques Polak (e.g. 1991) that the IMF was not concerned about long-term poverty problems in LDCs. That the IMF would later be criticized for trespassing on the objectives of the World Bank to tackle poverty made matters more confusing. (Finally, Garuda (2000) studied the distributional effects of IMF programs and the results do not show unambiguous deterioration in income inequality).

The IMF as an international lender of last resort?

In *Manias, Panics and Crashes*, Charles Kindleberger (1978, Chapter 12) was one of the first economists to weigh up arguments for and against the IMF formally assuming the role as ILLR. Earlier, Richard Cooper (1975, p.37) foresaw the need for an ILLR separate from the IMF. Kindleberger's point of departure was that an IFI acting in the collective interests of its members as an ILLR could reduce the impact of contagion crises. An ILLR can prevent the negative, cross-border spillover effects arising from liquidity or possibly even insolvency problems in parts of the international economy. Kindleberger made the ILLR proposal in the light of his knowledge of the interwar currency crises and 1930s Depression when there was no ILLR. At the time, the League of Nations attempted to take on the role in a very minor way and provided some stabilization loans on an experimental and *ad hoc* basis to some European countries. Kindleberger also appreciated Walter Bagehot's (1873) classic rules for a lender-of-last-resort in general. With the advent of the IMF, the BW Agreement determined that it would not be a credit-creating bank or have credit-creating powers, or produce its own international money. A classic Bagehot rule for a lender-of-last-resort is that it must have such powers. In strict principle then, the IMF could not be described as an ILLR. Nations, or groups of nations in a monetary union, have monetary sovereignty and would not readily relinquish sovereignty to a world central bank. Thus, for Kindleberger, while a world central bank with credit-creating powers could function as an ILLR it would be a highly unlikely institution given national preferences for monetary independence.

When Stanley Fischer (1999), then at the IMF, attempted to rehabilitate the proposal to establish the IMF as a genuine ILLR, we notice that he was in good company with other prominent economists at the time. It was nevertheless difficult to ascertain whether or not anything new was being offered in the light of what Kindleberger had already concluded. The IMF trajectory of thought on financial systems was by then well established: a high level of supervision and carefully framed legislation would reduce the risks of financial crisis but not eliminate them. Once crises occur – either standard currency crises, self-fulfilling currency crises, or cross-border contagion crises incorporating financial and banking problems – domestic monetary authorities can do little to reduce subsequent instability. They could act collectively as a coor-dinated group of monetary authorities in which case they might have a favourable impact. Otherwise the question of a single, all-powerful ILLR arises. Fischer explains how an ILLR can assist in reducing the frequency and scale of international financial crises. He outlines the main reasons for the IMF being able to act effectively in this role. First, it has large scale lending facilities. Second, it has become an experienced financial crisis manager by default. Third, it is strengthening its technical exper-tise for improving national financial systems. The IMF does not have the attribute of a bank in the sense of having money-creating capacity but that is not regarded as essential. Fischer cites many historical exam-ples of national lender-of-last resort experiences that are similar to problems faced in the international realm. These experiences

> make the point that the lender of last resort need not have the power to create money, as long as it can provide credit to the market or to institutions in trouble. It is possible to set up an agency to deal with potential banking sector problems [in the national economy realm] and endow it with sufficient funds. In dealing with banking crises, the lender of last resort has more often acted as crisis manager, as coor-dinator, without putting up its own funds, than as an outright lender (p.89).

Furthermore, apart from the historical record, Fischer was convinced on logical grounds that an international lender-or-last resort need not have the money creating attribute to be an effective crisis manager. Neverthe-less, the classic Bagehot rules for a lender-of-last-resort, cited by Fischer and many others, require a domestic LLR to lend virtually unlimited amounts of short-term finance to financial markets as a whole, against good collateral and at penalty interest rates. This original set of rules has been reinterpreted on the margin to include within its ambit the possibil-ity of lending to individual financial institutions that are 'too big to fail', that is, with very large liquidity problems relative to the size of the overall market. In cases where the demand on lender funds was extremely large, Fischer proposed that the IMF (acting as ILLR) could borrow to augment its resources and call on member governments to pool additional funds to assist in a crisis. In the latter event the IMF would act as an organizer and manager of rescue packages rather than a sole funder.

Fischer was especially committed to the Bagehot 'good collateral' rule. Thus, 'when financial institutions know that the lender of last resort will demand collateral, they have an incentive to reduce risk in their portfolios by holding assets that would be accepted as collateral' (p.90). Moreover, the lender must assess collateral in terms of asset values prevailing before a crisis, that is, in 'normal times' so as to bolster market confidence and avert panic in the sale of assets. The nature of such panics is so variable, however, that it is not possible, even if were desirable in principle, to set clear rules for the operation of the LLR or ILLR as the case may be. Indeed, a modicum of

> ambiguity is simply unavoidable: no central bank or lender of last resort will ever be able to spell out precisely in advance the circumstances under which it will act as either a crisis lender or crisis manager and the conditions it will lay down at the time. But unnecessary ambiguity is not constructive, for it implies that occasions will occur when...a lender of last resort is expected to take action, but...cannot or does not provide the function (pp.91–2).

Balanced against this danger is the requirement that the ILLR not make its terms of lending assistance so clear in advance as to create moral hazard. That is, the ILLR cannot make a country rely in advance on clear rules concerning a bailout because that potential borrower may then take excessive risks in the light of that fact and this behaviour just increases the probability of a bailout (Rogoff 1999, p.27).

Jeffrey Sachs (1995a) saw the essential feature of emerging market crises in the post-BW era in terms of unsustainable debt burdens – similar to burdens eventually giving rise to runs on domestic banks. In domestic banking crises, banks may have a liquidity problem rather than an insolvency problem. Similarly, this argument applies to whole countries facing a financial crisis. His view was developed from detailed research on the Latin American debt crisis in the 1980s (Sachs 1984, 1986, 1989). He was persuaded in favour of creating an ILLR that could, like a domestic central bank acting as a LLR, lend in a timely manner to avert an international financial crisis. Sachs' unpublished but widely cited Frank Graham Lecture at Princeton outlined the possible functions of a new IMF founded on ILLR principles, though not principles satisfying Bagehot's original rules (Sachs 1995a). Like Fischer, he maintained that when lending was forthcoming in a timely manner to countries as a whole – their governments or selected financial institutions – a financial panic could be thwarted. He was more precise than Fischer about the nature of a financial panic: it referred to

> a circumstance where the level of short-term indebtedness is very high relative to short-term liquidity and for whatever reason, a market

equilibrium unfolds in which the short-term debt is called. And the borrower has no recourse to refinance the short-term debt. From a theoretical point of view, this is the [same] kind of framework that we use to analyze bank runs in a domestic economy. It has also become one of the favorite vehicles for trying to understand a range of international crises (Sachs 1999, p.182).

When a financial panic was averted by the intervention of an ILLR, downward pressure on a currency would be reduced and the natural tendency for domestic bank lending to contract would be counteracted. In short, at once, a currency and banking crisis could be avoided. Additionally, sharp contraction in the domestic money supply in crisis countries will also be averted, thereby reducing the impact on output and employment.

A crucial prerequisite for Sachs' proposal was the need for an ILLR properly to identify a liquidity problem in a crisis (as opposed to a hopeless case of insolvency). The informational requirements to complete such a task were assumed to be surmountable. He then distinguishes three types of liquidity problem that an ILLR may have to address (Sachs 1989 and 1999, pp.182–3).

1. A financial panic when short-term indebtedness (e.g. to international capital markets) is high but short-term liquidity is relatively low. Panic occurs when borrowers are unable to refinance short-term liabilities perhaps because creditworthiness ratings either collapse or are rendered non-existent because of uncertainty and possibly because debt markets are incomplete, especially in LDCs.
2. A 'debt overhang' crisis. In this case bankrupt borrowers need short-term capital to carry on their operations otherwise they would not be able to generate income to service any debt whatsoever.

   It is quite possible under (1) above that borrowers may not be able to access finance even when the return on its use as working capital would exceed any market interest rate. In the USA, according to Sachs, the existence of a bankruptcy code allows financial assistance in such cases to an affected entity in order for it to remain a going business concern. Panic is not usually a feature of this situation. Access to credit is the principal problem. Hence, in the international realm the IMF acting as an ILLR would play a vital role in providing credit in preventing panic.
3. Sovereign debts or public sector enterprise collapse. Here debt overhang is not a preeminent concern. Governments and their enterprises usually have dominant market positions protected by law.

Governments also have powerful, enforceable tax raising capacity. Political and civil strife may prevent effective use of those government powers. With such social and political instability, private capital markets will not function well, so a ILLR would bring stability and credibility to the situation, refinance sovereign or government enterprise debts and restore their natural, enforceable, income-earning power to service that debt.

In all three types of liquidity crises distinguished by Sachs, the international economy needs an ILLR. A reconstituted IMF is suitable for the role even though it does not strictly meet Bagehot's criteria. In brief, the proposed use of the IMF as ILLR violates Bagehot's rules because the IMF cannot create credit, does not have near unlimited financial resources and is unable to enforce claims on 'good collateral' (i.e. seize assets) if something goes wrong. In practice the IMF was managing approximately seventy countries and their debt policies as of 1998 (Sachs 1999, p.188). Sachs asserted that the IMF was not needed in that role. In fact the

reason we have such an institution is that we have made no provision for discharge of unpayable debts. That keeps an endless routine of IMF programs going. We have also allowed the highly short-term capital to rule the system in [the post-BW era] through dangerous exchange rate and capital account policies. The combination has made...financial panics much more prevalent than they need to be (p.188).

The solution was to create the international equivalent of domestic bankruptcy laws administered by the IMF in its capacity as an ILLR. If debts are deemed immediately unpayable or expected to be so, an efficient system of financial workouts is usually established by bankruptcy courts in more developed economies. Debt resolution in LDCs does not follow orderly procedures, so the IMF during the post-BW era became entangled in *ad hoc*, uncertain arrangements in many countries (Sachs 1995b, pp.10–11 citing IMF 1995). If the IMF were reconstituted into (say) a quasi-ILLR this would lead to easy promulgation of an international bankruptcy code applying to all IMF loan recipients. Unfortunately there was no

literal bankruptcy court to move in the direction of such mechanisms. We could begin with a clear statement of IMF operating principles regarding each stage of the workout. We could search for ways to establish emergency priority lending from private capital markets, under IMF supervision. The IMF and governments could recommend model covenants for inclusion in future sovereign lending instruments that would allow for emergency priority lending and for efficient renegotiations of debt claims (Sachs 1995b, p.13).

Sach's trajectory of thought followed the sentiments originally expressed by Kindleberger; it was founded on the belief in the inherent, persistent and major inefficiencies of the IFS. These inefficiencies justified the existence, preferably *de jure*, though in fact at the time *de facto*, of the IMF acting as an ILLR. As a *de facto* ILLR, the IMF had been moderately effective in the 1980s and 1990s. If it assumed international bankruptcy adjudication as suggested by Sachs, it would then operate in the best interests of its members and create an atmosphere of cooperation between international creditors and debtors. This would mark another crucial step in the process of global financial integration but it would emphatically not be a form of integration that relied exclusively on untrammelled market processes.

Inefficiencies in financial markets and banking practices in LDC's could make ILLR operations more difficult.

As in any lender-of-last resort operation, the governing principle for emergency international support should be a combination of: ex ante prudential standards to avoid moral hazard; strong conditionality in the event of a bailout, timely lending to avert or stem a panic; and closure (or merger) of insolvent, as opposed illiquid, financial institutions. Probably the greatest shortcoming in proceeding with a general international system of support is the lack of adequate prudential supervision in most developing countries, and the lack of detailed attention at the level of the IMF and BIS to the state of banking regulation in developing countries (Sachs 1995b, p.15).

By contrast with developing countries, in the 1990s it was taken for granted that banking practices in highly developed industrialized nations were adequately supervised and regulated and the application of prudential standards had reached some optimal state. By the late 1990s, the advent of 'casino' banking practices carried out in highly sophisticated banking systems were soon to call in to question this standard presumption. Finally, given IMF resources, and despite the inadequate state of financial regulation in LDCs, if the IMF plays even a limited

ILLR role, it would actively 'bail in' private sector investors in a crisis containment and resolution phase. Altogether, Sachs believed that moral hazard problems would be reduced if his scheme was adopted.

In many ways the deliberations of Allan Meltzer and his International Financial Institution Advisory Commission (IFIAC) Report, mirrored Sachs' approach. The Commission included Sachs who endorsed the majority report (along with 8 other members including Meltzer as chair). The IFIAC (2000) produced a sweeping blueprint for IMF reform based on the idea of an ILLR. As mentioned earlier in this chapter, Meltzer was extremely critical of the IMF's functions in the post-BW era especially insofar as it contributed to moral hazard (Meltzer 1998). Earlier he had gone so far as to recommend abolition of the IMF on those grounds alone (Meltzer 1995). According to the IFIAC, the IMF needed a new mandate; it must set pre-qualifications centred on certain financial standards that become conditions for accessing the resources of the ILLR. Consistent with some of Bagehot's classic criteria, the IFIAC recommended that the IMF lend strictly on a short-term basis and not for longer-term purposes, and at penalty rates. Pre-qualification standards would presumably be a rough parallel to the 'good collateral' idea (Bagehot's third rule), even though such collateral was not easy to seize in the event of default. Pre-qualification incorporated IMF monetary and fiscal standards, and was predicated on good banking systems in which banks had adequate capital and liquid reserves in the country concerned. In other words, pre-qualification was an *ex ante* incentive system compared with the existing *ex post* conditionality requirements of the IMF that were based on the practice of lending immediately, followed later by use of an intrusive 'command and control' system to oversee loans. The import of the IFIAC approach, if it could be operationalized and implemented, was that excessive private sector lending by the IMF would become rare. Lending would be directed to sovereign governments and their monetary authorities; these had better collateral and were directly responsible for adopting pre-qualification standards – that is IMF approved banking, monetary and fiscal policies. At the very least, policymaker moral hazard would be reduced.

A member of the IFIAC, Charles Calomiris at Columbia University wrote prolifically in defense of the IFIAC report after it was published.[22] He saw the report as a reconstitution of the IMF that would remove its

---

[22]Later, Meltzer (2003, 2005) also reiterated and defended the majority report of IFIAC.

association with private sector, financial system bailouts. *Bona fide* liquidity crises would imply some concomitant balance of payments problem and/or a currency crisis, and the IMF would simply provide protection against market illiquidity as a whole by assisting monetary authorities in the first instance. The IMF would not act as a lender for macroeconomic counter-cyclical purposes, that is, it would not provide 'global counter-cyclical financial subsidies to its members'. Counter-cyclical policy was the duty of domestic monetary and fiscal authorities. Furthermore, long-term development assistance and structural reform financing were a matter for other IFIs such as regional development banks and the World Bank (Calomiris 2000, pp.96–7). The IFIAC blueprint brings the IMF closer to its original 1944 mission. The IMF would use its resources to target poorer, pre-qualifying LDCs; direct poverty alleviation would, if resources permitted, be disbursed by grants rather than loans. The latter could be a function of the IMF in addition to its ILLR role. This philosophy closely resembled Sachs' ideas (Sachs 1995a, 1995b, 1999, 2003). That the IMF should have a direct role in dealing with absolute poverty was not something widely shared by other economists mentioned in this chapter. Perhaps this implied residual or supplementary role of the IMF in the IFIAC report and in the writings of Sachs, was meant to compensate for the likelihood that the IMF (playing an ILLR role) would end up lending too little to the poorest, disorganized, non-qualifiers? As well, non-pre-qualifiers may ultimately produce damaging contagion crises (Bordo and James 2000). And what of the possibility that pre-qualifiers would be time-inconsistent in maintaining IMF approved monetary and fiscal standards? Would IMF 'command and control' then be necessary? Country circumstances – political, social, economic – may change, whereas pre-qualification is a one-time event.

Doctrinal differences on the IMF acting as an ILLR do not become clear if we immerse ourselves in its day-to-day operations. The ideas underwriting any set of operations are clarified when we consider major opponents of the ILLR. Here we might refer to the work of Anna Schwartz (1999) at the NBER. Schwartz denies the need for an international lender given the growth in international capital markets. The IMF does not have the essential attributes of a lender-of-last-resort of the kind national central banks possess. For Schwartz, the IMF 'is only a simulacrum' of an ILLR; it 'is not the real thing' (p.3). Apart from the reasons we have already adduced (and readily admitted by Sachs and Fischer) that do not make the IMF an ILLR along the strict lines required by Bagehot, Schwartz also doubts the international collective governance powers of the IMF. The IMF does not have 'independent authority' to create 'high-powered money' and has no real powers of enforcement (p.5). As well, it would require unrealistically large financial resources that are only available in private international capital markets. Schwartz concludes that the IMF had useful functions in the BW era when international capital markets were 'limited and repressed'. At the end of the 1990s those markets are 'deregulated and flush with funds' (p.5). What, then, was left for the IMF to do? In a subsequent article Schwartz (2000, p.24) proposed that the IMF should be downsized and function to coordinate national attempts to harmonize financial market regulations and prudential supervision of those markets. The other minor role for the IMF was in economic research, statistics gathering, and reporting on the financial policies of member governments. All this would serve to improve information flows in private capital markets.

Summary and conclusion

Ideas relating to changes in the role of the IMF in the process of international financial integration have addressed:

(i) the operation of that institution in response to post-BW changes in exchange rate policies, capital account convertibility, new types of financial crises and the recycling of international reserve assets through its lending programs;

(ii) the broader rationale for the existence, functions and scope of its activities that have been transformed in response to various post-BW developments under (i) above.

This chapter has concentrated largely on the larger background issues raised under (ii), and rather less on covering the detailed foreground issues under (i). Yet the foreground issues concerning various running repairs to existing IMF operations and detailed debate over IMF governance structures have preoccupied many economists in the period under review.

The ideas and policy suggestions we have reviewed are concerned with anchoring the IMF in principle. What have been the arguments for its existence and scope in principle? All too often this question was blurred by foreground issues to do with *ad hoc* operational adjustments to the IMF as it currently existed. Undoubtedly, these issues were important insofar as they were concerned with perceived immediate pressures emanating from day-to-day events in the IFS. Ralph Bryant at the Brookings Institution in Washington DC was a long time observer and commentator on the theory and practice of IFIs, international policymaking, policy coordination and developments in cross-border policy consultation (e.g. Bryant 1995). He avoided foreground issues, and distinguished three different approaches to the IMF (Bryant 1999, p.230):

1. the 'untrammelled markets' view;
2. the 'sweeping' reform view and
3. 'pragmatic incrementalism'.

Our discussion of thought trajectories, as we have called them in this book, can also be cast in terms of this tripartite division.

IMF economists attempted to produce a self-styled model – a rationale in other words – on which to base Fund programs. They formulated broad rules for policies applied to country debt and balance of payments problems. Critics contended that the monetary approach of the Polak model implied simple pro-market monetary rules and a fiscal austerity program. While by no means living up to Bryant's 'untrammelled markets' view, in the 1970s and 1980s the IMF was associated with the idea that market processes should be used heavily to assist with crisis-adjustment and debt problems. Hence the ideas of Polak, Fischer, Krueger, Rogoff and Obstfeld share a common trajectory of thought with the IMF policy line. There were differences between these economists but only on matters of detail as specific problems faced by the IMF altered over the post-BW era.

The 'sweeping' reformist group included Meltzer, Sachs, Stiglitz, Wade and Schwartz. However, there were marked doctrinal differences between some of them. Stiglitz, Wade (and Krugman) demanded a complete overhaul of IMF programs so that they could focus more on growth and distributional concerns than exclusively on stabilization at all costs, and on pandering to financial markets. Sachs, Meltzer (and Calomiris) emphasized a reconstitution of the IMF into an ILLR, with tight prequalification rules for its lending operations. The Sachs-Meltzer view was substantiated further in the IFIAC majority report which emphasized the development of a more formal rule-based IMF that would reduce the endemic moral hazard problem increasingly associated with its operations. Sachs added the international bankruptcy code of requirements in his deliberations on the scope of IMF functions. The Sachs-Meltzer line also recommended a distinct, separate set of IMF functions for the attack on world poverty. While Stanley Fischer was strongly associated with the pro-markets group, he too argued for the establishment of the IMF as an ILLR though

without too much formalization. He appeared to favour organic development of the IMF into a quasi-ILLR role, a position it had already seemed
to be assuming by the 1990s at least in a *de facto* sense.

Anna Schwartz is the only economist who might be referred to as an
'untrammelled', sweeping market reformer on IMF matters. Schwartz
was supremely optimistic about private international capital markets
acting as responsible lenders, even in crises. Rather than abolish the
IMF, Schwartz urged sweeping reductions in the scope of its lending
activities, reducing its role to a mere provider of economic intelligence
as a service to capital market participants. That the IMF could not out-
perform vast world capital markets and that its financial capacity was
too miniscule, are also views shared by Kenneth Rogoff. Accordingly,
he too was sceptical of the ILLR proposal.

There was also a long line of 'pragmatic incrementalists' on the IMF
who were broadly similar to the group we described as 'eclectics' in previous chapters. In this chapter that group included, as before, Eichengreen, and also Gregorio, Goldstein, Ito, and Wyplosz – an internationally
cosmopolitan group. These economists were not in favour of installing
the IMF in the formal ILLR role. They focused on foreground issues, on
amending operational activities and incremental reform of IMF practices.
They appreciated the political and practical feasibilities, thus concentrating on running repairs of the IMF as the evolution of events in the IFS
demanded. They reflected little on the overall existence or mission of the
IMF, losing sight of the big questions concerned with its existence, scope
and range of activities. Less charitable commentators would charge the
incrementalists with status quo bias. As well, in focusing on operational
activities they tended to lose sight of questions such as the long-term
significance of the IMF in the IFS as a whole relative to the dominance of
international capital markets.

In conclusion, this chapter has presented a rather mixed bag; the
doctrinal divisions are not so clear-cut as they were in previous chapters.
Nevertheless, most of the ideas outlined fitted distinct categorizations of
thought trajectories having much in common with those distinguished
in previous chapters. The IMF is a policymaking agency. Therefore much
of the discussion in this chapter was on policy matters rather than economic ideas *per se*. It could be said that IMF economists themselves, more
than any others, provided the most comprehensive ideational basis for
their role in the international economy through construction of the Polak
model. On other matters of principle such as those of conditionality
and surveillance – these necessarily changed with major changes in the
world economy in the post-BW era. While the pragmatic incrementalists

seemed generally resigned to political influences on the IMF, the sweeping reformers and pro-market economists fervently opposed any IMF politicization.

The proposition that there must be a place for global collective action on economic and financial matters to correct market failures is by no means incontrovertible. The fundamental doctrine of international collective action through IFIs such as the IMF, has not been well-developed despite extension of the 'public goods' idea to international institutions in the work of Charles Kindleberger (1986) and Joseph Stiglitz (1995). The division of thought trajectories on this subject in relation to the IMF for instance, is not so clear-cut. Some doctrines exposited in this chapter take a 'public choice' view suggesting that collective action can exacerbate the market failures it attempts to address, so the operations of IFIs should be minimized (e.g. Schwartz). Other economists accept the general point that IMF action can fail in a serious way, but that does not obviate the need for extensive IMF action; it only justifies major reforms so that it becomes a more focused agency treating major international market failures such as inadequate economic growth, periodic, economically damaging crises and distributional problems (e.g. Stiglitz). Still others (e.g. Sachs) agree with the public choice idea very provisionally, and they suggest that the IMF's major collective action role should be to operate in a formally rule-bound manner as an ILLR responding to catastrophic market failures; those rules might also remove the scope for *ad hoc* discretion, reduce moral hazard and excessive IMF politicization.

7
Currency Consolidation and Currency Unions

Introduction

In outlining the 'tripolar' options for exchange rate regimes in Chapter 3 we foreshadowed that we would consider controversies over the third polar option – the currency union, including full monetary union – in this chapter. Arguments for the widespread adoption of a common currency, or even a universal global currency, all turn on the idea of monetary internationalization, or international monetary integration. In short, they are arguments for increasing the extent of financial integration between nations and for finding optimal monetary standards. Single national currencies are a reflection of monetary independence, and while being advantageous as national symbols, they are an obstacle, in principle, to full international monetary integration. In this chapter we shall consider ideas and policies on system-wide issues – ideas and policies that feature multilateral approaches allowing countries actively to participate in the process of financial and economic integration by way of achieving some form of common money. The debates during the post-BW era over the process of transition to a common currency (such as the euro) will largely be avoided. The longer-term principles and associated policies required to create a common currency or choose to consolidate currencies in the first place, will be the focus of this chapter. Similarly, the comparatively short-term issue of the rise to dominance of one or other national currency in the international realm (e.g. dollar supremacy vs. yen vs. euro) will be set aside. Our attention will be accorded to broader issues of the international financial architecture: the purpose, rationale and place of common currencies, currency consolidation (e.g. dollarization), deliberate design of a universal global currency, and the potential for the spontaneous emergence of new currency arrangements, in that overall architecture.

One natural corollary of arguments for common currencies and monetary unions across national borders is enhanced international financial integration. Maintaining separate national currencies retards the 'globalization' of international finance and related institutions. As well, economic policies, especially monetary policies across national jurisdictions become harmonized or fully integrated with the adoption of monetary unions. One of the main general benefits of nationally independent currencies and market-determined exchange rate regimes is that national monetary authorities could be free to conduct monetary policies for domestic macroeconomic adjustment purposes, and allow their national currencies to be market-determined and flexible. Both monetary and exchange rate policy could then be used for countercyclical purposes, thereby contributing to the achievement of policy objectives such as high growth and lower unemployment (than might otherwise be the case). In general, if there is a common, cross-border agreement requiring monetary authorities to follow simple policy rules and commit to a common currency and a stable nominal framework for an integrated market economy, then the benefits of independent monetary policy and exchange rate policy would be relinquished. Proponents of a common currency and monetary union argue that such benefits are small relative to the long-term gains of monetary policy harmonization.

Sharing a common currency and monetary policy across national geo-political borders is just another way of resolving the problem of international policy coordination that might otherwise have to be confronted to deal with increasing cross-border economic interdependencies and interactions in finance, trade and the movement of capital and labour. However, the national decision to accept a common currency and monetary union may involve a trade-off between the microeconomic efficiency gains and the loss of policy independence for macroeconomic adjustment at the national level (Krugman 1992, p.xviii). Some economists, as we shall see in this chapter, maintain that there is no such trade-off; others accept its short-term validity but deny its existence over the long term. The extent of the trade-off, if any, probably depends on the country or region in question. While there may always be microeconomic gains from using a common currency – the transaction costs reductions being the most obvious – losses occurring from the lack of freedom to attack macroeconomic adjustment problems at the national level are not so assured or so obvious. What for instance might be the costs of relinquishing a market-determined exchange rate in favour of a fixed rate with other union members?

In respect of exchange rate regimes, Paul Krugman (1992, pp.194–5) observed that countries using such regimes can be incentivized to use restrictive monetary policy to disinflate faster than their trading partners and then gain greater long-term trade competitiveness even though such action may cause short-term exchange rate appreciation and recession. In Krugman's words,

> countries under floating rates have an incentive to engage in beggar-thy-neighbour disinflation: by pursuing a tight monetary policy, any individual country can appreciate its currency and thereby achieve a rapid reduction in inflation. Unfortunately, if all countries try to do this, they will have chosen a deeper recession (p.195).

By contrast, a more mutually acceptable 'collective inflation-output trade-off' could be chosen by adopting a common currency and monetary policy in which exchange rates are fixed by definition. Charles Wyplosz (1997, p.19) contended that independent monetary policies and freely floating exchange rates can also produce 'beggar-thy-neighbor', protectionist pressures. Such pressures would be a direct consequence of the kind of policies prosecuted under the conditions Krugman mentions above. Protectionist policies, in turn, are one way of responding to the impending 'deep recession' he suggests will be forthcoming. He thought the move to create the EMU and the associated Euro would help avoid all that.

In reviewing the arguments for different exchange rate regime choices in the post-BW era, including the option of monetary union with a common currency, Krugman warned that it is not easy to categorize the ideas and policy inclinations of economists into a simple binary grouping. Appealing to the beneficence of market processes can go hand-in-hand with the case for independent, national currencies, the values of which are determined by day-to-day market forces. Equally, a pro-market thinker could support a single, common currency of some kind in a particular economic region in which exchange rates are fixed within the region and market-determined against other currencies outside the region. As Krugman (1992, p.188) concludes: '[w]hich is more nearly a free market system: flexible exchange rates, fixed exchange rates, or a common currency? The answer is not obvious and even if we could decide on some ranking of freeness, no policy conclusions will follow'. In the following sections of this chapter we shall have the opportunity to review Krugman's conclusion.

Robert Mundell's ideas on common money in the post-BW era

At Columbia University, 1999 Nobel laureate Robert Mundell made a celebrated case for optimum currency areas (OCAs) in his research during the BW era.[23] During the post-BW era Mundell (1973b, 1973c, 1997a, 1997b, 1998) restated his arguments for OCAs. He accepted the trade-off between the two forces identified by Krugman – that micro efficiency gains trade-off against losses in a country's reduced freedom to use various macro policies in adjusting to localized macroeconomic disturbances. In his classic, well-known BW era case for OCAs, a common currency has the attributes of a common language; it enjoys economies of scale in use because the greater the range and scope of its use, the more people will want to use it. Moreover, as more countries join the OCA, the transactions domain is enlarged as is the domain for movement of goods, services, labour and capital. In principle, therefore, by reducing transaction costs, an OCA should be trade-enhancing. The OCA should also: improve the degree of financial integration between OCA members; and be most effective if it permits free trade, free capital and free labour mobility in the OCA. Other than transaction cost efficiencies, additional micro efficiency gains include, among other things, greater internal output market integration, lower information costs and correspondingly lower costs of economic calculation given the common unit of account.

In the BW era Mundell held much enthusiasm for fixed currency exchange rate regimes and he carried this view over into the post-BW era. He stated an 'iron law' of international economics: the ubiquitous fact of economic interdependence between nations which in turn implied and ongoing problem of adjusting to external, current account imbalances between them. That adjustment could not simply rely upon market forces – it required deliberate, planned multilateral exchange rate management (Mundell 1977, p.244). Like Friedrich Hayek (see Chapter 3 above pp.50–1), Mundell feared the worst from the adoption of market-determined exchange rates. Flexible exchange rates permitted national monetary independence and freedom to inflate. By comparison, fixed exchange rates provided a nominal barrier mitigating against policy

---

[23]On the development of his ideas in the BW era mostly in support of fixed exchange rate regimes, along with his attempt to salvage that aspect of the BW IFO, see Endres (2005, pp.188–203).

freedom to inflate come-what-may. Monetary policy under fixed exchange rates is subordinated to the maintenance of a credible exchange rate (Mundell 1997a, p.7). Speculation between inter-country (member) exchange rate regimes is no longer possible in an OCA. Trade and exchange between area members will not be subject to exchange rate uncertainty and to the sometimes prohibitive costs of forward exchange contracts. Compared with market-determined exchange rates, Mundell (1973b, pp.149–50) believed markets for goods and services, labour and financial capital integrate more smoothly in a world of fixed exchange rates. Of course, as we found in Chapter 3 above, most economists in the post-BW era agreed that it did not matter what currency regime was chosen if these markets were completely integrated, that is, if prices for all inputs and outputs were perfectly flexible in the world economy as a whole. For Mundell, the relative economic size of nations mattered. Flexible, market-determined exchange rates were only able to remain viable in the post-BW era – an era marked by considerable price and wage rigidities and barriers to the international movement of capital and labor – because smaller countries in economic terms were able to benchmark their currencies against the relatively stable, floating US dollar or another key currency. In doing so, in finding this route to measuring the value of national small-country currencies as units of account, the so-called free-market solution to exchange rate regime choice seems to have worked. Yet it was a precariously poised system dependent on very stable, key currency relationships.

In Mundell's case for monetary and currency union, a supranational monetary authority and a common fiat currency replaces national currencies. Ignoring transitional issues, all national currencies are demonetized and the supranational authority operates monetary policy; that authority would provide the nominal anchor for the OCA. Individual countries give up national sovereignty over monetary policy but may influence that policy by formal representation on the monetary authority's controlling board. Adopting a single, common currency is not strictly necessary for a monetary union and, conversely, monetary union need not require the abolition of national currencies, though in practice it usually does. In Mundell's (1997a, p.14) view, 'the best path toward monetary union is through irrevocably fixed exchange rates.' Currency areas are a half-way house on the way to fuller monetary union.

Mundell explains the main (unweighted) reasons why a particular nation might choose to enter an OCA. Here we paraphrase important sections of Mundell (1997a, pp.15–16; 1997b, 1997c and 1998). The choice of a common currency could be made to:

1. establish – a monetary anchor, a mechanism for monetary and fiscal guidance, an economic and political power bloc to function as a bigger cushion against external shocks, a competing international currency to rival key currencies such as the US dollar;
2. gain – seigniorage from sharing a more widely used currency that would potentially become more 'international' i.e. used more widely outside the OCA as a vehicle currency, investment currency, official reserve currency or an international unit of account; the inflation rate of the OCA; participation in the financial centers of the OCA;
3. reduce – transaction costs; currency production costs; the costs of cross-border economic calculation; the discretion of national monetary and fiscal policymakers; the sum of idle international reserves required previously by individual countries (gold, IMF reserve holdings, currencies).

At a deeper economic level, Mundell also extends his trajectory of thought on the 'right' exchange rate choices that he had in common with several other leading economists in the post BW era. He rails against the deleterious effects on economic policy and on the real economy of major currency fluctuations. The quality of a currency is important to him; that quality is enhanced by its widespread usage and low volatility in value against other currencies. By contrast, with a multiplicity of small currencies in a particular region such as in Europe, the

> expectations of exchange rate changes greatly unsettle the money markets, make planning difficult, and, in the long run, weaken the control a government has over economic policy...Europe could reap appreciable gains from establishing a centralized financial market, not in the sense of a single location but in the sense of unified rates on different currencies...The only way to establish a unified money market is to kill the sporadic and unsettling speculation over currency prices that have ravaged European markets. The exchange rate should be taken out of both national and international politics in Europe (Mundell 1973b, p.147).

Mundell disagreed with the pro-market approach that considered exchange rates as simple commodity prices like 'the price of cabbage'.

Exchange rates embody expectations of future policy stances linking the national currency to the world price level. A particular exchange rate reflects the credibility of the relevant monetary authority in maintaining the purchasing power of that unit of account. Thus, a fixed exchange rate between nations in a union is

> an expression of the monetary authorities' commitment to a monetary policy. Leaving the parity of the smaller national currencies to arbitrary and frequent changes is to make the exchange rate the hostage of any monopolistic attack, whether internal or external, on currency. The arguments for changing the exchange rate are short-run arguments based on a money illusion that is increasingly disappearing (Mundell 1973b, p.149).

Mundell was pragmatic about the viability of an OCA in practice; it need not require all the conditions to satisfy an 'optimum' in theory. It was 'enough' he believed, that in the case of the proposed European OCA, that the European countries in question possessed similar characteristics to the United States. Thus, the European countries could eliminate exchange fluctuations by choosing a common currency and allow free capital and labour mobility in the region, just as in the United States (Mundell 1973b, pp.166–72).

With the advent of the euro, the configuration of the post-BW IFS would change significantly. As before, Mundell (1998, p.3) championed the overall economic and political 'power' that would accrue to nations adopting the euro. It was his conviction that the

> collapse of the Bretton Woods arrangements did not alter the power configuration of the international system. Both before and after the breakdown, the dollar was the dominant currency. The introduction of the euro, on the other hand, will challenge the status of the dollar and alter the power configuration of the system. For this reason the introduction of the euro may be the most important development in the international monetary system since the dollar replaced the pound sterling as the dominant international currency soon after the outbreak of World War I (Mundell 1998, p.3).

In his Nobel lecture he repeats this point with an additional, bold prediction: the 'introduction of the euro will redraw the international monetary landscape' (Mundell 2000, p.337). For Mundell the euro added another element of stability to the IFS, giving the international economy a 'tri-polar' key currency structure around the US dollar, yen and euro. As long as the relative values of these currencies remained fairly stable, the world economy would prosper. In the long term, on the periphery of the tri-polar structure, new OCAs may be formed or smaller nations may join, or link themselves to, one of the three key currencies. The greatest challenge will be to manage the otherwise market-determined exchange rates between the three key currencies, especially the euro-US dollar rate. It is a formidable management task, preferably effected through formal international economic policy co-ordination and will be vital to the stability of the entire IFS (Mundell 1998). A concerted shift toward greater fixity of exchange rates would then be more sustainable, yielding greater price stability overall. For countries on the periphery, LDCs and small, developed, open economies, the 'volatility of exchange rates is especially disturbing', all the more so when they have responsibly adopted monetary policies ensuring domestic price stability. In the more flexible exchange rate world in the post-BW era, these countries had to contend with 'dysfunctional shifting [of resources] between domestic and international goods' production dictated by wide swings in their exchange rates. So Mundell (2000, p.338) concludes: 'flexible exchange rates are an unnecessary evil in a world where each country may achieve price stability'. That the nations choosing flexible rates had the monetary discipline to achieve price stability was one thing; fixing exchange rates in an OCA provides more consistent discipline.

Following a contrasting thought trajectory, with an equally long pedigree to that of Mundell's, Milton Friedman (1999, pp.37–8) demurred. In one of his very last statements on international monetary arrangements, he drew on long experience in observing the behaviour of central bankers. He was sceptical that the ECB would be sufficiently disciplined and apolitical. In a conference examining the subject he exclaimed: 'I'm impressed at how much of the discussion takes for granted that you can count on the Central Bank to do what it's supposed to do'. He doubted the political independence of central bankers in general, as well as their reliabilities and different personalities that occasionally may deviate from true independence. In the case of the ECB, it 'will have a governing body that represents the various nations of Europe. There's going to be differing advice. There's going to be nothing to rule out the central bank behaving like all banks have behaved from time to time, promoting inflation.' Friedman was not at all confident that the ECB could not at some point recklessly inflate without having very formal, binding monetary rules to control its conduct. Mundell's (1999, p.48) less than convincing answer exuded confidence in the German 'mark central countries' acting as dominant, even hegemonic, players in all ECB decisions: 'Germany will always be saying "tighten, tighten, tighten". The other countries are always going to be saying "loosen, loosen, loosen"'. He believed a political resolution to this stand-off would be found and that it would not result in the ECB giving way to inflationary pressures. Thus, 'there is no reason why an independent ECB, modelled partly on the Bundesbank, cannot be as effective a body as the Federal Reserve system in the United States' (Mundell 1997a, p.7). In this role, the ECB would have the delicate task of managing adjustment to sometimes unsynchronized macroeconomic disturbances in countries constituting the European currency area. The ECB would be supervising a system and issuing a currency that will develop a momentum of its own. Once the EMU 'gets going and successfully launches' Mundell (1999, p.47) predicted that 'more and more countries will want to get into it...[and the] more countries that join Europe, the more powerful European Monetary Union is going to be'. In the event he saw the euro as an eventual threat to the US dollar as the world's most favoured international money.

Altogether, by the end of the century, Mundell (2000, p.339) was pleased that the ongoing 'destruction' of the IFS in the post-BW era was coming to an end. There were positive signs by the end of the 1990s in the genuine attempts by many nations to formulate a multilateral agreement on reforming the IFS following the East Asian financial crisis. More importantly, establishment of the euro brought about 'three islands of monetary stability' between the three key world currencies. Yet there were two items of 'unfinished business': (i) how to deal with the 'dysfunctional' fluctuations in exchange rates between key currencies through a plan to coordinate monetary policies and (ii) the absence of a common world currency. Mundell always hankered after a more complete solution – a formal IFO incorporating a global optimum currency.[24] He made this position patently clear in the mid-1990s:

> The creation of a stable international currency would be a great benefit to the world community...A universal currency would be a

---

[24]In a later interview outside the period under review Mundell rued the absence of a global currency, claiming that it amounted to 'an international monetary crime'. He continued: 'why have globalization in everything except money?' (Vane and Mulhearn 2006, p.106).

great benefit to the lesser powers that, one by one, might stabilize and enter the world system. [Currently the] official system of managed flexible exchange rates is not adapted to the developing countries or to those new republics in Eastern Europe and the former Soviet union that are seeking ways to stabilize their currency (Mundell 1995, pp.492–3).

In this endeavour, Mundell did not underestimate the political obstacles and he did not disregard the dangers presented, and costs incurred, when a vast international bureaucracy had to accompany a scheme for the deliberate creation of a world currency. Nevertheless, regional OCAs, euroization, and dollarization were second best solutions. We turn next to consider the work of Richard Cooper who, throughout the post-BW era, relentlessly and unstintingly promoted what he thought was the 'first best' option – the single international currency.

The theoretical optimum: Proposals for a world currency

The demand for an international medium of exchange and unit of account separate from national and regional currencies was solved under the classical gold standard by spontaneous acceptance of gold in that role. It is well-known that no government planned to implement the gold standard. In the post-BW era, the US dollar remained preeminent as the most widely used (but not the only) international currency. The dollar's role was a concrete manifestation of the positive 'network externalities' and economies of scale in the use of a currency. The more market participants traded and used the US dollar the greater the network benefits accruing to its role (Dowd and Greenaway 1993). The 24 hour trade on the US dollar foreign exchange market, like the US Treasury bill market, resemble the operation of textbook-perfect markets. The US dollar was also widely used as a unit of account for most major traded commodities; it was a major vehicle currency for international trade; a widely held investment and central bank reserve currency.

What most worried some deep-thinking economists was precisely the predominance of the US dollar in its foregoing international functions. To substitute for the US dollar-gold standard that anchored currencies in the BW era, attempts were made to create an embryo of a world currency, namely the 'special drawing right' (SDR) managed by the IMF (Endres 2005, pp.180–4; Mundell 1995, pp.483–6). The main ideas underwriting the SDR had a long history insofar as they marked another attempt by economists to create synthetic international money, just as Keynes had tried to do in his plan originally presented at the BW conference.

Right up until his last contributions to published discussions on international monetary arrangements, Richard Cooper at Harvard University maintained a position he had held from the 1970s: exchange rates were a crucial price in a macroeconomic sense – a price that differed fundamentally from other prices. Specifically, flexible, market-determined exchange rates were like asset prices; they were highly volatile and their volatility had major consequences for decisions to produce internationally tradeable goods. So-called 'floating' exchange rates possessed two severe limitations. First, they produced so much uncertainty and this deterred trade. Second, they could be manipulated for purely domestic purposes through deliberate monetary policy targeting (echoing Krugman's point made earlier in this chapter, Cooper 1984b, pp.172–3). So Cooper concludes that the post-BW system of widespread flexible exchange rates would not be sustainable in the long term. He had always opposed market-determined exchange rate regimes, and saw little prospect of successfully coordinating exchange policy between key currency countries (Cooper 1999c). Unlike Milton Friedman, Cooper (1999b, pp.39, 101) considered the dearth of policy coordination coupled with market-determined exchange rates in the 1990s, as a 'serious institutional weakness' in the IFS.

In the 1980s Cooper was unimpressed with the properties of both market-determined and various fixed exchange rate regimes. He developed the idea of single, universal world currency and world monetary union (Cooper 1984a, 1984b). Here we shall ignore transition issues (from the existing post-BW IFS). Cooper thought it would take upwards of 25 years from the time the single currency was endorsed to full adoption by the world's major industrial nations (specifically he mentions the USA, Europe and Japan). The single world currency would enjoy many of the characteristics of a fixed exchange rate regime but avoid the worst problem of such regimes, namely fixed parities. He wanted to formulate a 'system of credibly fixed exchange rates' that would eliminate exchange rate uncertainty (Cooper 1984b, p.177; 1999d, p.117). One world currency achieves this aim in one-fell-swoop.

Cooper's one world money required one world monetary policy. The mechanism he proposed was quite simple in its initial, basic foundations. A world monetary authority would be established with an internationally representative governing board. The authority would issue currency on the basis of certain agreed rules. Its objective would be to stabilize the international economy and act as an ILLR to maintain liquidity in particular nations by lending to national central banks. It would use open market operations to buy and sell bonds denominated in the international currency as its main stabilizing instrument. He realized that the creation of a world monetary authority was 'radical' and faced political obstacles. This is why he thought the establishment of a single world currency would take several decades; it would involve much negotiation over details (Cooper 1984a, pp.183–4 and 1984b). He maintained that international monetary policy would in any case converge over the twenty five year period 1984-2009 because international financial markets would grow disproportionately relative to trade in goods and services. Financial market activities would therefore have major exchange rate impacts requiring joint action by monetary authorities in different countries. As well, real economic shocks would become internationalized along with growing international trade interdependencies and financial globalization. At the very least, under these conditions, the major economic disturbances 'would not be radically asymmetrical'; they would quickly be transmitted across borders and internationalized. Financial market contagions would become the norm rather than the exception as flexible exchange rates became less like real shock absorbers and more like instant transmitters of crises. In this context, strong international monetary policy coordination would be desirable, indeed inevitable to ensure the stability of the IFS (Cooper 1999b, p.117). It was only another step from this scenario to a common world monetary regime and a single currency.

With growing international financial integration, Cooper's proposal was tantamount to asserting that cross-border cyclical fluctuations will become more closely correlated. In that case the national gains from having an independent monetary policy, enjoyed with the choice of a market-determined exchange rate regime, become chimerical. Cooper therefore denies the existence of a long-term trade-off between the micro-efficiency gains of a currency union and the costs of relinquishing the tools of macroeconomic policy to deal with localized macroeconomic disturbances. In his single money regime, national 'balance-of-payments' adjustment problems would be similar to, and no more complex to deal with than, regional adjustments in a federal system such as the USA. No country would need to exercise control over its own monetary policy. Yet in order to maintain national economic and social identity, fiscal policy heterogeneity would be required. Fiscal policy would be formulated independently by each country. How would fiscal imbalances be financed? Cooper proposed that some pro-rata share of the world monetary authority's open market purchases (in the case of deficit financing) would be allocated to the country experiencing a fiscal deficit. Otherwise deficits would be financed, and indeed constrained, by the need and capacity respectively to borrow in international capital markets that used the common currency (Cooper 1984a, p.166). The availability of international capital for this fiscal purpose

> would be determined by a market assessment of the probability of repayment, which would assuredly be high within a plausible range of budgetary behaviour. Both receipts and expenditures would be made in the common currency, as would the borrowing. Each country could set its own course independently, with no need for formal coordination of fiscal policy. Financial markets would 'coordinate' to some extent, via interest rates, since if all governments decided to borrow heavily at once, in a period in which private demands for credit were also high, interest rates would rise and that would induce caution in borrowing (Cooper 1984b, p.33).

Cooper's vision was founded on a long-run view of the outcome of financial globalization in which markets for commodities, goods, services, factors of production including finance, were increasingly integrated on a world scale. Integration would occur mostly through market processes and relative prices and wages across borders would become highly flexible. Freer international trade was 'complementary' to his scheme but 'not entirely necessary' (p.166). That may be an understatement. Freer trade than in fact existed from his vantage point in 1984 would seem to be vital to ensure that any semblance of an 'optimum' in the world currency area could be achieved. Otherwise the prospect of increasing flexibility in cross-border relative prices and wages may diminish, and more complete world economic integration would not occur (Kawai 1987, p.742).

Apart from the obvious transitional and political difficulties with Cooper's proposal, of which he was well aware, some economists (though not Mundell) reacted dismissively. Barry Eichengreen (1999a, p.93) referred to Cooper's proposal as one of many 'castles in the air' imagined by different economists in the post-BW era. For Eichengreen, thinking about practical reforms of the existing IFS took priority over Utopian schemes for the IFO in the long run. However, Cooper's motivation was precisely to focus more debate on the overall IFO, whereas the pragmatists (including Eichengreen) were excessively preoccupied with day-to-day issues as they presented themselves in the post-BW era. Anna Schwartz (1987, p.400) appreciated Cooper's bold visionary stance though she could not find much merit in his scheme because it proposed no 'rule binding the world monetary authority' to a certain quantity of currency production. Moreover, Schwartz questioned, '[w]ould a single monopolistic monetary authority possess the information to govern the provision of the appropriate supply of money without a rule?' While in her view there was nothing controversial in the proposition that a single world money, produced in a stable non-inflationary manner, would realize major efficiencies, Cooper did not provide any suggestions for creating a rule-based international monetary constitution. Such a constitution would be critical to the durability of a world currency.

The post-Keynesians, led by Paul Davidson's (1992–3, 1997, 2000) contributions, also wanted to reform the IFO by creating a world-wide system of fixed exchange rates. Unlike Cooper or Mundell, these economists wanted to restrict the international movement of capital; they did not require the abandonment of national currencies, a supra-national monetary authority or a world monetary union. Davidson endorsed a slightly modified version of Keynes' clearing union plan proposed in the 1940s. Thus as Keynes argued:

> We need an instrument of international currency having general acceptability between nations...We need an orderly and agreed upon method of determining the relative exchange values of national currency units...We need a quantum of international currency...[which] is governed by the actual current [liquidity] requirements of world commerce, and is capable of deliberate expansion... We need a method by which the surplus credit balances arising from international trade, which the recipient does not wish to employ can be set to work...without detriment to the liquidity of these balances (Keynes quoted in Davidson 1997, p.680).

Davidson's (2000, pp.1127–8) 'architectural solution' showed some variation on Keynes' clearing union idea expressed in this passage.[25] Without delving into to fine details of his blueprint which contains eight major provisions and many subsidiary provisions, Davidson called for the creation of an international clearing unit of account – a

---

[25]For a modern attempt along post-Keynesian lines to rehabilitate the Keynes plan see Costabile (2009). On Davidson's plan see Gnos and Rochon (2004). On the post-Keynesian approach to international economic policy in general, see Arestis and Sawyer (1998).

synthetic reserve asset or equivalent for international liquidity held by central banks. The international clearing unit would be fixed in value at its inception at chosen rates against each national currency. The clearing unit would be used in

> a <u>closed</u>, double-entry bookkeeping clearing institution to keep the payments 'score' among the various trading regions plus some mutually agreed upon rules to create and reflux liquidity while maintaining the international purchasing power of the international currency (Davidson 1992–3, p.158, his emphasis).

The international payments adjustment mechanism in this system would place the onus on surplus nations automatically to recycle their international excess liquidity of clearing units. One prime concern was to prevent the deficiency of demand that could persist and show up in balance of payments disequilibria on the current account of a nation's balance of external payments; that persistent deficiency could not be remedied by relying on flexible exchange rates to correct the current payments imbalance. Davidson proposed that in the situation just described, other nations must be 'either holding excessive reserves or draining reserves from the system' (p.158). In his formulation of the ideal international financial architecture, those countries would be required to recycle their surpluses in a particular, controlled manner. At the center of the architecture would be an 'International Clearing Agency' which would be all-powerful in this respect. Lastly, national aggregate demand would also be protected in his system by permitting each nation to control capital outflows.

  Davidson's approach was long term and visionary in the sense of wanting to reconstitute the IFO and not fiddle with 'plumbing' issues associated with the post-BW IFS. He was focused on creating an international currency in the sense of a unit of exchange for clearing payments imbalances between nations. In his trajectory of thought it was undesirable that a national currency (such as the US dollar) should be used for this purpose. The hegemonic and financially imperialistic connotations of allowing one or other national currency to perform the international currency role seemed uppermost in his mind. Invariably by default in such an arrangement, surplus countries would place the burden of adjustment almost wholly on deficit countries. Furthermore Davidson did not, at least in principle, propose the creation of a single, optimal world currency along the lines of Cooper (and desired by Mundell). By comparison with Cooper's plan which accepted the inevitability of financial globalization in the post-BW era, Davidson's wished to turn back the clock (and the tide!) since it relied for its implementation on a full set of controls on private, international capital movements.

The sceptics on currency and monetary unification

James Tobin (1987) to some extent contributed to the post-Keynesian thought trajectory though he was not a proponent of a single world money or of regional monetary unification. He was generally in favour of high levels of international economic policy coordination in a world with converging macroeconomic objectives. Policy coordination reduced tendencies toward protectionism and promoted responses to macroeconomic disturbances while avoiding mutually destructive cross-border policies. While policy coordination between monetarily independent states was desirable, Tobin (1993) highlighted the macroeconomic costs of a common set of policies imposed on countries with quite heterogeneous economic structures and institutions including different degrees of wage and price flexibility. The impact of a common, harmonized monetary policy in these conditions is not uniform or neutral. In general, prominent economists who pronounced against fully fledged currency and monetary unification did so because they accepted the existence of a fundamental, enduring trade-off between enhanced micro-level efficiencies and the loss of macro policy instruments that could be specifically tailored to national circumstances.

One group of dissenters of whom Harvard economist Martin Feldstein (1988) is representative, doubted the value of constraints limiting sovereignty over monetary policies. He had always been sceptical of international economic policy coordination *per se* (Feldstein 1998b). The standard case for monetary union was equivalent to claiming that the benefits of coordination outweighed the costs. The risks and disadvantages of policy coordination, indeed perfect harmonization as far as monetary policy goes, were downplayed in this standard case. One major limitation concerned the prospects that nations could join a monetary union in order to avoid making necessary changes in monetary policy. Monetary unions can therefore insulate bad policies. For instance, pressure would be brought to bear on the proposed ECB to reduce the emphasis on price stability. And the proposed union 'arrangements could also affect the broader prospects of economic policy, including protectionist trade policies toward non-EMU countries and the policies that affect structural unemployment within the EMU area' (Feldstein 1997, p.32).

Feldstein assessed the net economic effects of the EMU in particular, as negative. National political and social interests in retaining a high degree of autonomy over countercyclical monetary and fiscal policies and exchange rates would be too strong and render the union infeasible (p.35). In terms of purely economic factors, firstly the structure of the European economy was significantly heterogeneous. Differences in trading patterns and the structure of GDP between countries meant that external shocks affecting Germany for instance, will be different from those affecting Portugal. Secondly, the EMU was constituted by economies with vastly different degrees of wage and price flexibility. Thirdly, factor mobility, especially labour mobility, was quite minimal because of major institutional barriers (e.g. language, culture, social security policy). Fourthly, there was a fiscal policy integration problem that could not be ignored. Prospects of making large fiscal transfers from one part of the union to another in order to counter a decline in demand, output and employment were unfavourable. Compared to the USA, there 'is no cyclical net transfer in Europe, since taxes and benefits are almost exclusively the responsibility of the national government' (p.36). Finally, the advantages of having a monetary anchor based on fixed exchange rates, so often trumpeted as a key anti-inflation mechanism in a monetary union, was not exclusive to fixed exchange rate regimes. A nation can reduce the rate and variability of inflation without fixing its exchange rate to another currency or abandoning its currency for another and without formal, cross-border macroeconomic policy coordination (p.37). In conclusion, in Feldstein's view, the scope for greater experimentation with monetary and currency policies and competition between European nations is reduced by the convergence of economic and social policies embodied in EMU membership. Persistently high levels of structural unemployment in parts of Europe would not, as a consequence of EMU, be much reduced at all.

Similarly, in Anna Schwartz's (1987, p.391) view, the only way to reach a viable common cross-border monetary arrangement was if 'individual countries adopt appropriate monetary and fiscal policies that stabilize their own economies'. Simply agreeing to adopt such policies after joining a monetary union is not a substitute approach. To a large extent, plans for the EMU as they evolved in the 1970s and 1980s were consistent with Schwartz's view. In that period economists did not really address whether or not the adopted, 'appropriate' policies *ex post* were going to be time-consistent, credible and sustainable.

At Stanford, Ronald McKinnon echoed Feldstein's concerns over the fiscal policy problem. McKinnon's case against a common monetary

standard in Europe was based on insufficient inter-governmental coordination that creates the fiscal policy dilemma. If a modicum of fiscal
integration between countries existed before a union was created then
economic shocks specific to one country or region could more easily
be dealt with by fiscal transfers from the unaffected regions to the
impacted region. This simple point had been made in the BW era
by Peter Kenen (1969) and McKinnon (1995) followed this line of
thought closely. While the EMU agreed on a vague mechanism for inter-
governmental transfers to deal with asymmetrical cyclical downturns
between member countries, such downturns may reach crisis proportions, creating not only high levels of unemployment; highly indebted
governments could also emerge. Thus, 'a country experiencing a fiscal
breakdown would, under a common currency, have great leverage on the
other member governments' (McKinnon 1995, p.474). That is to say,
other members would not wish a localized cyclical problem to spill
over and lead to a community-wide economic and financial crisis, and
associated bank failures, caused by one member-country threatening
debt default. This was indeed a plausible argument that had some
antecedents in the EU before full EMU had occurred. In McKinnon's
reading of the likely scenario, a distressed union member might put pressure on 'the solvent members...to bail it out, whether by asking the
ECB to buy the troubled government's bonds, or by direct government-
to-government lending. Knowing this *ex ante*, politicians in the errant
country might become even less willing to take resolute fiscal action.
Moral hazard would be uncomfortably high' (p.474). McKinnon's
views were consistent with Feldstein's; all general government debt
is not going to be consolidated at some federal level as it is in the
USA. Therefore large debt transfers would not automatically be made
(pp.475–6). There was an important implication in all this relating to
policy credibility in the union: it is not enough to adopt a common,
credible monetary policy and allow the pursuit of relatively independent fiscal policies. Countries in a union may well need to sacrifice
both monetary and fiscal policy independence, or at least formally
coordinate fiscal policies between members.

McKinnon concludes with a pessimistic outlook. In his view fiscal
sustainability was a serious, neglected issue. Fiscal integration problems
were insurmountable. While the EMU might be formed on the basis of
rules governing a common monetary policy regime, independent national
currencies should not, and need not, be abandoned. Moreover, independent currency exchange rate movements (in other words, the independent exchange rate policy instrument) would be necessary to assist

in adjusting to asymmetric economic shocks that could not otherwise be dealt with given the absence of a sufficient degree of fiscal integration.

Another group offering a somewhat different, yet sceptical perspective may broadly be characterized as economic historians. These economists, including Benjamin Cohen (University of California Santa Barbara), Barry Eichengreen (UCLA) and Michael Bordo (NBER), used long-run studies of the international economy and international monetary arrangements, in conjunction with selected aspects of economic theory. They explain in three steps (and at great length with supportive evidence) why:

(i)   monetary and currency unification are not inevitable
(ii) monetary and currency unions are not irrevocable or forever sustainable and that there exist
(iii) many other regional currency arrangements, such as parallel currencies which were observable and advantageous for some countries in the post-BW era.

Cohen (1998) discussed the broad pattern of 'deterritorialization' in the use of money in the twentieth century. He considered this phenomenon as a demand-driven process produced by rational market participants who anticipated certain microeconomic efficiency benefits in the use of money. Certainly the economic historians have documented how, in the post-BW era, small nations with uncompetitive currencies cannot rely on their national monetary authorities successfully to defend those currencies in a crisis, thereby creating another source of demand for currency consolidation. Yet, the obstacles to monetary unification and the sustainability of an associated currency consolidation depend as much on political factors as they do on economic imperatives (Cohen 2000). This view was shared by Paul Krugman (1992, p.viii). For example, on the issue of fiscal policy coordination and integration he remained sceptical, seeing any fiscal problems as essentially political rather than economic. As for the economics, 'active use of fiscal policy for stabilization purposes has become fairly rare'. For the EMU, he found it hard to envisage 'why it should become a major issue' since it was the level of aggregate demand in the EU as a whole that mattered and monetary policy could manage that variable. And he offered the practical example of the United States 'with its federal system: if fiscal coordination is so important, why has the United States found it unnecessary to police state and local budgets?' (pp.201–2). Taken in isolation, this argument is a highly controversial one that perhaps underestimates the degree of national political variability in the EU as opposed the United States. However, Krugman adds an important qualification: unification in an economic sense 'is almost surely a necessary adjunct of European political unification' (p.203). Major changes would be required in political institutions across borders. According to Krugman (1993b, p.260), a federalized fiscal system was needed in Europe, though that necessitated a 'massive change in European institutions'. Only then would the use of fiscal policy be workable, as necessary, to achieve regional stabilization. Thus Eichengreen (1992, p.48) warned that 'significant regional problems will continue to arise' after unification. Naturally, subsequent measures to reflate implemented 'by the depressed regions will be limited by the external constraint. Even in a currency union, member states will face sharply rising costs of debt finance.' We could legitimately expect the fiscal policy problem to loom large in the long run because monetary policy could not deal with demand shocks that may result from changes in consumer requirements and production technologies, particularly those specific to various regions.

Krugman was for the most part an economic theorist who appreciated the value of historical perspectives. He explains how there are no unequivocal answers available from economic theory justifying, once-and-for-all, a case for or against currency or monetary union in any real circumstances. Michael Bordo and Lars Jonung (1997, 2000) offer further rather sceptical conclusions derived from thorough historical work, strongly suggesting that concerted political will always dominate precise economic arguments in the decision whether or not to create common money. In this they were strongly supported by Barry Eichengreen (1997, pp.323–4):

> the case for monetary unification must be advanced on political-economy grounds rather than grounds of microeconomic efficiency... The political-economy argument for the single currency rests on the importance of avoiding exchange-rate instability and sustaining political support for Europe's internal market, and on the proposition that the only assured way of reaching this goal is by establishing a monetary union. Semifixed exchange rates being intrinsically fragile and easily destabilized by speculative attacks, the only directions for Europe are forward to EMU or backward to floating.

Further, in employing the concept of 'network externalities' in the use of money, Eichengreen (1999c, p.33) reflects on the historical lock-in effects that arise as a consequence. As we have seen in this chapter already, the analytical work by Kevin Dowd and David Greenaway (1993, p.1180) sheds light on monetary experience by explaining how 'network effects can influence the value of a particular currency – its value rises with the number of people who use it'. Thus, even when a currency is not well-managed, in the sense that it may be over-produced to the point of creating considerable inflation and loss of purchasing power, the demand for that currency does not fall completely to the point of abandonment; that demand 'is often still quite substantial' even when there is hyperinflation (p.1184). Currency users do not necessarily switch (or adopt new currencies) quickly. Historical lock-in effects have been widely observed. In short, the benefits of incumbency are important and valued by the market. Therefore, even though the standard microeconomic efficiency argument for abandoning a national currency in favour of joining a currency union may be overwhelming and outweigh any macroeconomic trade-offs, currency consolidation is not inevitable.

Other features of Eichengreen's vast historical research program raise doubts about the oft-made comparisons and parallels between the USA as a currency and monetary union, and the impending EMU and ECU (Eichengreen 1990, 1992). Eichengreen's expression of these doubts – focusing on whether or not Europe was an OCA before the advent of monetary unification at the turn of the century – were representative of a long line of historically minded economists (e.g. Krugman 1993). The main point of Eichengreen's contributions on this subject was that Europe was far from being integrated (in the sense of having highly integrated goods, services and factor markets) sufficiently to reap the theoretical benefits of union. While the logic of economic integration in Europe may be compelling there is no way economists could 'mount a general argument that monetary union is either essential or irrelevant' (Eichengreen 1996b, p.256). There was evidence of a central group of ECU member nations (Germany and its immediate neighbours) having much in common as far as macroeconomic symmetry was concerned – they generally experienced 'highly-correlated aggregate supply disturbances'. Another group was not so well-integrated so that previous economic experience indicated macroeconomic disturbances, especially supply shocks that were 'larger and more idiosyncratic' (Bayoumi and Eichengreen 1993, p.223). This evidence supported Rudiger Dornbusch's (1990b) position that there were 'two' quite different sets of countries intending to unionize and this justified a more cautious, practical approach if not a 'two-track' entry process to the EMU, with some countries joining more quickly than others. There were two other possibilities:

European economies could retain independent currencies and their exchange rate policy instruments, and market adjustments would take place in response to relative currency movements to 'moderate their impact on competitiveness'. However, the adjustments would rarely be complete so that cross-country complaints about competitive currency depreciations and 'exchange dumping' would not be avoided and thereby continue to destabilize the European economies. The second scenario was a system of fixed exchange rates in which labor markets in particular, and associated institutions, would adapt to prevent persistent unemployment in some regions, given sufficient time. This, of course, is the successful unification scenario. In the final analysis, Eichengreen's 'instinct is that monetary unification is the more stable long-run solution' (Eichengreen 1996b, p.256). The 'sufficient time' proviso was critical, however.

In Europe, at the University of Manheim, one of the more prominent public choice theorists, Roland Vaubel, also expressed strong scepticism about European currency and monetary union. There were several grounds for his negative position. Firstly, inflation in Europe was likely to be higher than otherwise because competition between national central banks and their respective currencies would be removed (Vaubel 1978b, 1983). Indeed, a single currency producer in an OCA amounts to having perfect collusion between central banks. Such collusion was the embodiment of full international standardization of monetary policies in a monetary union such that in the 'extreme case, it takes the form of fixed exchange rates, and an intentional holding-price cartel among money producers'.

Secondly, intending members of a monetary union do not all equally satisfy the conditions for joining an OCA. Countries differ in the way they meet certain aspects of an OCA (as originally outlined in principle by Mundell). These differences could not easily be weighed-up in some sort of scientific index or ranking of suitability (Vaubel 1990). Therefore, Vaubel recommended successively approximating unification using a half-way house. In the case of the EMU, he proposed that the euro be permitted to circulate as a parallel currency initially, allowing for continued competition between that currency and other competing European currencies. That way, financial market participants and currency users could choose the best currency in a drawn-out competitive process. Capital controls should be completely removed between intending ECU members in the interim so as to expand the choices in currency use. For the same reason, controls should also be removed between these intending ECU members and all other countries. If the euro proves eventually to be the most dominant currency in a particular country, it will mean that this country is a legitimate aspirant of the euro OCA (Vaubel 1978a). Vaubel applies the Hayekian notion of competition as a discovery procedure in the case of currency and monetary unions. Like Hayek he sees competition as a process rather than a one-time event. From a microeconomic standpoint,

> the efficiency of currency union depends on whether the information and transaction cost economies of scale in the use of money are sufficiently large to render money a natural monopoly good (or asset). If the supply of money was a natural monopoly in a certain region, currency competition would destroy itself, and a single producer of (real base) money would prevail. Thus, (potential) currency competition can serve as a discovery procedure. It is the only operational way of finding out whether currency union is efficient, and, if so, what sort of money is efficient, who is the most efficient supplier and which is the optimal money supply rule. The optimum may even vary over time (Vaubel 1990, p.939).

Thirdly, Vaubel (1990, pp.944–5 and 1997) shared Friedman's scepticism, which we reported earlier in this chapter regarding the idiosyncratic, sometimes partisan behaviour of central bankers. Ensuring central bankers' 'independence' was not a straightforward matter. For Vaubel, the behaviour, over a long period of history, of the Bundesbank in particular, offered little confidence in sustaining price level stability in the impending EMU. The public choice thought trajectory represented in Vaubel's work largely shared by other prominent international monetary thinkers including Anna Schwartz, had little faith in highly politicized policy coordination processes since they were affected by day-to-day political factors. Binding monetary and fiscal rules were required that set explicit bounds on the behaviour of policymakers. The positive micro efficiency gains of a currency and monetary union were outweighed by the sacrifice of competition in the production of money thereby leading, ultimately, to the greater prospect of higher and more variable rates of inflation at the macro level. As well, in this view, the microeconomic efficiency case for a single currency was not independent of retaining national autonomy over policy instruments used to respond to macroeconomic disturbances. In the long run, currency competition ensured lower inflation – the surest, most enduring way to counter macroeconomic disturbances in the first place. Monetary unions and currency consolidation of various kinds are by no means necessary and certainly not inevitable.

While not travelling along Vaubel's thought trajectory, Peter Kenen (1988, pp.391–2 and 1995, pp.454–5) and Charles Wyplosz (1988, 1997) were persuaded that EMU was going to be too reliant on a single, hegemonic nation, namely the Federal Republic of Germany, which would control and apply a conservative monetary policy and apply a rigid fiscal orthodoxy. It was evident to Wyplosz (1998, p.47) that 'Germany's emphasis on sound money and budgetary orthodoxy works as a contractionary restraint on the policy choices open to the other EMS countries'. Thus according to Wyplosz (1997, p.19), by the end of the 1990s it had become clear that 'the insistence on price stability' as a precondition for EMU membership 'along with the adoption of rigid and arbitrary criteria of fiscal rectitude', contributed to Europe's slow growth and unemployment experienced in the last decade of the twentieth century. The 'EMU's parenthood' resided in Germany and the credibility of its currency. The German policy approach of rigid price stability and fiscal conservatism was likely to alienate some intending member nations. This may especially be the case when one or other member is subject to: an external economic shock producing high unemployment and social upheaval or poor economic performance because of a series of major fiscal policy mistakes. Both events might call for exchange rate realignment in due course, though in a full currency and monetary union such realignment would not be possible. All the subsequent economic adjustment would fall on output and local employment. It might only be eased in the short term by an outflow of labour to other member countries if, that is, labour was sufficiently mobile. The latter requirement was hardly likely to be met in Europe.

Underwriting many positive opinions on the prospects for EMU was a simple monetary doctrine, embodied in many economists' standard models, and these could not be supported by events in the 1990s. That doctrine turned on the simple notion that 'a firm commitment to price stability is both necessary and sufficient for exchange-rate stability' (Kenen 1995, p.454). However, this doctrine required a very long time horizon if it was to work out in practice and a supportive economic system with significant flexibility in prices, common labour market institutions with a large degree of flexibility, and sufficient mobility of factors of production, including labour. Furthermore, as Peter Kenen points out, the standard doctrine neglects the possibility of major fiscal policy mistakes and the advent of temporary aggregate demand problems that are not common to all countries in a union. Little wonder that events in Europe in the 1990s were supportive of the euro sceptics.

Economic integration following monetary unification and the currency consolidation process

When the OCA literature was revisited by economists (other than Mundell) in the post-BW era, their 'new' theories and observations altered the way some economists looked at the movement toward international economic integration (Tavlas 1993, 2009). In the emerging economics literature in the 1990s the new ideas of policy credibility, time consistency and commitment appeared and they made the problem of choosing to adopt common money more intractable than before. For example, what if on joining a currency or monetary union, an individual nation had satisfied entry criteria on its macroeconomic (e.g. inflation) performance and policy settings but those policies (fiscal policy in particular) were not adhered to upon joining the union? What was the enforcement mechanism, or what were the excuse clauses for that matter, that were put in place in any common money arrangement? And what were the costs of dissolving the monetary and currency linkages? Were the linkages irrevocable?

Compared with the various costs of monetary and currency unionization, the size of the microeconomic efficiency benefits of unionization were not easy to estimate (Krugman 1993a, p.20). Attempts to quantify the costs and benefits were 'frustrating' and 'useless' (Wyplosz 1997, p.318). The OCA issue could not be settled by measurement just as it could not be solved by the logic of pure economic theory. Some of the costs and benefits were hidden – they could not be fully known in advance. Thus Krugman (1993a, p.22): '[c]onceivably, the hidden microeconomic benefits of a common currency are so overwhelming in the United States that Europe should follow suit even though the macroeconomic costs could be much greater. We just don't know.' Quantifying costs and benefits was made more difficult, if not impossible when, following adoption of common money, the degree of economic integration between member countries changes. While on the one hand many economists in the 1980s believed that greater economic integration between intending members of a monetary union would realize greater benefits and increase the union's effectiveness, there was on the other hand a potential *ex post* set of integration outcomes not predictable in advance. Krugman (1993b) always viewed the proposed EMU sceptically and came down on the side of expecting greater regional economic heterogeneity and specialization following unification. The macroeconomic outcomes would then be significant for some regions within the union and a policy adjustment problem would arise. Specific regional shocks would be more commonly observed and regional growth rates would diverge. Accordingly, greater business cycle asymmetry would prevail between member countries and regions. Moreover, as we have already observed, by comparison with the USA, a negative regional shock in Europe would not normally be adjusted to by the movement of labour to other regions because of various institutional barriers to labour mobility. Large and persistent increases in unemployment could be expected in those regions. The immobility of labour was a crucial factor in cementing Krugman's scepticism over the merits of EMU. Nevertheless, he was not implacably opposed to EMU. It was only that '[s]ome advocates of EMU seem to suggest...that <u>every</u> aspect of policy management will become easier. But as virtually any US state governor can attest, an integrated continental market does not solve all local problems, and can even make some of them worse' (Krugman 1993b, p.260, his emphasis).

The more guarded optimists, notably Paul de Grauwe (1993, p.269) at the Catholic University of Leuven, thought that the extent to which countries would have to sacrifice policy instruments upon joining the EMU were exaggerated. First, as for fiscal policy, he took a liberal Keynesian line in believing that national budgetary discipline would be maintained and that automatic fiscal stabilizers would respond adequately and in a timely manner to region-specific shocks well before they became too big to manage. Even accommodating a large negative shock would be possible 'at least if governments are sensible enough not to take the Maastricht requirements of no more than a 3% budget deficit too seriously'. He predicted that EMU governments would not be governed by the dictates of conservative central bankers. Second, the European economy had one advantage over US economic conditions: while the economies would become more integrated with union, the degree of labour mobility would never reach the level found in the US partly for cultural reasons. So this 'means that when one country faces a negative shock, there will not be a major outward migration'. Adjustments through a significant national real wage reduction (relative to other regions in the EMU) would then normally follow. Krugman's prediction of mass unemployment following a region-specific shock was not regarded as plausible. Fourth, European policymakers possessed another advantage over US policymakers that was not often identified: they had the experience and the inclination to adopt incomes polices in different regions of the type that were used to respond to shocks in the Netherlands and Belgium in the 1980s. Incomes policies purportedly spread the burden of adjustment more widely in the region affected without the need to place the whole stabilization burden on automatic fiscal policy responses.

Another group of optimists, including Jeffrey Frankel and Andrew Rose (1997, 1998) at the UCLA, thought the EMU would be more justified *ex post* rather than *ex ante*. When new monetary and currency consolidation regimes are given time to work, they may result in countries experiencing more rather than less symmetry or synchronization in the periodic fluctuations of output and employment. As the OCA evolves for instance, economic integration develops endogenously (i.e. within the area) (Frankel 1999, p.23). Economic structures are expected to change in response to joining a union. As trade links and thence income generation are progressively strengthened within the union (via reduced transaction costs, removal of trade policy barriers, reduced costs of economic calculation and so forth), economic cycles would be harmonized. At the very least, with greater inter-country and inter-industry trade between union members, economic shocks exclusive to one member would not be so frequent or asymmetric. It may well be, as McKinnon (1963) pointed out in an earlier contribution in the BW era, that the extent of pre-existing openness to trade between potential union members might be set as a crucial, prime criterion for an OCA. This more optimistic thought trajectory, bolstered by sophisticated empirical research, claimed that the

> criteria for optimum currency areas include the intensity of trade links and the magnitude of income correlations. Small political units that have tight economic links with their neighbors are too small to float. If the boundaries of a geographic area are drawn large enough that the trade links and income links among its constituent parts are strong compared to the trade links and income links with its neighbors, then it is the optimal size to constitute an independent currency area...[W]hen a political unit adopts the currency of a neighbor, the creation of the monetary union promotes trade over time between the neighbors, which in turn has a positive effect on the correlation in incomes (Frankel 1999, p.30).

If the OCA varies in time and across countries as Frankel maintains, there are not only important endogenous growth outcomes remaining unaccounted for before unification; a country may gain inflation – fighting credibility in the process, especially if it has had a previous history of high and accelerating inflation. Altogether, overall economic performance will be enhanced. The loss of monetary independence may work in favour of particular countries intending to import the credibility and sustained commitment to price stability in a monetary union. This argument applies widely to other forms of currency consolidation such as dollarization.

Currency consolidation as (ultimately) a market-driven process

The increasing consolidation of currencies observed in the post-BW era may be sufficient, indeed the optimal process in its own right. Ongoing experimentation with different currency arrangements may be the appropriate, if not the optimal, approach in the international economy taken as a whole. A universal global currency may not be the Holy Grail as supposed by some economists we have mentioned in this chapter. This view was advanced by Kenneth Rogoff and Maurice Obstfeld in the post-BW era (and summarized nicely in Rogoff 2001) and was consistent with Rogoff's earlier work discussed in previous chapters. That work highlighted the potential counterproductive aspects of international economic policy coordination and, by implication, of full policy coordination in a currency and monetary union. Rogoff's contribution depended for its strong conclusions on the policy coordinating central banks exploiting 'the existence of nominal wage contracts to systematically raise employment' rather than target price stability. He continued:

> [o]f course, in a time-consistent equilibrium, wage inflation will [eventually] be high enough so that the central bank's efforts will be futile. International monetary cooperation may raise the rate of wage inflation because wage setters recognize that a noncooperative regime contains a built-in check on each central bank's incentives to inflate. The reason is that when a central bank expands its money supply unilaterally, it causes its country's real exchange rate to depreciate thereby reducing the employment gains and increasing the CPI inflation costs. Cooperation may remove this disincentive to inflate, and thus raise time-consistent wage growth (Rogoff 1985, p.200).

A supportive line of thought, instanced in the work of Roland Vaubel, which does not depend on the nature of wage-setting in any national jurisdiction, proposes that the maintenance of competition between the world's key currencies (when the value of those currencies are largely market-determined) provides a strong rein on inflation. It would then be counterproductive to favour policy coordination and completely unnecessary on economic grounds to pursue currency consolidation to the final point of a single world currency. Competition between currency producers can have valuable stabilizing consequences. These consequences are not easily observed; they are dispersed throughout the markets in which currencies are used.

Earlier in Chapter 3 above (pp.45, 52) we referred to Friedrich Hayek's criticisms of the idea that a single, optimal international currency could be deliberately designed. The emerging post-BW hierarchy of key fiat currencies is more optimal because it reflects the working-out of a long process of competition involving the following factors:

1. Demand-side factors – for example, what are now recognized as network externalities in the use of currencies; the associated depth and scale of currency markets which reduce transaction costs.
2. Supply-side factors – the dominance of particular currencies in the international economy (US dollar, yen, and later the euro) must reflect long-run supply forces, namely inflation risk and the associated behaviour of monetary authorities in the respective currency issuing nations.
3. Interrelated demand-supply factors – there is an interconnection between demand and supply when there is international currency competition and the transnational use of currencies. The market confers 'reputation' on the producers of national currencies, as well as the institutions available for trading in them (such as sophisticated financial products and established financial centers).

Hayek's, Vaubel's, and Rogoff's perspectives do not rule-out currency consolidation, including the deliberate design of currencies such as the euro (and the US dollar long before that), and the choice of dollarization. The market test is ultimately critical in determining the durability of any form of currency consolidation.

Complete or partial abandonment of a national currency by way of adopting the euro (or US dollar) as an international currency is conceivable so long as ongoing currency use is market determined. Even the emergence of the euro possessed Hayekian elements: it was surely designed on the reputation and international competitiveness of the Deutsche mark, particularly in its extensive use as a vehicle and investment currency (Tavlas 1991). The transition to the euro is consistent with Hayek's (1978b, p.187) invocation to allow 'choice in currency'; choice takes place in a competitive process that does not exclude the possibility of currency consolidation. The market tests for common currency such as the euro are that they are supplied under the constraints introduced by other currencies also being supplied with a range of actual or potential transnational services (vehicle, investment or quotation services). Market tests are continuous; they are applied in a long historical process. Likewise, the Hayekian perspective endorses parallel currency developments in which national and regional currencies circulate and compete in particular geographic domains (as in recent trends observed in Asian currency integration). Fundamental to such trends is not deliberate engineering of a regional currency, but the market test: currency users would have freely to adopt such currencies and continue to use them over time.

Benjamin Craig (1996) provides evidence implicitly in support of a Hayekian perspective when documenting the Russian currency experience in the 1990s; dollars were increasingly held and used (illegally) by residents for a range of purposes and this induced the monetary authority producing national fiat currency to produce a more stable currency (i.e. targeting a lower level inflation). Dollarization is more sustainable if it is freely chosen rather than imposed by governments. Restrictions in the use of currency within national jurisdictions are obviously important in limiting currency substitution and are reinforced by government receipts and outlays denominated in the government-sanctioned and produced currency. Yet the Russian case illustrates how legal tender is continually under threat so long as market participants have some currency choice. Correspondingly therefore, legal tender currency does not strictly deny an ongoing process of currency competition.

Three general conditions are required to meet Hayek's standard for a viable currency regime: (i) absence of capital and exchange controls, (ii) greater trust in an internationally reputed issuer of money than in one domestic producer, and (iii) potential for competition that was 'nearly as effective as competition *in esse*' (Hayek 1978b, pp.214–15). Here the potential for currency competition rests on an ever-present element of contestability. Contestability acts inter temporally to check incumbent major government suppliers of currency such as the US dollar, euro, and yen. Potential entrants could be chosen over time to play more active international medium of exchange, quotation, and investment roles, if the reputation of one or other currency declines. Production costs of entry will be low since currency manufacture is cheap and the production techniques relatively unsophisticated. The international currency market is conceivably contestable though it is not equivalent to William Baumol's (1982, pp.3–4) benchmark case of perfect contestability. Hayek offers insights into the broad dynamics involved in currency contestability when currencies are interdependent and market participants act on a continuous flow of information about the performance of currency issuers.

The prospect was raised in the post-BW era that national monetary policies would be unable to manage the international order in a world characterized by currency competition and the trans nationalization of currency. Benjamin Friedman (1999) conjectured that central banks would be reduced to armies with only a signal corps. The possible diminishing loyalty in demand for any single central-bank-issued money, the growth of non-bank credit, technological advances that are making international financial clearing mechanisms cheaper and more efficient, and the vast array of assets regarded and traded as currency in modern financial markets, are all placing limits on the effectiveness of national monetary policies.

> As firms and households, and therefore banks, use currencies other than that of their own country, the country's geographical space becomes less relevant for indicating over what financial transactions and nonfinancial behavior the central banks' actions have efficacy (Friedman 1999, p.335).

Benjamin Friedman's conclusions would not have surprised Hayek whose thought trajectory chartered the course away from monetary nationalism in the 1970s in a manner completely different from Mundell.

The choice in currency behaviour referred to by Benjamin Friedman occurred in the post-BW era without deliberate government planning – precisely what Hayek (1978b, p.235) predicted would be essential for the emergence of 'good money' in the international economy. In this view, the notion of imposing a single currency or a single 'optimal design' (Black 1985, p.1185) on the IFS, or some region in the IFS, is not appropriate or feasible. The IFS evolved in the post-BW era to a large extent in a self-organized manner with the IMF's interventionist functions greatly diminishing in proportion to the world's private capital markets, and with some national currencies and key financial centers playing a prominent role. Therefore, the idea that the IFS needed new currencies, or that new rounds of currency consolidation should be planned and deliberately prosecuted by governments, had to be treated with caution, all the more so if it meant deliberately planning a new IFO (i.e. a 'new international financial architecture' as it became more popularly known in the 1990s, e.g. Eichengreen 1999a).

Given the path of events in the international economy, those taking the Hayekian thought trajectory (e.g. Richard Vaubel and to some extent Milton Friedman) drew the following kinds of conclusions about currency consolidation. These eight conclusions were based on allowing more room for market processes. Moreover, in reducing the scope for planned, formal international economic policy coordination among the producers of major currencies as suggested by Obstfeld and Rogoff, what broad outcomes might be predicted that bear the marks of an ongoing market-driven process of currency consolidation? The following eight broad possibilities arise:

   (i) Currency competition will proceed, concomitantly with: the erosion of legal restrictions requiring the monopolization of fiat currency production and use within national jurisdictions, advancement in technology, and more timely communication of information about the credibility of currency issuers.

  (ii) Competitive pressure will be sustained on government currency issuers in the long run with the currency market focusing on inflation performance within national jurisdictions.

 (iii) Parallel currencies may become more popular among small open economies participating significantly in trade and payments arrangements within particular regions.

 (iv) The IFS will not work well if it is planned once-and-for-all by a single monetary authority; monetary authorities will continue to be rivals in a market for reputation over the transnational services provided by their brand of currency.

  (v) Key international currencies (U.S. dollar, euro, yen) may remain prevalent as transnational mediums of exchange or lose relative market share in an ongoing imperfectly contestable process. Market share changes for different currency services will be affected by transaction costs of substitution, convenience, and the credibility of the currency issuer in part indicated by risk adjusted yield preferences.

 (vi) National monetary policies will rendered less effective within national boundaries, especially in small open economies producing relatively lower volumes of less reputable currency.

(vii) Currency consolidation will become more prevalent as a result of prediction vi.

(viii) In the long run, expect more discoveries made by 'free experimentation' (Hayek 1980, p.240) with different currencies in the international realm: for instance, new currency areas perhaps in the Middle East and Asia, the use of parallel currencies in some regions, electronic money, and the rise of new key currencies such as the Chinese RMB.

Conclusion

We began this chapter elaborating on Krugman's contention that different assessments of the magnitude of micro-macro trade-offs are inherent in arguments about various forms of currency consolidation. The core trade-off turned on the broadly agreed micro efficiency gains of currency consolidation versus the not so widely agreed losses due to an individual nation's inability to use monetary policy, and rely on a flexible exchange rate, in response to localized macroeconomic disturbances.

Mundell and Cooper appreciated the short-term prevalence of this trade-off, but they saw no reason why it should endure after unification at the regional (Mundell) or world (Cooper) level. Policy coordination and harmonization would assist in the short term in reducing the macroeconomic costs component of the supposed trade-off. McKinnon considered the trade-off so fundamental given the fiscal policy harmonization problem, that OCAs coupled with full monetary unions were not viable. The economic historians, Eichengreen, Bordo and others, as well as Paul Krugman, believed the micro-macro trade-off was real, enduring, though variable in its impact depending on the country and the relevant region in which the OCA was either operating or being proposed. Therefore, currency consolidations were possible, sometimes fruitful but certainly not always desirable or inevitable.

Frankel and Rose among others, explained how the micro-macro trade-off might be real in the short term but diminish significantly in the long term as economic integration in the OCA improved over time such that business cycles became more synchronized. The Keynesians, Davidson and Tobin, held that the trade-off was enduring and unavoidable; it was endemic to all types of currency consolidation.

A final group, loosely congregating along a 'more-market' thought trajectory, regarded the micro-macro trade-off in a completely sceptical manner. Vaubel and Hayek championed the power of continuous currency competition, of currency contestability, between government money producers. Such contestability produced less visible, dispersed microeconomic benefits in the international economy as a whole; it also produced long-term macroeconomic gains at the national level. At the micro-level, currency users were able to choose a currency for a variety of different purposes in the international realm so long as cross-border, foreign exchange convertibility restrictions did not exist. One of the principal macroeconomic gains of currency competition was lower inflation. There was no need to worry about having the power to control macro policy instruments so long as currency competition was assured. Currency consolidation was acceptable so long as there was sufficient competition among currency producers (the market test), in which case there was no discernible trade-off between micro gains and the loss of macro policy independence. Currency competition led to the creation of 'good money' as Hayek called it, money freely chosen by market participants. Those choices were made in an evolving, open-ended process of currency experimentation and discovery.

In the Hayek-Vaubel view, competition between fiat money producers led to low inflation without the need for detailed, formal plans for monetary and fiscal policy coordination. Any suggestion of such coordination as Rogoff and Feldstein demonstrated, could lead to the retention of undisciplined, inflationary monetary policies and profligate fiscal policies. Since central bankers were unreliable, currency competition kept them in check. Moreover, fiscal policy needed to be the handmaiden of monetary policy and not vice versa. Friedman and Schwartz took a similar view in the post-BW era, with Schwartz underscoring the need to create binding, formal monetary constitutions to control the conduct of monetary policymakers.

So what may we make of Krugman's assertion that economic thought on exchange rate regimes and various currency arrangements does not divide neatly or simply into a 'more market' versus 'less market' grouping? Certainly we can agree with him but with some qualifications. Keynesians (and here we tentatively include McKinnon) generally favoured greater policy coordination between nations and the retention of national autonomy over fiscal policy. If the latter could not be guaranteed, there was no point in adopting a currency and monetary union. The risks of eventual fiscal collapse or default were too great. The pragmatists and eclectics (and here we include Krugman, Eichengreen, Cohen, Bordo) were equivocal about the prospects for currency consolidation in different parts of the world economy given the sheer variety of economic and political structures in existence. Of course, these pragmatists rejected Utopian and radical plans of the kind promoted by Cooper and Davidson and to a lesser extent, also favoured in the post-BW era work of Mundell. Finally, there was a pro-market group (and here we include Friedman, Hayek, Rogoff, Schwartz, Vaubel) favouring continued currency competition in a world of flexible exchange rates. This group was negative about any planned trend toward monetary unions and the creation of a universal international money; it denied the substantive value of international monetary policy coordination and was positive about maintaining the freely evolving 'competition and choice-in-currency' environment characterizing the international economy in the 1990s.

8
Epilogue

Historical structures in the IFS: The limits of reasoning by historical analogy

In this book's opening chapter we made a case for the study of comparative 'trajectories of thought' on international financial integration. We also foreshadowed a distinction between various intellectual trajectories – paths along which ideas may alter and develop over time in response to contemporary circumstances and in the light of applying the key ideas associated with those trajectories to practical problems. The 'trajectories of thought' approach embodies three principal assumptions:

1. ideas on the subject of international financial integration, for example how to conceive, effect, retard or manage economic interdependencies between nations, will incorporate deep core philosophical beliefs, economic methodologies (styles of reasoning and evidence collection), grand generalities, core propositions and so forth, that are not easily refutable;
2. ideas change and evolve on the periphery to the extent that inferences are drawn and redrawn to form core propositions in an iterative, interactive feedback process as evidence is gathered from contemporary or past circumstances and as an idea clashes with competing ideas;
3. different 'trajectories' of thought may be identified over a time period (in this case the post-BW era from 1971–2000) along which clusters of economists may be aligned and compared; these economists will bear allegiance to common core propositions (doctrines as we have called them), about how the international economy works and how it should work. These clusters of economists will imitate one another or innovate on the periphery of the core proposition in

responding to prevailing problems identified in the IFS and to associated controversies over those problems.

The comparative ideas approach employed in the foregoing chapters may also enlarge our understanding of different ways of seeing the international economy, the economic interdependencies between nations and the process of international financial integration. There is no presumption made here that a comparative ideas approach can set out to resolve current problems in the international economy or major differences between competing ideas (and associated policies). Moreover, the chosen approach in this book does not draw definite conclusions about prospects for the present configuration of the IFS. Instead, our approach involves a mapping of competing trajectories of thought on the organizational shape, coherence, reform and management of the IFS or particular aspects of that system.

In the light of the foregoing chapters which have discussed some of the main aspects and issues raised in the literature of international finance in the post-BW era, it is possible to illustrate how our approach differs from other popular methodologies in the field. We have some common ground with economic historians in believing that historical research matters. Economic historians generally think about the prospects for the IFS by reflecting on long-run historical trends, past events and past successes and failings with policies applied in different historical epochs. These historians also favour comparing events and policies in the current IFS with previous systems such as the classical gold standard, interwar currency experience, the Depression years, the BW system and so forth. In short, economic historians approach the subject using the technique of historical analogy. Sometimes, additionally, economic historians employ counterfactuals in the light of evidence from reasoning by historical analogy (e.g. Eichengreen 2007, pp. xiii, 18–22; Bordo and James 2008a, 2008b). By using historical insights, extensive historical and institutional research, economic historians possess powerful tools that enable deep reflection on the workings and failing of the IFS (the work of Charles Kindleberger is exemplary in this regard). As with all economists they are nevertheless apt to read evidence and historical experiences in different ways – historical analogy is not a full-proof method and analogies are never perfect so that researchers are not normally able to press them too hard. As with other economists, economic historians will align themselves with like-minded researchers on an underlying thought trajectory. Take, for instance, Robert Skidelsky's remarks at a 2003 conference on international economic policy. He suggests, by analogy, that the world economy is 'returning to the historical conditions when it will be possible to stabilize exchange rates of the three main currencies: the dollar, the euro and the yen' (Skidelsky 2005, p.80). Reading the historical parallels from a particular viewpoint he finds the international monetary conditions in 2003 to be similar to those evident in 1936 when the Tripartite Monetary Agreement between France, Great Britain and the United States was established. Under the Agreement, key currencies were permitted to move only within narrow target bands. Skidelsky favoured a return to predominantly fixed exchange rates supported by international agreement to maintain the stability of the world's major currencies and their associated financial centres, while at the same time permitting liberal policies on capital mobility (p.77).

By contrast, another economic historian, Barry Eichengreen, read the historical experience differently. As we saw in the foregoing chapters, Eichengreen was responsible for contributing to a trajectory of thought emphasizing the bi-polar exchange rate regime choice (market-determined or fixed in a currency union); either option was acceptable subject to supporting macroeconomic policies. He also flirted with a Tobin tax on capital movements to dampen the movement of fast flowing international finance. In Eichengreen's (2007, p.xiii) perspective, 'the power of analogy resides not just in drawing out the parallels between two historical settings but also in highlighting the differences between them'. Thus he builds a compelling case against a modern line of thinking on the current IFS, represented by Michael Dooley et al. (2004, 2009). The latter have drawn parallels between the confluence of circumstances, policies and global imbalances in the BW era and what they refer to as the present 'BW II' era. The following summary statement of their position should suffice to indicate the substance of this attempt to reason by historical analogy in relation to issues facing the twenty-first century IFS:

> The economic emergence of a fixed exchange rate periphery in Asia has re-established the United States as the centre country in the Bretton Woods international monetary system. We argue that the normal evolution of the international monetary system involves the emergence of a periphery for which the development strategy is export-led growth supported by undervalued exchange rates, capital controls and official capital outflows in the form of accumulation of reserve asset claims on the centre country. The success of this strategy in fostering economic growth allows the periphery to graduate to the centre. Financial liberalization, in turn, requires floating exchange rates among the centre countries. But there is a line of

countries waiting to following the Europe of the 1950s/60s and Asia today sufficient to keep the system intact for the foreseeable future (Dooley et al. 2004, p.2).

Economic historians are still debating whether or not the international economic conditions referred to in the above passage warrant calling the present IFS a 'BW II system'. Be that as it may, it should be noticed that Eichengreen's rejection of the Dooley et al. argument turns on substantial differences between his reading of current and past (especially BW) international financial conditions and theirs. Skidelsky's exchange rate policy recommendations ignored the growing economic significance of diverse emerging market economies in the twenty-first century and the vast, ever-accumulating surpluses being built, for example, in China (under a fixed-adjustable exchange rate regime with a currency of increasing international significance). By comparison, Dooley et al. miss not only the heterogeneous nations on the so-called periphery; they underestimate the speed of integration in modern, sophisticated world financial markets such that the financial 'centres' have become partly dependent upon the 'periphery'; and they underestimate (at the time of writing) the move away from export-led growth strategies in Asia, due to slackening demand from western developed economies. Greater emphasis is now being placed on internal, domestic-led economic expansion (especially in China and India). The message here is that events often conspire, sometimes quickly, making the use of historical analogies much less plausible if not rendering them redundant. Correspondingly, attempting to assess the prospects for the present IFS, or to make predictions on the basis of historical analogy is a precarious undertaking. It is without doubt a popular pastime among economic historians wishing to demonstrate the relevance of history and related institutional conditions, and it draws applause when the variously distilled 'prospects' or predictions turn out to be corroborated – if only for a short period or over a narrow range or events.

Studying the contours of previous international financial structures in different epochs, their benefits, costs, successes and failings can be helpful in improving our understanding of emerging, contemporary arrangements. However, historical research prosecuted along these lines is not sufficient. Historical research on the international economy, or research on country experiences within a particular IFS, can produce evidence for quite different generalizations and predictions some of which will be contrary to each other depending on the time period chosen, research methodologies and the case in question. In short, and stated trivially, the history of the international economy will be read in different ways. In this respect, we need only recall the contrast in Chapter 5 above on under-standing the causes and proposed policy responses to a preeminent event in the post-BW era IFS – the 1990s Asian financial crisis. Joseph Stiglitz's view on that event (supported by Robert Wade) differed markedly from that of Stanley Fischer (supported by Lawrence Summers). Similarly, in searching for practical, operational reforms of the IFS in response to the Asian crisis, Barry Eichengreen's (1999a) now classic work on the crisis compares starkly with the ideas of Jane D'Arista (2000) or Paul Davidson (2000) on the same event, at about the same time. Likewise, in the pre-sent twenty-first century circumstances, readings of international finan-cial history and the analysis of the IFS by D'Arista (2009), Robert Wade (2009) and Lilia Costabile (2009) promote fundamental, activist inter-national monetary reform contrasting with the status quo bias (or, more charitably stated, the spontaneous evolution perspective) evident in Dooley et al. (2009).

Contemporary views of international financial integration may agree on the need for change in the IFS but differ fundamentally on how change is best effected. Some economists will favour change in the IFS that is delib-erately planned and managed by (say) governments, monetary authorities or an IFI in the interests of achieving broad economic and social goals. In this view, the evolution of the IFS needs strongly to reflect collective attempts to steer integration in certain directions otherwise an ongoing struggle between separate nations will produce, in Tobin's terms, inter-national economic and monetary 'anarchy'. Other economists will favour change that does not ignore the dynamic, spontaneous structure of the present IFS where in-built economic incentives contribute largely to the shape and coherence of that structure. The IFS, as it is presently configured, is only marginally controlled by governmental supervision, financial regu-lation and collective international policy actions. Broader economic and social outcomes of ongoing international financial integration in the present IFS are by-products, and not insignificant ones, of this spontaneously evolving system. Economists of this persuasion often agree that, periodic-ally, these by-products are negative for many participants in the inter-national economy though sometimes they blithely proceed to take for granted that the net by-product is positive for all in the long run.

Intellectual structures: Why the contest of ideas on the IFS matters

Rather than drawing selectively on particular events or historical struc-tures, this book has concentrated on alternative intellectual structures used for thinking about problems in the IFS, and in some cases for complete, formal reconstruction of the IFO. Indeed, it has been a central contention in previous chapters that changes in intellectual structures and the conflict between divergent intellectual structures are worthy of consideration in their own right. To be sure, often such ideational changes and conflicts are wrought by the impact of circumstances and surprising events (Endres 2000 and Wade 2009, p.560). As Paul Krugman (1993a, p.2) noted in connection with the evolution of economic ideas and controversies over the IFS:

> [i]t is slightly shameful...that economists interested in policy find themselves pleasantly stimulated by economic crises, just as professional military men are somewhat cheered by the prospect of war. This is particularly true when the events are dramatic without being too threatening in a personal sense.

A complete historical analysis which informs our understanding of the IFO and IFS, including the plans and schemes that have been part of the making of the present IFS or that help rationalize the IFS, must include a study of relevant intellectual history. The ideas of economists are often formulated in response to opposing intellectual structures as much as they are constructed in response to pressing historical contingencies in the IFS. Accordingly, these ideas, competing theories, plans and schemes of the kind reviewed in this book, were never formulated without an existing state or structure of ideas in view. Obviously, modest reform proposals were concerned with day-to-day operational issues and policies – the existing state of things such as exchange rate regimes, capital account convertibility issues, IMF lender-of-last-resort functions and so forth. We discussed some examples of intellectual structures in which grand schemes for wholesale international financial reorganization were advanced. Here the work of Cooper, Davidson, Mundell and McKinnon looms large in the post-BW era. Even in these instances, these economists built on, and referred to, an existing IFS and their idealistic policy proposals also drew upon economic doctrines already available in the literature of economics (e.g. Davidson's promotion of Keynes' clearing union scheme with modifications for international economic relationships in the 1990s).

In emphasizing the importance of intellectual structures making for the rationalization of an existing IFS, for incremental changes in that IFS or for grand reform in the IFO, the foregoing chapters asserted that doctrinal roots run deep. Doctrines take hold irrespective of circumstances, of the plethora of data sets and new measurement techniques that are brought to bear on issues pertinent to international financial integration. The contention that doctrinal history matters, is not to say that the ideas of economists are dogmatic, or are necessarily doctrinaire. The matter is more complex. Core propositions guiding what we have called 'thought trajectories' are defended by highly sophisticated inferences and supportive arguments, both logical and empirical. And empirical methods during the post-BW era exhibited major technical advances. Thus, the strong differences between doctrines on the place of controls on international capital flows – one group broadly favouring workable restrictions and another demonstrating that restrictions would be inefficient and ineffective – marshalled substantial evidence and cogent arguments in support of their respective propositions. The same point may be made over different doctrines on exchange rate choices; on the role of the IMF as ILLR; on the net returns from international macroeconomic policy coordination, and many other opposing doctrinal positions. On many of these major issues concerning the IFS, an eclectic, pragmatic position is also evident in the post-BW era. This position asserted that the efficacy of one or other policy or IFS reform proposal depended on the time and case. Jeffrey Frankel's view on exchange rate choices, that 'no single currency regime is right for all countries or at all times' epitomizes this position. The eclectic, pragmatic approach was nevertheless based on a definite doctrine, mostly founded on very short-run operational considerations in the post-BW IFS rather than on grand system-wide visions. So the eclectic economists were usually 'sequentialists' when it came to issues of domestic and international financial liberalization; they were alive to short-term differences in national economic structures; attuned to a country's stage of economic development, degree of openness and the state of economic governance structures in any particular case. Finally, the eclectics were often comfortable with incremental changes in the arrangement of the IFS (such as proposing marginal changes in the operations of the IMF or staged entry into the ECU).

A major advantage in taking an intellectual history approach is that it allows us to retain a degree of scepticism towards the use of terminology that is often disguised as value-neutral when it is really value-loaded. Take, for example, the original claim by John Williamson, implicitly accepted by James Tobin and largely supported by Robert Mundell, that the IFS in the post-BW era was in fact a 'non system'. Lately this widely-held belief is repeated by Barry Eichengreen (2007, p.15) who referred to the 'current non system'. In a slightly different vein Stanley Fischer (1999a, p. F557) maintained that 'we need a new international financial architecture'.

Some economists would respond that we already, currently, have both a 'system' and an 'architecture' and that both the supposition that we have a 'non system' and the invocation to find a new 'architecture' carry the implication that deliberate planning is required to come up with a blueprint for an overall IFO. Certainly Eichengreen and Fischer could use historical analogy to point out that the current IFS, or the one evident in the post-BW era up to 2000, are nothing like the deliberately designed BW IFO. That it needs to be deliberately designed is a definite doctrinal proposition. All the economists' ideas reviewed in early chapters of this book in fact took for granted that they were dealing with an existing, evolving international financial structure of some kind whether or not they regarded it as a genuine system. Yet their use of the term 'non system' suggests otherwise.

We noticed in the last section of Chapter 7 that market participants generally believed that the post-BW IFS was a 'system' insofar as it provided a structure in which to pursue their interests. The case in question was the choice of currencies to use as international vehicle, reserve and investment instruments. Hayek, Friedman and Vaubel proposed that market participants, not governments, ultimately choose the appropriate currency consolidations that occasionally take place in the IFS. The euro may have been deliberately planned, but its ongoing acceptance and use is dependent on the market test. More generally, there is a 'system' at work in currency choice – in the choice of the euro for example – in which the market test is continuously applied to give the euro its geographic reach, maintain its functions in the EMU and expand its role as an international currency.

The twenty-first century interest in international financial integration has to some extent been stimulated by occasional financial crises – crises that appear more easily transmitted across borders than in the BW era. In a contribution to the study of global capital market integration, Maurice Obstfeld and Alan Taylor (2003, pp.4–5) acknowledge the 'alternative perspectives' from which policymakers have tried to deal with capital flows. Obstfeld and Taylor deliver on a promise to discuss the 'vicissitudes' of these attempts 'quantitatively' and explain them. However, they retreat from any proposal definitively to cast judgement on, or directly confront, the 'alternative perspectives' at a deeper doctrinal (including philosophical and methodological) level. They proceed by asserting that 'economic theory and economic history together can provide useful insights into the events of the past and deliver relevant lessons for today' (p.5). The point of this book has been to add the comparative ideas approach or in other words, the history of modern economic thought, to the list of relevant sub disciplines that may provide 'useful insights' and 'relevant lessons'. In response to Obstfeld and Taylor, intellectual historians might ask which 'economic theory' in particular provides 'useful insights'? Economic theory in general will not do. We need to distinguish theories in some manner; trace their pedigree; outline the trajectories of thought in question; identify the economists who broadly follow these trajectories and the inferences and policy conclusions they derive from them at different times. Economic theory may indeed provide 'useful insights' into the workings of the IFS and predict the impact of events affecting any particular set of international financial arrangements in the world economy. Yet we should expect that different theories often produce divergent interpretations that are not easily reconciled.

The states of knowledge or conventionally accepted knowledge (given the uncertainties attached to economic and financial relationships in the international economy), as well as the interests of economists, can influence what policies are adopted in the IFS. Interests may be identified in the way economists frame problems in the international economy and the way they view the operation of particular elements in the IFS. Whilst economists' interests (or ideologies) are suppressed in formal economic analysis, the limits on economic knowledge still loom large. Paul Krugman often made this point in the post BW era. For instance: '[w]e are kidding ourselves...if we think that we can settle the optimum-currency-area problem' (Krugman 1993a, p.21). At other times economists are not as self-effacing. Take for example the following position, enunciated in the 1990s on the choice of exchange rate regimes:

> I conclude that <u>the best international monetary system for the world today</u> would necessarily have to be a hybrid system, not too different from the present system, under which nations would agree on some set of soft currency target zones and each nation would intervene in the foreign exchange market (Salvatore, 1995a, p. 447, emphasis added).

A doctrinal study would classify this view as typical of the trajectories of thought originally advanced by Roy Harrod and Robert Mundell in the later BW years; it was a view that desired to salvage the fixed exchange rate structure and a view that was deeply suspicious of market-determined currency values. As we saw in Chapter 5 above, John Williamson, Paul Davidson and Paul Krugman carried forward this thought trajectory in the post-BW era. This doctrine was aided by the new-found power of official sterilized exchange market interventions and empirical evidence mustered by sympathetic economists in favour of the effectiveness of exchange market interventions. Two further comments can be made about Dominic Salvatore's 'best' system in the light of our survey of economists' ideas in previous chapters. First, the 'world today' as Salvatore apprehended it, was characterized by a very temporally contingent IFS rather than a set of the 'best' monetary arrangements. He considered reform was necessary along the lines of a formal agreement among nations to limit the movement of exchange rates. The 'best' system was one in which exchange rate changes were controlled presumably because these changes reduced the ability of the IFS to deliver desired outcomes. Ongoing trends toward increasing international financial integration and a global economy increasingly open to freer capital movements seem to have been set aside – their importance is certainly minimized. Secondly, Salvatore's remarks, as well as many other proposals for international financial reforms in the post-BW era, remind us of Fritz Machlup's (1966, p.1) warning:

> It would be unreasonable to expect that anyone could devise an international monetary system serving all purposes optimally. Since people's aims are different, and to some extent incompatible with one another, no system can be 'objectively' called the best (his emphasis).

Intellectual structures in the fields of international monetary reform and financial integration have a tendency to be recycled oftentimes because of fads and fashions in the discipline of economics more generally (Bronfenbrenner 1966). Those structures also change and develop with advances in economists' analytical and empirical techniques and in response to pressing problems presented by the operation of the IFS. Just as there are parallel concrete historical situations in the international economy, so too are there ideas that run parallel with, or are substantially equivalent to, ideas and proposals on international monetary reform in previous eras and epochs. Indeed, just there are a variety of historical experiences with such phenomena as IMF lending practices, capital flows, or floating exchange rates, so there are varieties of intellectual constructs designed to reason over, and respond to them. This book's focus on intellectual structures has used the notion of thought trajectories to represent developments and changes within those structures over time. Among other things, this approach invites reasoned reflection on the divergences of views on key questions and dimensions of international financial integration, and it accepts that a pluralistic range of answers (rather than a definitive answer) will be forthcoming.

Like historical structures and patterns, ideas repeat themselves with variation. Thus the inferences, operational and practical implications drawn from core economic doctrines in the foregoing chapters, were different from time-to-time in the post-BW era because specific problems demanded variations especially in policy design. There are many examples of this phenomenon encountered in other foregoing surveys. Here we shall recall only three. Economists favouring fixed exchange rates in the BW era carried over that preference to the 1970s. Triffin, Williamson and McKinnon come to mind in this connection. Yet their policy reform proposals differ markedly. Similarly, economists favouring market-determined exchange rates can trace their ideas to Graham, Friedman and Johnson in the BW era – the last two carrying their views over to the post-BW era. This thought trajectory is reinforced by Obstfeld, Rogoff, Mussa and Fischer in the 1980s and 1990s, though these later contributors were often placed in a position of explaining why a reversion to some form of fixed exchange rate would not be desirable after a market-determined regime had been chosen. And, unlike their predecessors, they were inclined to believe that the transition to a choice of fully flexible exchange rates could take some time in some cases. James Tobin always favoured capital controls because of a belief that short-term capital flows were destabilizing to output and employment. Later in the post-BW era he came to accept the co-existence of taxes on capital flows and market-determined exchange rates (rather than more intrusive controls).

Some typical thought trajectories on the IFS in the post-BW era

The principal core beliefs embodied in various thought trajectories on international financial reform deserve some elaboration. For each trajectory there are distinguishing marks in the specific policy implications that are derived since there are indicative of a view on the way some aspect of the IFS should be arranged. From the outset of the post-BW era in 1971, we saw in Chapter 2 how divergences between different approaches quickly came into view (see column 2 Table 8.1 below). First there emerged grand, sweeping reformers (Mundell, Triffin) wishing to create a synthetic international money to replace the BW gold-dollar standard. Charles Kindleberger continued to apply his historical approach just as he had done during the BW era. Using historical

Table 8.1 Broad Thought Trajectories on Dimensions of International Finance 1971–2000

Trajectories	Initial Responses to BW Collapse	Exchange Rate Regime	Capital Account Regime	Crises	IMF	Currency Consolidation
1. Long-Run Historical Analogies	Kindleberger	Bordo Eichengreen		Kindleberger	Kindleberger	
2. Untrammelled Markets, Chicagoan, Public Choice, Austrian	Johnson	Friedman Johnson	Hayek Lucas	Schwartz	Schwartz	Friedman Hayek Rogoff Vaubel
3. Pro-Market Reformers	Haberler Machlup	Meade Mussa Obstfeld Rogoff	Feldstein Fischer Obstfeld	Feldstein Frankel Obstfeld Summers	Fischer Krueger Mussa Polak	Frankel Feldstein
4. Ecletics, Pragmatists, Sequentialists	Samuelson	Dornbusch Frankel Goldstein	Cooper Dornbusch Edwards McKinnon Rodrik	Dornbusch Eichengreen Sachs	Eichengreen Feldstein Rodrik	Cohen Dornbusch Eichengreen Krugman Wyplosz
5. Grand Schemes	Mundell Triffin	McKinnon Cooper			Davidson Krugman Meltzer Sachs Stiglitz	Cooper Mundell
6. Mainstream 'Keynesian'	Cooper Fleming Meade	Krugman Tobin Williamson	Eichengreen Stiglitz Tobin Wyplosz	Krugman Stiglitz		
7. Other 'Keynesian'		Davidson Eatwell Taylor Wade	Davidson	Wade Minsky		Davidson

analogies, he criticized all idealistic schemes deliberately aimed at creating new international money, adopting sweeping changes in exchange rate regimes such as market-determined rates, and the implementing whole-sale liberalization of capital accounts. The Keynesians (Cooper, Fleming, Meade, Williamson) were aligned to a thought trajectory that drew similar conclusions, though Meade stood-out with his pro-market stance on choice of exchange rate regime (provided that choice could be made after national macroeconomic policies, including possibly incomes policy, could be satisfactorily formulated and coordinated across the major industrialized economies). Economic thought at the IMF, represented by J. Marcus Fleming, followed the prevailing orthodoxy in academic economics. During the post-BW era, mostly from the mid-1980s onwards, IMF economists (e.g. Fischer, Mussa) joined the new orthodoxy aligned to the neoliberal, pro-market thought trajectories. This line of thinking was represented in the work of Haberler and Machlup at the beginning of the period under review. Harry Johnson represented the 'untrammelled markets' perspective, while Paul Samuelson emerged from the early expert discussion on the demise of BW as a sceptic on matters of international finance; he saw some good reasons to allow much greater exchange rate flexibility than under the BW system (even paying royal tribute to Friedman's early work on the subject).

Progressively as the post-BW era developed, patterns of thought coalesced around specific topics in the emerging IFS such as capital account convertibility issues, new roles for the IMF, and European Union. Initial post-BW discussion among leading economists focused on bigger, systemic issues; though later only McKinnon, Cooper and Mundell kept these matters at the forefront of their contributions. When financial crises and the place of the IMF (in a world of market-determined exchange rates and capital account liberalization) became more popular topics of discussion, a larger group of economists began to revisit systemic issues (see Table 8.1, line 5, 'Grand Schemes' column 6).

It should be emphasized that just because we have aligned economists with particular thought trajectories that indicate their doctrinal persuasions, this does not mean that the individuals concerned were doctrinaire advocates of certain policies. Take for example the capital account regime choice and associated programs for financial market liberalization discussed in Chapter 4. Economists divided neatly into various groups according to whether or not they thought capital account liberalization was (i) never a good idea, (ii) not generally a good idea, (iii) only advantageous in conjunction with a planned sequencing program including domestic financial market reform, and (iv) desirable in general. As our review indicated, all the economists grouped in these categories bolstered their positions with sophisticated arguments, carefully designed policy suggestions and empirical evidence. In relation to capital account openness, all the economists mentioned in Chapter 4 were favourable to cross-border foreign direct investment flows though some would have applied more stringent monitoring to those flows than others.

Chapter 5 on financial crises and the following chapter on the IMF presented some approaches which were not easily categorized. Anna Schwartz came closest to representing the 'untrammelled markets' trajectory on these issues, whereas Robert Wade represented the 'other Keynesian' approach recommending or at least strongly implying, that the operation and reach of markets should be tightly controlled and limited respectively. Hyman Minsky presented a highly original perspective on crises, though his intellectual debts (but not the only ones) owe much to Keynes and the Keynesians. Therefore, for want of a better characterization, we have located him along the 'other Keynesian' trajectory in Table 8.1. We had no difficulty categorizing the IMF's self-styled monetary approach to balance-of-payments adjustment initiated in the work of Jacques Polak. The IMF model was decidedly pro-market in orientation; it was a model with a very short-run horizon not easily equated with Chicago-style monetarism, though it was a working, rule-of-thumb model which applied a blunt, rule-based monetary policy approach to effect macroeconomic stabilization and especially current account adjustment in LDCs.

Generally, most of the IMF economists (e.g. Fischer, Mussa) were positioned along the pro-market trajectory; they favoured market-led, accelerated liberalization on exchange rate policy, capital account convertibility, currency competition and consolidation. In this endeavour, they were supported in the 1990s by Anne Krueger, Maurice Obstfeld and Kenneth Rogoff. These economists were openly critical of IMF policies applied to countries in a 'one-size-fits-all' framework. Yet their general viewpoint was biased toward removing restrictions on market processes in the international economy; they formulated recommendations favouring market-based economic adjustment and financial liberalization. While often mentioning the right preconditions for liberalization, noting the danger of premature or indiscriminate financial liberalization especially in LDCs, and the financial fragility of LDCs in the short run, these thoughts were mostly caveats; they were protective inferences around an overall doctrinal outlook that had a definite pro-market orientation. According to vocal critics of this doctrine, including the 'Keynesian' and 'Other Keynesian' groups and some of the 'Eclectics' (Dornbusch, Sachs) in Table 8.1, the right preconditions for market-based liberalization in the post-BW era were not discovered as absent until after a financial crises had taken hold. Both Keynesian groups subsequently proposed grand schemes for IMF reform (Table 8.1, column 6).

Often economists at the IMF stated generalities that virtually all economists may agree with. However, when they drew specific policy inferences their underlying doctrinal approach was revealed. Later in the post-BW era, for example, Michael Mussa (1995, p.494), then an Economic Counsellor and Director of Research at the IMF, confidently supported national monetary policies that were rule-based and exclusively set to target 'reasonable price stability' and 'sustainable rates of growth over the medium and longer term'. While many of the economists whose ideas we have reviewed in this book could equally have used these generalities to define policy goals, Mussa's policy inferences would not have been accepted in the last two thought trajectories at the base of Table 8.1. Mussa's normative inference was that with 'national monetary policies devoted to these goals, a regime of <u>floating exchange rates</u> among the world's most important currencies is...a fundamental and desirable feature of the international monetary system' (emphasis added).

On crises, Krugman and Stiglitz were major contributions to the broadly labelled 'Conventional Keynesian' trajectory. Their approach was analytically deepened by advances in empirical techniques and in Stiglitz's case, by his celebrated work on the economics of information. The 'other Keynesian' group, Davidson, Eatwell, Taylor and Wade generally paralleled the views of Krugman and Stiglitz, although they drew more interventionist policy inferences across most dimensions of the IFS. Needless-to-say, this Keynesian trajectory was orthogonal to the untrammelled markets trajectory.

The Chicago line, coupled with the public choice and Austrian economists, generally favoured market processes in the IFS. This trajectory has its intellectual roots in the work of Simons, Graham and Friedman in the BW era. The 'untrammelled markets' idea is more sharply distinguished from other thought trajectories on subjects such as choice of exchange regime (e.g. Friedman) capital account regimes (Lucas, Hayek), crises and the IMF in which Anna Schwartz played a leading role, and in the field of currency choice, currency competition and consolidation where Hayek's ideas are most prominent.

Table 8.1 outlines seven broad thought trajectories that constitute only general characterizations. The table summarizes intellectual tendencies rather than perfect alignments. Some prominent economists are associated with different trajectories depending on the IFS dimension. For example in the early 1980s, Eichengreen, like Kindleberger, initially contributed extensive historical analysis of the IFS, providing unique insights into the workings of the global economy under different systemic arrangements, including the classical gold standard system. When turning to policy issues in the 1990s, such as crises, IMF reform and currency consolidation, Eichengreen becomes a cautious incrementalist and pragmatist. And on the issue of capital movements he took a position in line with the mainstream Keynesians. Similarly, when we consider the work of Martin Feldstein and Jeffrey Frankel, we find a general pro-market line, though Feldstein was a pragmatist on IMF reform, and Frankel held an eclectic view of exchange rate regime choice.

Enough has now been said about Table 8.1 to imply that we have, at the very least, some grounds for distinguishing broad, contrasting trajectories of thought on international financial integration and problems of IFS reform. Categorizations of the kind attempted in Table 8.1 are hazardous exercises. To repeat a point made earlier: the categorizations are meant to indicate the intellectual tendencies of economists – their inclination generally to adopt certain underlying doctrines.

Let us now follow some of the illustrative 'core' doctrinal statements in the boxes at the end of Chapter 1, and ignore qualifications, nuances and unique inferences elicited by individual economists. We can then report that the economists aligned with the trajectories 2 and 3 in Table 8.1 generally accepted the following statements as workable, intellectual benchmarks.

1. The IFS is self-stabilizing.
2. Exchange rates are like other commodity prices.
3. International financial markets are inherently stable and beneficent when allowed to function in tandem with open capital accounts, floating exchange rates and open current accounts.
4. The IMF is perennially subject to policy failure given moral hazard and enforcement problems.
5. The IMF, if it continues to exist, should promote pro-market policy reform at the national level.
6. Post-BW era financial crises have not been a convincing indication of the deleterious consequences of increasing market-based international financial integration; they have more often been caused by policies that thwart integration.

Progressively as we descend Table 8.1, from trajectory 1 through 7, more of these doctrinal statements are hedged about by major qualifications (e.g. by eclectics, scepticists, and pragmatists). These statements are roundly rejected by the time we reach trajectory 7.

Postscript: The IFS and the significance of economists' ideas

Taking an overall system standpoint, Robert Mundell (1977, p.242) opined that the IFS should be arranged in a manner that would pursue 'full employment, price stability, and moderate growth, freedom of international commerce and lending, and wiser global conservation policies'. He was mindful at the time that, in principle, economists would agree with these lofty objectives but, in practice, their views on how to achieve these objectives would only converge under very rare circumstances. Mundell added that economists would have to agree in the first place on how the IFS would 'evolve' over the longer term, presuming that full control of that evolutionary process was not possible. In terms of the making of both the overall, formal IFO (in some cases) and the management of the day-to-day operations of the IFS, several clear divisions of thought become evident in the post-BW era.

Some economists believed that the total set of background, international monetary arrangements in both the IFO and day-to-day arrangements in any particular IFS – should be strongly guided by a coherent set of international rules and national economic policies consistent with those rules (as in the BW IFO). Policies should be reformed continuously in the light of the overarching IFO rules. Incremental changes in the workings of the IFS would be required in response to short-run problems that require correction or amelioration (such as exchange rate misalignments, financial problems in LDCs etc). Another approach common among economists is to ignore the possibility of forming a blueprint for the whole international monetary order and concentrate on deliberately containing problems as they arise in the evolving IFS. There would be set guidelines for containment, perhaps established by IFIs, in order for example, to effect changes in the levels of world output and employment; shelter LDC's from short-term capital flows; create regional monetary and currency unions; respond to financial contagion crises or currency crises; provide lender-of-last resort protection; and redistribute the gains from ongoing advances in international economic integration (arising from freer trade and freer capital movements).

Another view takes comfort in the fact that economists, monetary authorities, IFIs and other international and national regulatory agencies cannot fully know how the IFS is going to evolve. What changes in the IFS might emerge after a global credit crisis such as that experienced in 2008–9, despite regulatory changes wrought by governments attempting to remedy that situation? What will be the unforeseen consequences of the latest crisis in terms of its impact on individual behaviour, and the unintended outcomes of the reactive policy responses? To pose these questions is to appreciate the limits of economists' knowledge; they put into more realistic proportion the ideas, international financial plans and schemes advanced by economists in the post-BW era. The IFS is an emergent, spontaneously organized phenomenon in which reform is mostly the outcome of a self-organizing process rather than being predominantly the result of deliberate design. No government, IFI, or set of policy rules can steer the IFS in any obvious direction over an extended period of time. While the evolution of the IFS is not independent of existing attempts to contain or steer certain parts or dimensions of the system (e.g. plan currency unions, regulate exchange rate setting or control capital movements), these attempts are not, ultimately, decisive. Here Friedrich Hayek's advice in his Nobel Memorial Lecture commends itself.

> If man is not to do more harm than good in his efforts to improve the social order, he will have to learn that in this, as in all other fields where essential complexity of an organized kind prevails, he cannot acquire the full knowledge which could make mastery of the events possible. He will therefore have to use what knowledge he can achieve, not to shape the results as the craftsman shapes his handiwork, but rather to cultivate a growth by providing the appropriate environment, in the manner in which the gardener does this for his plants (Hayek 1974, p.7).

Future architects of the international financial system might do well to heed this advice.

Bibliography

Aliber, R.Z. (1987) 'Exchange Rates' in J. Chipman, J. Eatwell and M. Milgate (eds) *The New Palgrave: A Dictionary of Economics VOL. 1* (London: Macmillan).

Arestis, P. and Sawyer, P. (1998) 'Keynesian Economic Policies for the New Millenium', *Economic Journal*, 108(446), 181–95.

Bagehot, W. (1873) *Lombard Street* (London: William Clowes and Sons).

Bank For International Settlements (1998) *Reports on Strengthening the International Financial Architecture* (Basel: BIS).

Basu, K. (2003) 'Globalization and the Politics of International Finance', *Journal of Economic Literature*, 41(3), 885–99.

Baumol, W.E. (1982) 'Contestable Markets: An Uprising in the Theory of Industry Structure', *American Economic Review*, 72, 1–15.

Bayoumi, T. and Eichengreen, B. (1993) 'Shocking Aspects of European Monetary Integration' in F. Torres and F. Giavazzi (eds) *Adjustment and Growth in the European Monetary Union* (Cambridge: Cambridge University Press).

Belassa, B. (1969) 'Toward a Theory of International Economic Integration', *Kyklos*, 22, 1–15.

Best, J. (2005) *The Limits of Transparency: Ambiguity in the History of International Finance* (Ithaca: Cornell University Press).

Bhagwati, J. (1998) 'The Capital Myth: The Difference Between Trade in Widgets and Dollars', *Foreign Affairs*, 77(3), 7–12.

Black, S.W. (1985) 'International Money and International Monetary Arrangements' in P.B. Kenen and R.W. Jones (eds) *Handbook of International Economics II* (Amsterdam: North-Holland).

Blaug, M. (1992) *Methodology of Economics or How Economist Explain*, 2nd edn (Cambridge. Cambridge University Press).

Blejer, M.I. and Frenkel, J.A. (1987) 'Monetary Approach to the Balance of Payments' in J. Chipman, J. Eatwell and M. Milgate (eds) *The New Palgrave: A Dictionary of Economics VOL. 3* (London: Macmillan).

Bordo, M. (1993) 'The Bretton Woods International Monetary System: A History and Overview' in M. Bordo and B. Eichengreen (eds) *A Retrospective on the Bretton Woods System* (Chicago: University of Chicago Press).

Bordo, M. and James, H. (2000) 'The International Monetary Fund: Its Role in Historical Perspective', U.S. Congressional International Financial Institution Advisory Commission.

Bordo, M. and James, H. (2008a) 'The Past and Future of IMF Reform: A Proposal' (mimeo).

Bordo, M. and James, H. (2008b) 'The US Dollar and Its Role in the International Monetary Order' (mimeo).

Bordo, M. and Jonung, L. (1997) 'The History of Monetary Regimes: Some Lessons for Sweden and EMU', *Swedish Economic Policy Review*, 4(2), 285–358.

Bordo, M. and Jonung, L. (2000) *Lessons for EMU From the History of Monetary Unions* (London: Institute of Economic Affairs).

Boughton, J.M. (2001) *Silent Revolution: The International Monetary Fund, 1979–1989* (Washington D.C.: International Monetary Fund).

Bronfenbrenner, M. (1966) 'Trends, Cycles and Fads in Economic Writing', *American Economic Review*, 56, 538–52.

Bryant, R.C. (1987) *International Financial Intermediation* (Washington D.C.: Brookings Institution).

Bryant, R.C. (1995) *International Coordination of National Stabilization Policies* (Washington D.C.: Brookings Institution).

Bryant, R.C. (1999) 'Policymaking in an Integrated World: Discussion' in J.S. Little and G.P. Olivei (eds) *Rethinking the International Monetary System* (Boston: Federal Reserve Bank of Boston).

Calomiris, C.W. (2000) 'When Will Economics Guide IMF and World Bank Reforms?', *Cato Journal*, 20(1), 85–103.

Calvo, G.A., Leiderman, L. and Reinhart, C.M. (1994) 'The Capital Inflows Problem: Concepts and Issues', *Contemporary Economic Policy*, 12, 54–66.

Calvo, G.A., Leiderman, L. and Reinhart, C.M. (1996) 'Inflows of Capital to Developing Countries in the 1990s', *Journal of Economic Perspectives*, 10(2), 129–39.

Calvo, G.A. and Mendoza, E.G. (2000a) 'Rational Contagion and the Globalization of Securities Markets', *Journal of International Economics*, 51, 79–113.

Calvo, G.A. and Mendoza, E.G. (2000b) 'Contagion, Globalization and the Volatility of Capital Flows' in S. Edwards (ed.) *Capital Flows and Emerging Market Economies: Theory, Evidence and Controversies* (Chicago: University of Chicago Press).

Chrystal, K.A. (1984) 'On the Theory of International Money' in J. Black and G. Dorrance (eds) *Problems of International Finance* (London: Macmillan).

Citrin, D. and Fischer, S. (2000) 'Strengthening and International Financial System: Key Issues', *World Development*, 28(6), 1133–42.

Cohen, B.J. (1998) *The Geography of Money* (New York: Cornell University Press).

Cohen, B.J. (2000) 'Beyond EMU: The Problem of Sustainability' in B. Eichengreen and J. Friedin (eds) *The Political Economy of European Monetary Integration*, 2nd edn (Boulder: Westview Press).

Cohen, B.J. (2008a) *International Political Economy: An Intellectual History* (Princeton: Princeton University Press).

Cohen, B.J. (2008b) *Global Monetary Governance* (London and New York: Routledge).

Cooper, R.N. (1972) 'Eurodollars, Reserve Dollars, and Asymmetries in the International Monetary System', *Journal of International Economics*, 2, 325–44.

Cooper, R.N. (1975) 'Prolegomena to the Choice of an International Monetary System', *International Organization*, 29(1), 63–97.

Cooper, R.N. (1984a) 'Is There Need for Reform?' in Federal Reserve Bank of Boston, *The International Monetary System: Forty Years After Bretton Woods* (Boston: Federal Reserve Bank of Boston).

Cooper, R.N. (1984b) 'A Monetary System For the Future', *Foreign Affairs*, 63(1), 166–84.

Cooper, R.N. (1985) 'Economic Interdependences and the Coordination of Economic Policies' in R. Jones and P. Kenen (eds) *Handbook of International Economics VOL. I* (Amsterdam: North-Holland).

Cooper, R.N. (1998) 'Should Capital Account Convertibility Be a World Objective?' in S. Fischer et al., *Should the IMF Pursue Capital Account Convertibility?* (Princeton University: International Finance Section).

Cooper, R.N. (1999a) 'Should Capital Controls be Banished?', *Brookings Papers on Economic Activity*, 1, 89–141.

Cooper, R.N. (1999b) 'European Monetary Union, Dollar and International Monetary System' in P.J. Zak (ed.) *Currency Crises, Monetary Union and the Conduct of Monetary Policy* (Cheltenham U.K.: Edward Elgar).

Cooper, R.N. (1999c) 'Key Currencies After the Euro', *World Economy*, 22(1), 1–23.

Cooper, R.N. (1999d) 'Exchange Rate Choices' in J.S. Little and G.P. Olivei (eds) *Rethinking the International Monetary System* (Boston: Federal Reserve Bank of Boston).

Corden, W.M. (1983) 'The Logic of the International Monetary Non-System' in H. Giersch, F. Machlup, G. Fels and H. Muller-Groeling (eds) *Reflections on a Troubled World Economy: Essays in Honor of Herbert Giersch* (New York: St. Martin's Press).

Corden, W.M. (1994) *Economic Policy, Exchange Rates and the International System* (Oxford: Oxford University Press).

Costabile, L. (2009) 'Current Global Imbalances and the Keynes Plan: A Keynesian Approach for Reforming the International Monetary System', *Structural Change and Economic Dynamics*, 20, 77–89.

Craig, B. (1996) 'Competing Currencies: Back to the Future', *Federal Reserve Bank of Cleveland Economic Commentary*, October, 1–8.

D'Arista, J. (2000) 'Reforming the Privatized International Monetary and Financial Architecture', *Challenge*, 43(3), 44–82.

D'Arista, J. (2009) 'The Evolving International Monetary System', *Cambridge Journal of Economics*, 33, 633–52.

Davidson, P. (1992–93) 'Reforming the World's Money', *Journal of Post Keynesian Economics*, 15(2), 153–79.

Davidson, P. (1997) 'Are Grains of Sand in the Wheels of International Finance Sufficient to do the Job When Boulders are Often Required?', *Economic Journal*, 107, 671–86.

Davidson, P. (1998) 'Volatile Financial Markets and the Speculator', *Economic Issues*, 3, 1–18.

Davidson, P. (2000) 'Is a Plumber or a New Financial Architect Needed to End Global International Liquidity Problems?', *World Development*, 28(6), 1117–31.

De Grauwe, P. (1989) *International Money: Post-War Trends and Theories* (Oxford: Oxford University Press).

De Grauwe, P. (1993) 'Discussion' in F. Torres and F. Giavazzi (eds) *Adjustment and Growth in the European Monetary Union* (Cambridge: Cambridge University Press).

Dominiguez, K. and Frankel, J.A. (1993) 'Does Foreign-Exchange Intervention Matter? The Portfolio Effect', *American Economic Review*, 83(5), 1356–69.

Dooley, M.P. (1996) 'A Survey of Literature on Controls Over International Capital Transactions', *International Monetary Fund Staff Papers*, 43(4), 639–87.

Dooley, M.P., Folkerts-Landau, D. and Garber, P.M. (2004) 'The Revived Bretton Woods System: The Effects of Periphery Intervention and Reserve Management on Interest Rates and Exchange Rates in Center Countries', *National Bureau of Economic Research Working Paper*, No. 10332, March.

Dooley, M.P., Folkerts-Landau, D. and Garber, P.M. (2009) 'Bretton Woods II Still Defines the International Monetary System', *National Bureau of Economic Research Working Paper*, No. 14731, February.

Dopfer, K. and Potts, J. (2008) *The General Theory of Economic Evolution* (London and New York: Routledge).

Dornbusch, R. (1980) 'Exchange Rate Economics: Where Do We Stand?', *Brookings Papers on Economic Activity*, 1, 143–85.

Dornbusch, R. (1986) 'Flexible Exchange Rates and Excess Capital Mobility', *Brookings Papers on Economic Activity*, 1, 209–26.

Dornbusch, R. (1987) 'Exchange Rate Economics 1986', *Economic Journal*, 97, 1–18.

Dornbusch, R. (1988a) 'Doubts About the McKinnon Standard', *Journal of Economic Perspectives*, 2(1), 105–12.

Dornbusch, R. (1988b) 'The European Monetary System, the Dollar and the Yen' in F. Giavazzi, S. Micossi and M. Miller (eds) *The European Monetary System* (Cambridge: Cambridge University Press).

Dornbusch, R. (1990a) 'From Stabilization to Growth', *National Bureau of Economic Research Working Paper*, No. 3302, March.

Dornbusch, R. (1990b) 'Two-Track EMU, Now!' in K.O. Pohl (ed.) *Britain and EMU* (London: Centre for Economic Performance).

Dornbusch, R. (1991) 'International Financial Crises' in M. Feldstein (ed.) *The Risk of Economic Crisis* (Chicago: University of Chicago Press).

Dornbusch, R. (1997) 'Cross-Border Payments Taxes and Alternative Capital-Account Regimes' in *International Monetary and Financial Issues for the 1990s. Research Papers for the Growth of Twenty-Four* (New York and Geneva: United Nations Conference on Trade and Development).

Dornbusch, R. (1998) 'Capital Controls: An Idea Whose Time is Past' in S. Fischer et al., *Should the IMF Pursue Capital-Account Convertibility?* (Princeton University: International Finance Section).

Dornbusch, R. and Fischer, S. (1994) *Macroeconomics* (New York: McGraw Hill).

Dornbusch, R., Goldfajn, I. and Valdes, R.O. (1995) 'Currency Crises and Collapses', *Brookings Papers on Economic Activity*, 2, 219–70.

Dornbusch, R. and Werner, A. (1994) 'Mexico: Stabilization, Reform and No Growth', *Brookings Papers on Economic Activity*, 1, 253–97.

Dowd, K. and Greenway, D. (1993) 'Currency Competition, Network Externalities and Switching Costs: Toward an Alternative View of Optimal Currency Areas', *Economic Journal*, 103(420), 1180–9.

Eatwell, J. and Taylor, L. (2000) *Global Finance at Risk* (New York: New Press).

Eatwell, J. and Taylor, L. (2002) 'A World Financial Authority' in J. Eatwell and L. Taylor (eds) *International Capital Markets: Systems in Transition* (Oxford: Oxford University Press).

Edwards, S. (1989a) *Real Exchange Rates, Devaluation and Adjustment: Exchange Rate Policy in Developing Countries* (Cambridge Mass: MIT Press).

Edwards, S. (1989b) 'International Monetary Fund and the Developing Countries' in K. Brunner and L. Meltzer (eds) *Carnegie-Rochester Conference Series on Public Policy VOL.31* (Amsterdam: North-Holland).

Edwards, S. (1992) 'The Sequencing of Structural Adjustment and Stabilization', *CEPR Occasional Paper*, No. 34.

Edwards, S. (1998) 'Capital Flows, Real Exchange Rates and Capital Controls: Some Latin American Experiences', *NBER Working Paper*, No. 6000.

Edwards, S. (1999) 'International Capital Flows and Emerging Markets: Amending the Rules of the Game?' in J.S. Little and G.P. Olivei (eds) *Rethinking the International Monetary System* (Boston: Federal Reserve Bank of Boston).

Edwards, S. (2000) 'Introduction' in S. Edwards (ed.) *Capital Flows and the Emerging Economies: Theory, Evidence and Controversies* (Chicago: The University of Chicago Press).

Eichengreen, B. (1990) 'Is Europe an Optimum Currency Area?' reprinted in B. Eichengreen (2005) *European Monetary Unification: Theory, Practice and Analysis* (Cambridge Mass: MIT Press).

Eichengreen, B. (1992) 'One Money for Europe? Lessons From the US Currency Union' reprinted in B. Eichengreen (2005) *European Monetary Unification: Theory, Practice and Analysis* (Cambridge Mass: MIT Press).

Eichengreen, B. (1994) *International Monetary Arrangements for the 21ˢᵗ Century* (Washington D.C.: Brookings Institution).

Eichengreen, B. (1996a) *Globalizing Capital: A History of the International Monetary System* (Princeton: Princeton University Press).

Eichengreen, B. (1996b) 'A More Perfect Union? On the Logic of Economic Integration' reprinted in B. Eichengreen (2005) *European Monetary Unification: Theory, Practice and Analysis* (Cambridge Mass: MIT Press).

Eichengreen, B. (1997) *European Monetary Unification: Theory, Practice and Analysis* (Cambridge Mass: MIT Press).

Eichengreen, B. (1999a) *Toward a New International Financial Architecture: A Practical Post-Asia Agenda* (Washington D.C.: Institute for International Economics).

Eichengreen, B. (1999b) 'Policymaking in an Integrated World: From Surveillance to ...?' in J.S. Little and G.P. Olivei (eds) *Rethinking the International Monetary System* (Boston: Federal Reserve Bank of Boston).

Eichengreen, B. (1999c) 'European Monetary Union, the Dollar and the International Monetary System' in P. Zak (ed.) *Currency Crises, Monetary Union and the Conduct of Monetary Policy* (Cheltenham U.K.: Edward Elgar).

Eichengreen, B. (2000) 'Taming Capital Flows', *World Development*, 28(6), 1105–16.

Eichengreen, B. (2007) *Global Imbalances and the Lessons of Bretton Woods* (Cambridge Mass: MIT Press).

Eichengreen, B., Mussa, M., Dell'Ariccia, G., Detragiache, E., Milesi-Ferretti, G. and Tweedie, A. (1999) *Liberalizing Capital Movements: Some Analytical Issues* (Washington D.C.: International Monetary Fund).

Eichengreen, B. and Portes, R. (1989) 'The Anatomy of Financial Crises', *NBER Working Paper*, No. 2126, August.

Eichengreen, B. and Rose, A.K. (1999) 'Contagion Currency Crises: Channels of Conveyance' in T. Ito and A. Krueger (eds) *Changes in Exchange Rates in Rapidly Developing Economies* (Chicago: University of Chicago Press).

Eichengreen, B., Rose, A.K. and Wyplosz, C. (1995) 'Exchange Market Mayhem: The Antecedents and Aftermath of Speculative Attacks', *Economic Policy: A European Forum*, 21, 249–96.

Eichengreen, B., Rose, A.K. and Wyplosz, C. (1996) 'Contagious Currency Crises: First Tests', *Scandinavian Journal of Economics*, 98, 1–22.

Eichengreen, B., Tobin, J. and Wyplosz, C. (1995) 'Two Cases For Sand in the Wheels of International Finance', *Economic Journal*, 105(1), 162–72.

Eichengreen, B. and Wyplosz, C. (1996) 'Taxing International Financial Transactions to Enhance the Operation of the International Monetary System' in M. ul Haq, I. Kaul and I. Grunberg (eds) *The Tobin Tax: Coping with Financial Volatility* (Oxford and New York: Oxford University Press).

Emminger, O. (1984) 'Adjustments in World Payments: An Evaluation' in Federal Reserve Bank of Boston *The International Monetary System: Forty Years After Bretton Woods* (Boston: Federal Reserve Bank of Boston).

Endres, A.M. (2000) 'Rethinking the International Monetary System (review)', *Journal of Economic Literature*, 38, 954–6.

Endres, A.M. (2005) *Great Architects of International Finance: The Bretton Woods Era* (London and New York: Routledge).

Endres, A.M. (2008) 'Frank Graham's Case for Flexible Exchange Rates: A Doctrinal Perspective', *History of Political Economy*, 40(1), 133–62.

Endres, A.M. (2009) 'Currency Competition: A Hayekian Perspective on International Financial Integration', *Journal of Money, Credit and Banking*, 41(6), 1251–64.

Endres, A.M. and Fleming, G.A. (2002) *International Organisations and Analysis of Economic Policy 1919–1950* (Cambridge: Cambridge University Press).

Feldstein, M. (1993) 'Why Maastricht Will (Still) Fail', *The National Interest*, 32, 19.

Feldstein, M. (1997) 'The Political Economy of European Economic and Monetary Union: Political Sources of an Economic Liability', *Journal of Economic Perspectives*, 11(4), 23–42.

Feldstein, M (1998a) 'Reforming the IMF', *Foreign Affairs*, 77(2), 20–33.

Feldstein, M. (1998b) 'Distinguished Lecture on Economics in Government: Thinking About International Policy Coordination', *Journal of Economic Perspectives*, 2, 3–13.

Feldstein, M. (1999) 'International Capital Flows: Introduction' in M. Feldstein (ed.) *International Capital Flows* (Chicago: The University of Chicago Press).

Fellner, W. (1972) 'The Dollar's Place in the International System: Suggested Criteria for the Appraisal of Emerging Views', *Journal of Economic Literature*, 10(3), 735–56.

Ferreira, F. and Litchfield, J. (1999) 'Calm After the Storm: Income Distribution and Welfare in Chile 1887–1994', *World Bank Economic Review*, 13(3), 509–38.

Fischer, S. (1998) 'Capital Account Liberalization and the Role of the IMF' in S. Fischer et al., *Should the IMF Pursue Capital Account Convertibility?* (Princeton University: International Finance Section).

Fischer, S. (1999a) 'Reforming the International Financial System', *Economic Journal*, 109, F557–F576.

Fischer, S. (1999b) 'On the Need for an International Lender of Last Resort', *Journal of Economic Perspectives*, 13(3), 85–104.

Fischer, S. (2001) 'Distinguished Lecture on Economics in Government: Exchange Rate Regimes: Is the Bi Polar View Correct?', *Journal of Economic Perspectives*, 15(2), 3–24.

Fischer, S. (2003a) 'Financial Crises and Reform of the International Financial System', *Review of World Economics*, 139(1), 1–37.

Fischer, S. (2003b) 'Globalization and its Challenges', *American Economic Review Papers and Proceedings*, 93(2), 1–30.

Fisher, I. (1933) 'The Debt-Deflation Theory of Great Depressions', *Econometrica*, 1(3), 337–54.

Fleming, J.M. (1972) 'Towards a New Regime For International Payments', *Journal of International Economics*, 2, 345–73.

Folkerts-Landau, D. and Ito, T. (1995) *International Capital Markets: Development, Prospects and Policy Issues* (Washington D.C.: IMF).

Frankel, J.A. (1999) *No Single Currency is Right For All Countries or at All Times* (Princeton University: International Finance Section).

Frankel, J.A. and Goldstein, M. (1989) 'Exchange Rate Volatility and Misalignment: Evaluating Some Proposals for Reform' in Federal Reserve Bank of Kansas City, *Financial Market Volatility* (Kansas City: Federal Reserve Bank of Kansas).

Frankel, J.A. and Rose, A.K. (1997) 'Is EMU More Justifiable *Ex Post* or *Ex Ante?*' *European Economic Review*, 41, 753–60.

Frankel, J.A. and Rose, A.K. (1998) 'The Endogeneity of Optimum Currency Area Criteria', *Economic Journal*, 108, 1009–25.

Frankel, J.A. and Rose, A.K. (1996) 'Currency Crashes in Emerging Markets: An Empirical Treatment', *Journal of International Economics*, 41, 351–66.

Frenkel, J. (1991) 'Intervention, Coordination and Crises' in M. Feldstein (ed.) *The Risk of Economic Crisis* (Chicago: University of Chicago Press).

Frenkel, J., Goldstein, M. and Masson, P.R. (1996) 'International Coordination of Economic Policies' in J. Frenkel and M. Goldstein (eds) *The Functioning of the International Monetary System* (Washington D.C.: International Monetary Fund).

Frenkel, J. and Johnson, H.G. (1976) 'The Monetary Approach to the Balance of Payments: Essential Concepts and Historical Origins' in J. Frenkel and H.G. Johnson (eds) *The Monetary Approach to the Balance of Payments* (London: George Allen and Unwin).

Friedman, B. (1999) 'The Future of Monetary Policy: The Central Bank as an Army with Only a Signal Corps?', *International Finance*, 2, 321–38.

Friedman, M. (1953) 'The Case For Flexible Exchange Rates', *Essays in Positive Economics* (Chicago: Chicago University Press).

Friedman, M. (1984) 'Currency Competition: A Skeptical View' in M. Salin (ed.) *Currency Competition and Monetary Union* (The Hague: Martinus Nijhoff Publishers).

Friedman, M. (1999) 'European Monetary Union, the Dollar and International Monetary System' in P.J. Zak (ed.) *Currency Crises, Monetary Union and the Conduct of Monetary Policy* (Cheltenham U.K.: Edward Elgar).

Friedman, M. and Schwartz, A.J. (1963) *A Monetary History of the United States* (Princeton University: Princeton University Press).

Furman, J. and Stiglitz, J.E. (1998) 'Economic Crises: Evidence and Insights From East Asia', *Brookings Papers on Economic Activity*, 2, 1–135.

Garber, P. and Taylor, M.P. (1995) 'Sand in the Wheels of Foreign Exchange Markets: A Sceptical Note', *Economic Journal*, 105, 173–80.

Garuda, G. (2000) 'The Distributional Effects of IMF Programs: A Cross-Country Analysis', *World Development*, 28(6), 1031–51.

Ghosh, A.R., Gulde, A. and Wolf, H. (2000) 'Currency Boards: More Than a Quick Fix?', *Economic Policy*, October, 270–335.

Gilbert, M. (1980) *Quest For World Monetary Order: The Gold-Dollar System and its Aftermath* (New York: Wiley).

Giovannini, A. and Turtelboom, B. (1994) 'Currency Substitution' in F. van der Ploeg (ed.) *International Macroeconomics* (Oxford: Blackwell).

Gnos, G. and Rochon, L. (2004) 'Reforming the International Financial and Monetary System', *Journal of Post Keynesian Economics*, 26(4), 613–29.

Goldstein, M. (1989) 'The International Monetary Fund and the Developing Countries: A Critical Evaluation – A Comment' in K. Brunner and A. Meltzer (eds) *Carnegie Rochester Conference Series on Public Policy VOL. 31* (Amsterdam: North-Holland).

Goldstein, M. (1994) 'Improving Economic Policy Coordination: Evaluating Some New and Some Not-So-New Proposals' in P.B. Kenen, F. Papadia and F. Saccomanni (eds) *The International Monetary System* (Cambridge: Cambridge University).

Goldstein, M. (1995) *The Exchange Rate System and the IMF: A Modest Agenda* (Washington D.C.: Institute for International Economics).

Graham, F.H. (1943) *Fundamentals of International Monetary Policy* (Princeton: International Finance Section).

Gray, H.P. (ed.) (2005) *Globalization and International Economic Stability* (Cheltenham: Edward Elgar).

Greenwald, M. and Stiglitz, J.E. (1986) 'Externalities in Economies with Imperfect Information and Incomplete Markets', *Quarterly Journal of Economics*, 101(2), 229–64.

Gregorio, J. de, Edwards, S. and Valdes, R.O. (2000) 'Controls on Capital Flows: Do They Work?', *Journal of Development Economics*, 63, 59–83.

Gregorio, J. de, Eichengreen, B., Ito, T. and Wyplosz, C. (1999) *An Independent and Accountable IMF* (London: International Center for Monetary and Banking Studies).

Group of Seven (1998) 'Declaration of G7 Finance Ministers and Central Bank Governors', October.

Group of Ten (1996) *The Resolution of Sovereign Liquidity Crises* (Washington D.C.: International Monetary Fund).

Guitian, M. (1981) *Fund Conditionality: Evolution of Principles and Practices* (Washington D.C.: International Monetary Fund).

Guitian, M. (1995) 'Conditionality: Past, Present and Future', *IMF Staff Papers*, 42, 792–835.

Haberler, G. (1964) 'Integration and the Growth of the World Economy in Historical Perspective', *American Economic Review*, 54(2), 1–22.

Haberler, G. (1973) 'Prospects For the Dollar Standard' in C.F. Bergsten and W.G. Tyler (eds) *Leading Issues in International Economic Policy* (Lexington Mass: D.C. Heath).

Haberler, G. (1980) 'Flexible-Exchange-Rate Theories and Controversies Once Again' in J.S. Chipman and C.P. Kindleberger (eds) *Flexible Exchange Rates and the Balance of Payments: Essays in Memory of Egon Sohmen* (Amsterdam: North-Holland Publishers).

Haggard, S. and Maxfield, S. (1996) 'The Political Economy of Financial Internationalization in the Developing World', *International Organization*, 50, 35–68.

Hartmann, P. (1999) *Currency Competition and Foreign Exchange Markets* (Cambridge: Cambridge University Press).

Hayek, F.A. (1974) 'The Pretence of Knowledge', *American Economic Review*, 79, 3–7.

Hayek, F.A. (1978a) 'Choice in Currency' reprinted in S. Kresge (ed.) (1999) *The Collected Works of F.A. Hayek VOL. IV* (Chicago: University of Chicago Press).

Hayek, F.A. (1978b) 'The Denationalization of Money' reprinted in S. Kresge (ed.) (1999) *The Collected Works of F.A. Hayek VOL. IV* (Chicago: University of Chicago Press).

Hayek, F.A. (1979) 'Toward a Free Market Monetary System' reprinted in S. Kresge (ed.) (1999) *The Collected Works of F.A. Hayek VOL. IV* (Chicago: University of Chicago Press).

Hayek, F.A. (1980) 'The Future Unit of Value' in S. Kresge (ed.) (1999) *The Collected Works of F.A. Hayek VOL. IV* (Chicago: University of Chicago Press).

Hayek, F.A. (1994) *Hayek on Hayek: An Autobiographical Dialogue* (London: Routledge).

Hellman, T.F., Murdock, K.C. and Stiglitz, J.E. (1996) 'Deposit Mobilization Through Financial Restraint' in N. Hermes and R. Lensik (eds) *Financial Development and Economic Growth: Theory and Experiences From Developing Economies* (London and New York: Routledge).

Henderson, D.W. and Sampson, S. (1983) 'Intervention in Foreign Exchange Markets: A Summary of Ten Staff Studies', *Federal Reserve Bulletin*, 69, 830–6.

Henry, P.B. (2007) 'Capital Account Liberalization: Theory, Evidence and Speculation', *Journal of Economic Literature*, 45, 877–935.

IFIAC (2000) *Meltzer Commission: Report of the International Financial Institution Advisory Commission* (Washington D.C.: US Treasury).

IMF (1972) *Reforming the International Monetary System: Report of the Executive Director to the Board of Governors* (Washington D.C.: International Monetary Fund).

IMF (1974) 'Outline of Reform' in *International Monetary Reform: Documents of the Committee of Twenty* (Washington D.C.: International Monetary Fund).

IMF (1987) *Theoretical Aspects of the Design of Fund-Supported Programs* (Washington D.C.: International Monetary Fund).

IMF (1995) *International Capital Markets: Developments, Prospects and Policy Issues* (Washington D.C.: International Monetary Fund).

IMF (1997) *Theoretical Aspects of the Design of Fund-Supported Programs* (Washington D.C.: International Monetary Fund).

IMF (1999) *Involving the Private Sector in Forestalling and Resolving Financial Crises* (Washington D.C.: International Monetary Fund).

Independent Task Force (1999) *Safeguarding Prosperity in a Global Financial System: The Future of the International Financial Architecture* (Washington: Institute for International Economics and Council on Foreign Relations).

Isard, P. (2005) *Globalization and the International Financial System* (Cambridge: Cambridge University Press).

James, H. (1996) *International Monetary Cooperation since Bretton Woods* (New York: Oxford University Press).

Johnson, H.G. (1969) 'The Case for Flexible Exchange Rates, 1969', *Further Essays in Monetary Economics* (London: George Allen and Unwin).

Johnson, H.G. (1972a) 'Political Economy Aspects of International Monetary Reform', *Journal of International Economics*, 2, 401–23.

Johnson, H.G. (1972b) 'A General Commentary' in A.L. Acheson, J.F. Chant and M.F. Prachowny (eds) *Bretton Woods Revisited* (London: Macmillan).

Johnson, H.G. (1977) 'The Monetary Approach to the Balance of Payments: A Nontechnical Guide', *Journal of International Economics*, 7, 251–68.

Jurgenson Report (1983) *Report of the Working Group on Exchange Market Intervention* (Washington: U.S. Treasury).

Kawai, M. (1987) 'Optimum Currency Areas' in J. Chipman, J. Eatwell and M. Milgate (eds) *The New Palgrave: A Dictionary of Economics* (London: Macmillan).

Kenen, P.B. (1969) 'The Theory of Optimum Currency Areas: An Eclectic View' in R. Mundell and K. Swoboda (eds) *Monetary Problems of the International Economy* (Chicago: University of Chicago Press).

Kenen, P.B. (1988) *Managing Exchange Rates* (London and New York: Routledge).

Kenen, P.B. (1995) 'What Have We Learned From EMS Crises?', *Journal of Policy Modeling*, 17(5), 449–61.

Kenen, P.B. (1998) 'Panel Discussion: Reflection on the EMS Experience' in F. Giavazzi, S. Micossi and M. Miller (eds) *The European Monetary System* (Cambridge: Cambridge University Press).

Keynes, J.M. (1936) *The General Theory of Employment, Interest and Money* (London: Macmillan).

Keynes, J.M. (1937) 'The General Theory of Employment', *Quarterly Journal of Economics*, 51(1), 209–23.

Kindleberger, C.P. (1967) *The Politics of International Money and World Language* (Princeton University: International Finance Section).

Kindleberger, C.P. (1972) 'The Benefits of International Money', *Journal of International Economics*, 1, 425–42.

Kindleberger, C.P. (1978) *Manias, Panics and Crashes: A History of Financial Crises* (New York: John Wiley & Sons).

Kindleberger, C.P. (1986) 'International Public Goods without International Government', *American Economic Review*, 76(1), 1–13.

Kindleberger, C.P. (1989) *Economic Laws and Economic History* (New York: Cambridge University Press).

Kindleberger, C.P. (1991) 'International (and Inter Regional) Aspects of Financial Crises' in M. Feldstein (ed.) *The Risk of Economic Crisis* (Chicago: University of Chicago Press).

Kindleberger, C.P. (2005) *Manias, Panics and Crashes: A History of Financial Crises*, 5th edn (New York: John Wiley & Sons).

Kresge, S. (1999) 'Introduction' in S. Kresge (ed.) *The Collected Works of F.A. Hayek VOL. IV* (Chicago: University of Chicago Press).

Krueger, A.O. (1998) 'Whither the IMF and the World Bank?', *Journal of Economic Literature*, 36, 1983–2020.

Krueger, A.O. (2000) 'Conflicting Demands on the International Monetary Fund', *American Economic Review Papers and Proceedings*, 90(2), 38–42.

Krugman, P. (1979) 'A Model of Balance-of-Payments Crises', *Journal of Money, Credit and Banking*, 11, 311–25.

Krugman, P. (1989a) *Exchange Rate Instability* (Cambridge: MIT Press).

Krugman, P. (1989b) 'The Case For Stabilizing Exchange Rates', *Oxford Review of Economic Policy*, 5(3), 61–72.

Krugman, P. (1991a) 'Target Zones and Exchange Rate Dynamics', *Quarterly Journal of Economics*, 106, 669–92.

Krugman, P. (1991b) 'International Aspects of Financial Crises' in M. Feldstein (ed.) *The Risk of Economic Crisis* (Chicago: University of Chicago Press).

Krugman, P. (1992) *Currencies and Crises* (Cambridge Mass.: MIT Press).

Krugman, P. (1993a) *What Do We Need to Know About the International Monetary System?* (Princeton University: International Finance Section).

Krugman, P. (1993b) 'Lessons of Massachusetts for EMU' in F. Torres and F. Giavazzi (eds) *Adjustment and Growth in the European Economy* (Cambridge: Cambridge University Press).

Krugman, P. (1996) 'Are Currency Crises Self-Fulfilling?', *NBER Macroeconomics Annual*, 11, 345–78.

Krugman, P. (1998a) 'The Confidence Game', *New Republic*, 5, October, 23–5.

Krugman, P. (1998b) 'Saving Asia: It's Time to Get Radical', *Fortune*, 138(5), 74–80.

Krugman, P. (1999) *The Return of Depression Economics* (New York: Norton).

Krugman, P. (2000) 'Fire-Sale FDI' in S. Edwards (ed.) *Capital Flows and the Emerging Economies: Theory, Evidence and Controversies* (Chicago: University of Chicago Press).

Latsis, S. (ed.) (1976) *Method and Appraisal in Economics* (Cambridge: Cambridge University Press).

Leijonhufvud, A. (1976) 'Schools, "Revolutions" and Research Programmes' in S. Latsis (ed.) *Method and Appraisal in Economics* (Cambridge: Cambridge University Press).

Levine, R. (1997) 'Financial Development and Economic Growth: Views and Agenda', *Journal of Economic Literature*, 35, 668–726.

Lucas, R.E. (1990) 'Why Doesn't Capital Flow From Rich to Poor Countries?', *American Economic Review, Papers and Proceedings*, 90, 92–6.

Machlup, F. (1966) *International Monetary Systems and the Free Market Economy* (Princeton University: International Finance Section).

Machlup, F. (1972) *The Alignment of Foreign Exchange Rates: The First Horwitz Lectures* (New York: Praeger Publishers).

Machlup, F. (1977) *A History of Economic Thought on Economic Integration* (London: Macmillan).

Machlup, F. and Malkiel, B.G. (1964) *International Monetary Arrangements: The Problem of Choice* (Princeton University: International Finance Section).

Mair, D. and Miller, A. (1991) *A Modern Guide to Economic Thought: An Introduction to Comparative Schools of Thought in Economics* (Aldershot U.K.: Edward Elgar).

McKinnon, R.I. (1963) 'Optimum Currency Areas', *American Economic Review*, 53, 717–25.

McKinnon, R.I. (1973) *Money and Capital in Economic Development* (Washington D.C.: Brookings Institution).

McKinnon, R.I. (1974) *A New Tripartite Monetary System or a Limping Dollar Standard* (Princeton University: International Finance Section).

McKinnon, R.I. (1979) *Money in International Exchange: The Convertible Currency System* (New York: Oxford University Press).

McKinnon, R.I. (1981) 'The Exchange Rate and Macroeconomic Policy: Changing Postwar Perceptions', *Journal of Economic Literature*, 19(2), 531–57.

McKinnon, R.I. (1982) 'The Order of Economic Liberalization: Lessons From Chile and Argentina', *Carnegie-Rochester Conference Series on Public Policy*, 17, 159–86.

McKinnon, R.I. (1988) 'Monetary and Exchange Rate Policies for International Financial Stability: A Proposal', *Journal of Economic Perspectives*, 2(1), 83–103.

McKinnon, R.I. (1993) *The Order of Economic Liberalization*, 2nd edn (Baltimore: Johns Hopkins University Press).

McKinnon, R.I. (1995) 'Intergovernmental Competition in Europe With and Without a Common Currency', *Journal of Policy Modeling*, 17(5), 463–78.

McKinnon, R.I. (1996a) *The Rules of the Game: International Money and Exchange Rates* (Cambridge Mass.: MIT Press).

McKinnon, R.I. (1996b) 'Direct and Indirect Concepts of Currency Substitution' in P. Mizen and E. Pentecost (eds) *The Macroeconomics of International Currencies* (Cheltenham: E. Elgar).

McKinnon, R.I. and Pill, H. (1996) 'Credible Liberalizations and International Capital Flows' in T. Ito and A. Krueger (eds) *Financial Deregulation and Integration in East Asia* (Chicago: University of Chicago Press).

McKinnon, R.I. and Pill, H. (1997) 'Credible Liberalizations and Overborrowing', *American Economic Review Papers and Proceedings*, 87(2), 189–93.

Meade, J.E. (1955) 'The Case For Flexible Exchange Rates', *Three Banks Review*, 27, 3–27.

Meade, J.E. (1993) 'The Meaning of "Internal Balance"', *American Economic Review*, 83(6), 3–9.

Mehrling, P. (1999) 'The Vision of Hyman P. Minsky', *Journal of Economic Behavior and Organization*, 39, 129–58.

Meltzer, A.H. (1995) 'End the IMF', Paper Presented at the Cato Institute's Annual Monetary Conference, May.

Meltzer, A.H. (1998) 'Asian Problems and the IMF', *Cato Journal*, 17(3), 267–74.

Meltzer, A.H. (2003) 'The Future of the IMF and World Bank Panel Discussion', *American Economic Review Papers and Proceedings*, 93(2), 46–7.

Meltzer, A.H. (2005) 'New Mandates for the IMF and World Bank', *Cato Journal*, 25(1), 3–16.

Minsky, H.P. (1972) 'Financial Instability Revisited: The Economics of Disaster' in Board of Governors, Federal Reserve System, *Reappraisal of the Federal Reserve Discount Mechanism* (New York: Federal Reserve Bank).

Minsky, H.P. (1975) *John Maynard Keynes* (New York: Columbia University Press).

Minsky, H.P. (1980a) 'Capitalist Financial Process and the Instability of Capitalism', *Journal of Economic Issues*, 14(2), 505–22.

Minsky, H.P. (1980b) 'Money, Financial Markets and the Coherence of a Market Economy', *Journal of Post Keynesian Economics*, 3(1), 21–31.

Minsky, H.P. (1982) *Can "It" Happen Again?* (New York: M.E. Sharpe).

Minsky, H.P. (1984) 'The Potential for Financial Crises' in T. Agmon, R.G. Hawkins and R.M. Levich (eds) *The Future of the International Monetary System* (Lexington MA.: Lexington Books).

Minsky, H.P. (1986) *Stabilizing an Unstable Economy* (New Haven: Yale University Press).

Minsky, H.P. (1991) 'The Financial Instability Hypothesis: A Clarification' in M. Feldstein (ed.) *The Risk of Economic Crisis* (Chicago: University of Chicago Press).

Montiel, P. (1985) 'A Monetary Analysis of a Small Open Economy with a Keynesian Structure', *IMF Staff Papers*, 32, 179–210.

Mundell, R.A. (1969a) 'Toward a Better International Monetary System', *Journal of Money, Credit and Banking*, 1, 625–48.

Mundell, R.A. (1969b) 'Problems of the International Monetary System' in R.A. Mundell and A.K. Swoboda (eds) *Monetary Problems of the International Economy* (Chicago: University of Chicago Press).

Mundell, R.A. (1972) 'The Future of the International Monetary System' in A.L. Acheson, J.F. Chant and M.F. Prachowny (eds) *Bretton Woods Revisited* (London: Macmillan).

Mundell, R.A. (1973a) 'The Monetary Consequences of Jacques Rueff: A Review Article', *Journal of Business*, 46, 384–95.

Mundell, R.A. (1973b) 'A Plan For a European Currency' in H. Johnson and A.K. Swoboda (eds) *The Economics of Common Currencies* (London: George Allen and Unwin).

Mundell, R.A. (1973c) 'Uncommon Arguments for Common Currencies' in H. Johnson and A.K. Swoboda (eds) *The Economics of Common Currencies* (London: George Allen and Unwin).

Mundell, R. (1977) 'Concluding Remarks' in R. Mundell and J.J. Polak (eds) *The New International Monetary System* (New York: Columbia University Press).

Mundell, R.A. (1993) 'Panel Session II: Implications for International Monetary Reform' in M. Bordo and B. Eichengreen (eds) *A Retrospective on the Bretton Woods System* (Chicago: University of Chicago Press).

Mundell, R.A. (1994) 'Discussion' in P.B. Kenen, F. Papadia and F. Saccomanni (eds) *The International Monetary System* (Cambridge: Cambridge University Press).

Mundell, R.A. (1995) 'The International Monetary System: The Missing Factor', *Journal of Policy Modeling*, 17(5), 479–92.

Mundell, R.A. (1997a) 'Optimum Currency Areas', Conference on Optimum Currency Areas, Tel-Aviv University, December. Downloaded from http://www.columbia.edu/~ram15/eOCATAVIV4.html

Mundell, R.A. (1997b) 'Currency Areas, Common Currencies, and EMU', *American Economic Review*, 87(2), 214–16.

Mundell, R.A. (1997c) 'Updating the Agenda for Monetary Union' in M. Blejer, J.A. Frenkel, L. Leiderman, and A. Razin (eds) *Optimum Currency Areas* (Washington D.C.: International Monetary Fund).

Mundell, R.A. (1998) 'The Euro and The Stability of the International Monetary System'. Paper Presented at a Conference sponsored jointly by the Luxembourg Institute for European and International Studies and the Pierre Werner Foundation, December.

Mundell, R.A. (1999) 'European Monetary Union, the Dollar and International Monetary System' in P.J. Zak (ed.) *Currency Crises, Monetary Union and the Conduct of Monetary Policy* (Cheltenham U.K.: Edward Elgar).

Mundell, R.A. (2000) 'A Reconsideration of the Twentieth Century', *American Economic Review*, 90(3), 327–40.

Mussa, M. (1977) 'IMF Surveillance', *American Economic Review Papers and Proceedings*, 87(2), 28–31.

Mussa, M. (1995) 'The Evolving International Monetary System and Prospects For Monetary Reform', *Journal of Policy Modeling*, 17(5), 493–512.

Mussa, M., Goldstein, M., Clark, P., Mathieson, D. and Bayoumi, T. (1994) *Improving the International Monetary System: Constraints and Possibilities* (Washington D.C.: IMF).

Nayyar, D. (2002) 'Capital Controls and the World Financial Authority: What Can We Learn From the Indian Experience?' in J. Eatwell and L. Taylor (eds) *International Capital Markets: Systems in Transition* (Oxford: Oxford University Press).

Nurkse, R. (1944) *International Currency Experience* (Geneva: League of Nations).

Obstfeld, M. (1994a) 'The Logic of Currency Crises', *Cahiers Economiques et Monetaires*, 102, 624–60.

Obstfeld, M. (1994b) 'Risk-Taking, Global Diversification and Growth', *American Economic Review*, 85, 1310–29.

Obstfeld, M. (1995) 'International Capital Mobility in the 1990s' in P.B. Kenen (ed.) *Understanding Interdependence: The Macroeconomics of the Open Economy* (Princeton: Princeton University Press).

Obstfeld, M. (1996a) 'Models of Currency Crises with Self-Fulfilling Features', *European Economic Review*, 40, 1037–48.

Obstfeld, M. (1996b) 'Comment', *NBER Macroeconomics Annual*, 11, 393–403.

Obstfeld, M. (1998) 'The Global Capital Market: Benefactor or Menace?', *Journal of Economic Perspectives*, 12(4), 9–30.

Obstfeld, M. and Rogoff, K. (1995) 'The Mirage of Fixed Exchange Rates', *Journal of Economic Perspectives*, 9(4), 73–96.

Obstfeld, M. and Rogoff, K. (1996) *Foundations of International Macroeconomics* (Cambridge Mass.: MIT Press).

Obstfeld, M. and Taylor, A.M. (1998) 'The Great Depression as a Watershed: International Capital Mobility over the Long Run' in M.D. Bordo, C.D. Goldin and E.N. White (eds) *The Defining Moment: The Great Depression and the American Economy in the Twentieth Century* (Chicago: University of Chicago Press).

Obstfeld, M. and Taylor, A.M. (2003) *Global Capital Markets: Integration, Crisis and Growth* (Cambridge: Cambridge University Press).

Ocampo, J.A. (2002) 'Recasting the International Financial Agenda' in J. Eatwell and L. Taylor (eds) *International Capital Markets: Systems in Transition* (Oxford: Oxford University Press).

Patinkin, D. (1982) *Anticipations of the General Theory?* (Oxford: Basil Blackwell).

Pauly, L.W. (1997) *Who Elected the Banker? Surveillance and Control in the World Economy* (New York: Cornell University Press).

Polak, J.J. (1991) *The Changing Nature of IMF Conditionality* (Princeton University: International Finance Section).

Polak, J.J. (1996) 'The Contribution of the International Monetary Fund' in A.W. Coats (ed.) *The Post-1945 Internationalization of Economics* (Durham N.C.: Duke University Press).

Polak, J.J. (1998) 'The Articles of Agreement of the IMF and the Liberalization of Capital Movements' in S. Fischer et al., *Should the IMF Pursue Capital-Account Convertibility?* (Princeton University: International Finance Section).

Polak, J.J. (1999) *Streamlining the Financial Structure of the International Monetary Fund* (Princeton University: International Finance Section).

Prasad, E.S. and Rajan, R.G. (2008) 'A Pragmatic Approach to Capital Account Liberalization', *Journal of Economic Perspectives*, 22(3), 149–72.

Quinn, D.P. (1997) 'The Correlates of Changes in International Financial Regulation', *American Political Science Review*, 91(3), 531–51.

Rabin, A.A. and Yeager, L.B. (1982) *Monetary Approaches to the Balance of Payments and Exchange Rates* (Princeton University: International Finance Section).

Rhomberg, R.R. and Heller, R.H. (1977) 'International Survey' in IMF *The Monetary Approach to the Balance of Payments* (Washington D.C.: International Monetary Fund).

Rodrik, D. (1997) *Has Globalization Gone Too Far?* (Washington D.C.: Institute for International Economics).

Rodrik, D. (1998) 'Who Needs Capital Account Convertibility?' in S. Fischer et al., *Should the IMF Pursue Capital Account Convertibility?* (Princeton University: International Finance Section).

Rodrik, D. (2000) 'How Far Will International Economic Integration Go?', *Journal of Economic Perspectives*, 14(1), 177–86.

Rodrik, D. and Velasco, A. (1999) 'Short Term Capital Flows', *NBER Working Papers*, No. 734.

Rogoff, K. (1984) 'On the Effects of Sterilized Intervention: An Analysis of Weekly Data', *Journal of Monetary Economics*, 14, 133–50.

Rogoff, K. (1985) 'Can International Monetary Policy Cooperation be Counterproductive?', *Journal of International Economics*, 18, 199–217.

Rogoff, K. (1999) 'International Institutions for Reducing Global Financial Instability', *Journal of Economic Perspectives*, 13(4), 21–42.

Rogoff, K. (2001) 'Why Not a Global Currency?', *American Economic Review Papers and Proceedings*, 91(2), 243–7.

Roosa, R. (1984) 'Exchange Rate Arrangements in the Eighties' in Federal Reserve Bank of Boston, *The International Monetary System: Forty Years After Bretton Woods* (Boston: Federal Reserve Bank of Boston).

Sachs, J.D. (1984) *Theoretical Issues in International Borrowing* (Princeton University: International Finance Section).

Sachs, J.D. (1986) 'Managing the LDC Debt Crisis', *Brookings Papers on Economic Activity*, 2, 397–431.

Sachs, J.D. (1989) 'The Debt Overhang of Developing Countries' in G. Calvo (ed.) *Debt, Stabilization and Development: Essays in Memory of Carlos Diaz Alejandro* (Oxford: Blackwell).

Sachs, J.D. (1995a) 'Alternative Approaches to Financial Crises in Emerging Markets', paper prepared as background for discussion, Basel, December 9–10.

Sachs, J.D. (1995b) 'Do We Need a Lender of Last Resort?', unpublished manuscript, Frank D. Graham Lecture, Princeton University, April.

Sachs, J.D. (1998) 'General Discussion', *Brookings Papers on Economic Activity*, 2, 123–7.

Sachs, J.D. (1999) 'The International Lender of Last Resort: What are the Alternatives?' in J.S. Little and G.P. Olivei (eds) *Rethinking the International Monetary System* (Boston: Federal Reserve Bank of Boston).

Sachs, J.D. (2003) 'The Future of the IMF and World Bank Panel Discussion', *American Economic Review Papers and Proceedings*, 93(2), 47–8.

Sachs, J.D., Tornell, A. and Velasco, A. (1996a) 'The Collapse of the Mexican Peso: What Have We Learned?', *Economic Policy: A European Forum*, 22, 13–56.

Sachs, J.D., Tornell, A. and Velasco, A. (1996b) 'Financial Crises in Emerging Markets, the Lessons from 1995', *Brookings Papers on Economic Activity*, 1, 147–98.

Sachs, J.D. and Warner, A. (1995) 'Economic Reform and the Process of Global Integration', *Brookings Papers on Economic Activity*, 1, 1–118.

Salvatore, D. (1995a) 'The International Monetary System: Are Present Arrangements Optimal? Editor's Introduction', *Journal of Policy Modeling*, 17(5), 443–8.

Salvatore, D. (1995b) 'The Operation and Future of the International Monetary System', *Journal of Policy Modeling*, 17(5), 513–30.

Samuelson, P.A. (1972) 'Heretical Doubts About the International Mechanisms', *Journal of International Economics*, 1, 443–53.

Scammell, W.M. (1975) *International Monetary Policy, Bretton Woods and After* (London: Macmillan).

Schumpeter, J.A. (1954) *History of Economic Analysis* (London: Allen and Unwin).

Schwartz, A.J. (1986) 'Real and Pseudo-Financial Crises' in F. Capie and G. Wood (eds) *Financial Crises in the World Banking System* (New York: St. Martin's Press).

Schwartz, A.J. (1987) *Money in Historical Perspective* (Chicago: University of Chicago Press).

Schwartz, A.J. (1998) 'International Financial Crises: Myths and Realities', *Cato Journal*, 17(3), 251–6.

Schwartz, A.J. (1999) 'Is There a Need For an International Lender of Last Resort?', *Cato Journal*, 19(1), 1–6.

Schwartz, A.J. (2000) 'Do We Need a New Bretton Woods?', *Cato Journal*, 20(1), 21–5.

Skidelsky, R. (2005) 'Lionel Robbins Lecture' in R.A. Mundell, P.J. Zak and D.M. Schaeffer (eds) *International Monetary Policy After the Euro* (Cheltenham U.K.: Edward Elgar).

Solomon, R.S. (1977) *The International Monetary System 1945–76: An Insider's View* (New York: Harper and Row).

Solomon, R.S. (1999) *Money on the Move: The Revolution in the International Finance since 1980* (Princeton: Princeton University Press).

Stiglitz, J.E. (1989) *The Economic Role of the State* (Oxford: Basil Blackwell).

Stiglitz, J.E. (1995) 'The Theory of International Public Goods and the Architecture of International Organizations', Paper Presented at the Meeting of the High Level Group on Development Strategy and Management of the Market Economy, Helsinki, July.

Stiglitz, J.E. (1996) 'Some Lessons From the East Asian Miracle', *World Bank Research Observer*, 11(2), 151–77.

Stiglitz, J.E. (1998) 'More Instruments and Broader Goals: Moving Towards the Post-Washington Consensus' 1998 Wider Lecture, Helsinki University, reprinted in H.J. Chang (ed.) *The Rebel Within* (London: Wimbledon Publishing Company).

Stiglitz, J.E. (1999) 'Reforming the Global Economic Architecture: Lessons From Recent Crises', *Journal of Finance*, 54(4), 1508–21.

Stiglitz, J.E. (2000) 'Capital Market Liberalization, Economic Growth and Instability', *World Development*, 28(6), 1075–86.

Stiglitz, J.E. (2002a) 'Capital Markets Liberalization and Exchange Rate Regimes: Risk Without Reward', *Annals of the American Academy of Political and Social Science*, 579, 219–48.

Stiglitz, J.E. (2002b) 'Globalization and the Logic of Collective Action: Re-examining the Bretton Woods Institutions' in D. Nayyar (ed.) *Governing Globalization: Issues and Institutions* (Oxford: Oxford University Press).

Stiglitz, J.E. (2002c) *Globalization and its Discontents* (New York: W.W. Norton).

Stiglitz, J.E. (2008) 'Is there a Post-Washington Consensus?' in N. Serra and J. Stiglitz (eds) *The Washington Consensus Reconsidered: Toward a New Global Governance* (Oxford: Oxford University Press).

Stiglitz, J.E. and Uy, M. (1996) 'Financial Markets, Public Policy and the East Asian Miracle', *World Bank Research Observer*, 11(2), 249–76.

Summers, L. (1991) 'Planning For the Next Financial Crises' in M. Feldstein (ed.) *The Risk of Economic Crisis* (Chicago: University of Chicago Press).

Summers, L. (2000) 'International Financial Crises: Causes, Prevention and Cures', *American Economic Review Papers and Proceedings*, 90(2), 1–16.

Tavlas, G.S. (1991) *On the Use of International Currencies: The Case of the Deutsche Mark* (Princeton University: International Finance Section).

Tavlas, G.S. (1993) 'The "New" Theory of Optimum Currency Areas', *World Economy*, 6, 663–85.

Tavlas, G.S. (2009) 'Optimum-Currency-Area Paradoxes', *Review of International Economics*, 17(3), 536–51.

Taylor, L. (1991) *Income Distribution, Inflation and Growth* (Cambridge Mass.: MIT Press).

Taylor, L. (1993) *The Rocky Road to Reform: Adjustment, Income Distribution, and Growth in the Developing World* (Cambridge Mass.: MIT Press).

Taylor, L. (2002) 'Global Macroeconomic Management' in D. Nayyar (ed.) *Governing Globalization* (Oxford: Oxford University Press).

Taylor, L. and Eatwell, J. (2000) *Global Finance at Risk: The Case for International Regulation* (New York: New Press).

Tobin, J. (1974) *The New Economics One Decade Older*. The Eliot Janeway Lectures on Historical Economics in Honour of Joseph Schumpeter, 1972 (Princeton: Princeton University Press).

Tobin, J. (1978) 'A Proposal For International Monetary Reform', *Eastern Economic Journal*, 4, 153–9.

Tobin, J. (1982) 'The State of Exchange Rate Theory' in R. Triffin and R. Cooper (eds) *The International Monetary System Under Flexible Exchange Rates* (Cambridge Mass.: Ballinger Publishing).

Tobin, J. (1987) 'Agenda for International Coordination of Macroeconomic Policies' in P. Volcker (ed.) *International Monetary Cooperation: Essays in Honor of Henry C. Wallich* (Princeton University: International Finance Section).

Tobin, J. (1989) 'On the Efficiency of the Financial System' in C. Johnson (ed.) *The Market on Trial* (London and New York: Pinter Publishers).

Tobin, J. (1993) 'International Currency Regimes, Capital Mobility, and Macroeconomic Policy' in A.S. Courakis and G.S. Tavlas (eds) *Financial and Monetary Integration* (Cambridge: Cambridge University Press).

Tobin, J. (1996) 'Prologue' in M. ul Haq, I. Kabul and I. Grunberg (eds) *The Tobin Tax: Coping with Financial Volatility* (New York and Oxford: Oxford University Press).

Tobin, J. (2000) 'Financial Globalization', *World Development*, 28(6), 1101–4.

Triffin, R. (1972) 'International Monetary Collapse and Reconstruction in April 1972', *Journal of International Economics*, 2, 375–400.

Vane, H.R. and Mulhearn, C. (2006) 'Interview with Robert A. Mundell', *Journal of Economic Perspectives*, 20(4), 89–110.

Vaubel, R.I. (1983) 'Coordination or Competition Among National Macroeconomic Policies?' in F. Machlup, G. Fels and H. Müller-Groeling (eds) *Reflections on a Troubled World Economy* (London: Macmillan).

Vaubel, R.I. (1978a) *Strategies For Currency Unification: The Economics of Currency Competition and the Case for a European Parallel Currency* (Tübingen: Mohr).

Vaubel, R.I. (1978b) 'The Money Supply in Europe: Why EMS May Make Inflation Worse', *Euromoney*, 139–42.

Vaubel, R.I. (1990) 'Currency Competition and Monetary Union', *Economic Journal*, 100, 936–46.

Vaubel, R.I. (1997) 'The Bureaucratic and Partisan Behaviour of Independent Central Banks: German and International Evidence', *European Journal of Political Economy*, 13, 201–24.

Wade, R. (1998–9) 'The Coming Fight Over Capital Flows', *Foreign Policy*, 113, 41–54.

Wade, R. (2009) 'From Global Imbalances to Global Reorganisations', *Cambridge Journal of Economics*, 33, 539–62.

Whitman, M. (1980) 'Comments by Marina V. Whitman', *Brookings Papers on Economic Activity*, 1, 195–202.

Willett, T.D. (2000) *International Financial Markets as Sources of Crises or Discipline: The Too Much, Too Late Hypothesis* (Princeton University: International Finance Section).

Williamson, J. (1973) 'Surveys in Applied Economics: International Liquidity', *Economic Journal*, 83, 685–746.

Williamson, J. (1976) 'The Benefits and Costs of an International Monetary Non System' in E.M. Bernstein et al. (eds) *Reflections on Jamaica* (Princeton University: International Finance Section).

Williamson, J. (1977) *The Failure of World Monetary Reform* (Sunbury-on-Thames: Nelson Publishers).

Williamson, J. (1985a) 'On the System in Bretton Woods', *American Economic Review, Papers and Proceedings*, 75(2), 74–9.

Williamson, J. (1985b) *The Exchange Rate System* (Washington D.C.: Institute for International Economics).

Williamson, J. (1986) 'Target Zones and the Management of the Dollar', *Brookings Papers on Economic Activity*, 1, 165–74.

Williamson, J. (1990) *Latin American Adjustment: How Much Has Happened?* (Washington D.C.: Institute for International Economics).

Williamson, J. (1994) 'The Rise and Fall of the Concept of International Liquidity' in P.B. Kenen, F. Papadia and F. Saccomanni (eds) *The International Monetary System* (Cambridge: Cambridge University Press).

Williamson, J. (1999) 'The Case For a Common Basket Peg For East Asian Economies' in S. Collignon, J. Pisani-Ferry and Y.C. Park (eds) *Exchange Rate Policies in Emerging East Asian Countries* (London and New York: Routledge).

Williamson, J. (2003) 'The Washington Consensus and Beyond', *Economic and Political Weekly*, 38(15), 1475–81.

Williamson, J. (2008) 'A Short History of the Washington Consensus' in N. Serra and J.E. Stiglitz (eds) *The Washington Consensus Reconsidered: Towards a New Global Governance* (Oxford: Oxford University Press).

Williamson, J. and Miller, M. (1987) *Targets and Indicators: A Blueprint for the International Coordination of Economic Policy* (Washington D.C.: Institute for International Economics).

World Bank Development Research Group (2008) *Lessons from World Bank Research on Financial Crises* (Washington D.C.: World Bank).

Wyplosz, C. (1997) 'EMU: Why and How it Might Happen', *Journal of Economic Perspectives*, 11(4), 3–22.

Wyplosz, C. (1998) 'Discussion' in F. Giavazzi, S. Micossi and M. Miller (eds) *The European Monetary System* (Cambridge: Cambridge University Press).

Index